Justifying State Welfare

To my parents

Justifying State Welfare

The New Right versus The Old Left

David Harris

with a Foreword by
David Miller

Basil Blackwell

Basil Blackwell Ltd
108 Cowley Road, Oxford, OX4 1JF, UK

Basil Blackwell Inc.
432 Park Avenue South, Suite 1503
New York, NY 10016, USA

British Library Cataloguing in Publication Data

Harris, David
　　Justifying state welfare: the new right
　　versus the old left.
　　1. Welfare state—Political aspects
　　I. Title
　　361.6′5　　HN28
　　ISBN 0-631-14858-2

Library of Congress Cataloging in Publication Data

Harris, David (David C.)
　　Justifying state welfare.
　　Bibliography: p.
　　Includes index.
　　1. Public welfare—Great Britain.　2. Public
　　welfare—United States.　3. Right and left (Political
　　science)　4. Welfare state.　I. Title
　　HV248.H28　1987　361.6′5′0941　86-31772
　　ISBN 0-631-14858-2

Typeset in 10½ on 12 pt Ehrhardt
by Cambrian Typesetters, Frimley, Surrey
Printed in Great Britain by
T.J. Press Ltd, Padstow

Contents

Foreword

No politically alert person can fail to be aware that public expenditure on welfare services in the Western democracies has increased steadily as a proportion of gross domestic product (GDP) in the post-war period, and even the right-wing governments of Mrs Thatcher and President Reagan have found it difficult to reverse this trend. The welfare state, it seems, is here to stay, and few would wish it otherwise. None the less, we may respond to its existence in sharply opposed ways. For some of us, its presence is a sign that we have passed beyond the competitive struggle for survival to a higher stage in which we acknowledge a collective responsibility to meet the essential needs of everyone in our society. The welfare state, then, is a development of positive moral value. For others, it is no more than an unfortunate necessity, no doubt unavoidable as a safety net to catch the weak and unfortunate, but an incubus that we would be better off without. Morally speaking, a society of sturdy and self-reliant individualists would be preferable by far. Which of these opposing views we take makes a great difference to our attitude on many practical questions of policy, for instance the questions raised by private medical insurance or the various possible ways of financing unemployment benefit.

It is the first great merit of David Harris's book that he sets out the parameters of this debate in a most lucid way. He demonstrates that between the neo-liberal critics of extensive state welfare – the so-called 'new right' – and the older social democratic tradition of support, there is systematic disagreement over a whole gamut of questions. The debate is not merely about the cost-effectiveness of the welfare state, or the extent to which it succeeds in redistributing benefits between classes (important though these questions are), but about more fundamental issues of freedom, justice and rights. He shows, too, how weak many of the neo-liberal assumptions turn out to be when subjected to critical examination.

Harris's larger achievement, however, lies in his reconstruction of the foundations of the social democratic view. Enthusiasts for state welfare such as Tawney, Titmuss and Marshall were characteristically more confident in their policy recommendations than in articulating the premises from which these recommendations were derived. Harris disentangles their often cloudy pronouncements and extracts a coherent basis from which to justify the welfare state. The central idea, he argues, is that of citizenship, interpreted as full membership of a political community, and carrying with it a guarantee that the citizens will enjoy all those rights (including welfare rights) which full membership presupposes. The value of citizenship lies in the fundamental equality of status that it confers on all citizens, this in turn bolstering their self-respect. From this point of view, two other ideas which are often regarded as fundamental to the social democratic position, equality and need, can be shown to be derivative. In an acute piece of analysis, Harris shows that the equality that carries moral weight, in this tradition, is precisely the equality of status that citizenship provides. The idea of need, he further argues, presupposes some communally defined standard of an adequate life against which any particular person's needs can be measured. I find his case against my own earlier defence of a context-independent criterion of need entirely convincing.

An interesting consequence of Harris's argument is that, by drawing out the communitarian character of the welfare statists' thought, he allows us to forge connections between these earlier writers and the more recent revival of communitarian thoughts in the writings of Walzer, Taylor, Sandel and others. The relationship between them might be described in the following way. The recent communitarians have certainly achieved a more sophisticated understanding of the philosophy of community, in particular by putting forward a theory of the self in which the self is (partly) constituted by its communal attachments. On the other hand, they have far less to say about the practical implications of the communitarian position, and it is precisely for this reason that Harris's recovery of the social democratic tradition becomes so important. Tawney, Titmuss and Marshall were in no one's book first rate philosophers, but as social theorists they had a firm grasp of the kind of social policy that was required by their (often implicit) moral ideals. By bringing the techniques of contemporary political philosophy to bear on their work, Harris has provided the groundwork of a communitarian theory that is both philosophically sophisticated and practically relevant.

Of the difficulties facing the citizenship approach to the welfare state, one in particular may deserve more attention than it receives here. If citizenship theory relies on the idea of full membership as a status enjoyed equally by all, it is important that we should be able to identify, for any society, a 'way of life' which forms a benchmark against which needs can be judged. In societies that contain a number of diverse subcultures – based on ethnicity, religion and so forth – this may be a harder task than Harris supposes. Even if we could identify a minimum level of physical provision (of food, housing, etc.) that was a matter of common agreement across all subcultures, we might be hard put to discover a similar consensus in areas such as education, where ideas of 'adequate schooling', for example, would be more closely bound up with culturally specific beliefs about the purposes of education. If this is so, the idea of citizenship may have built into it some pressure in the direction of cultural uniformity, setting it more sharply at odds with liberal pluralism than Harris is willing to concede.

Other readers will find different aspects of this stimulating book with which to disagree, but none can fail to be impressed by the clarity and vigour of Harris's treatment of the subject. I know of no book which sets out better the fundamental issues at stake in the debate over the welfare state. Since this debate will continue to occupy a central place in the politics of the Western democracies in the years to come, it deserves – and will, I am sure, obtain – the widest possible audience.

David Miller

Preface

Inevitably, in an enterprise of this kind, more debts accumulate than can be individually acknowledged or ever repaid. Whatever merit this book has is principally the result of the moral and intellectual support of the friends I made at Nuffield College, Oxford, and my supervisors Bill Weinstein, John Gray and David Miller, from whose critical talents I benefited greatly. I owe them much.

Most of the work for this book was done while I was a student and then a Junior Research Fellow at Nuffield College. Without the encouragement and assistance of the Warden and Fellows this project could not have been completed. Some final research was made possible by the Social Sciences and Humanities Research Council of Canada which kindly awarded me a Private Scholar's grant for the summer of 1985. I am grateful for their generosity. Mrs Doreen Greig very kindly stepped in and typed the last chapter when it seemed impossible to meet my deadline.

I am especially indebted to my friends David and Sue Miller who, on walks around Stanley Park in Vancouver and in a car park in Victoria, persuaded me to take up this topic once again. Without their efforts the thesis would never have been translated into a book. Peter and Corinne Selby, with their characteristic generosity, lent me a personal computer to compose upon and did not complain when month after month I failed to return it. My thanks to them for their technical support but more especially for their friendship. Maria, my wife, devoted innumerable hours to editing and preparing the manuscript. Her unfailing good humour and grace as I wrote the book were more than I could expect or deserve. Our son, Anthony, delayed the completion of the manuscript by at least two months. His infectious giggle made concentration impossible and unwanted. Finally, my parents have always provided me with the support and encouragement to pursue my intellectual interests. This book is the fruition of their nurturing. I dedicate it to them.

David Harris

Introduction

In recent years, broad academic support for the welfare state has been shattered. Today it is fashionable to decry its achievements. The welfare state, we are reliably informed, is in 'crisis'. Far from being the institutional means for forging a reconciliation in the class war through the civilization of capitalism, the welfare state turns out to be the source of our current difficulties. The notion that the stark choice between capitalism and socialism can be avoided has been demonstrated to be fatuous. Politics without pain is not a practical option. It is time to choose.

But to choose what? If there really is no middle way in which social justice circumscribes economic liberty, we are faced with an unattractive choice. On the one hand, we are offered the freedom of the market place with the disruptive influence of democracy suitably confined in a constitutional strait-jacket; and on the other, the freedom of political participation with economic liberty banished as a bourgeois conceit. Stripped to its essentials, the choice is between laissez-faire or state socialism: inequality and insecurity or bureaucracy and regimentation. It may seem that we must decide whether we want 'freedom' without justice or 'justice' without freedom.

Powerful reasons exist, moreover, to persuade us that the choice cannot be evaded. Critics of both the right and left share a remarkably similar diagnosis of the political economy of the welfare state, even if their respective prescriptions diverge sharply. Social democratic politics, which encompasses the view that social justice can correct the market, rests, they allege, upon a mistaken understanding of the possible relationship between the political and economic systems. Distribution cannot be divorced from production. That attempted separation has undermined the foundations of an efficient and productive economy. Economic success has been destroyed by the combined growth of government spending and regulation. High taxation and social policies have overturned the incentive structure of the economy. Institutional rigidities stemming from the power of trade unions constrain the allocative efficiency of the market.

The mechanisms producing these results vary. But whether the emphasis is on the generation of excessive expectations by political competition, the pursuit of unprincipled group interests, the quest for an egalitarian chimera, or the inability of the state to provide the necessary conditions for the accumulation of capital and simultaneously maintain the legitimacy of the system, the consequence is the same. The liberalism of the market and the sovereignty of political democracy are fundamentally incompatible. No mixed system is stable in the long run. After 30 years of apparent success, the tensions between capitalism and democracy have re-emerged; the principles of social democracy, and with it those of the welfare state, that great social democratic achievement, have been exposed as fundamentally and irretrievably incoherent.

As if this were not enough the apparent successes of the welfare state in reducing inequality, distributing life chances more fairly and eradicating poverty have increasingly been subject to critical reappraisal. Poverty was rediscovered as far back as the 1960s and recent studies estimate that anywhere between six and twelve million Britons can be defined as poor, indeed, are kept poor by the combined operation of the tax and benefit system resulting in a poverty trap in which the state taxes away with the one hand welfare benefits it has given with the other. Moreover, it has become increasingly evident that little, if any, redistribution of the benefits and burdens of social life has occurred as the result of state intervention through social policy. The class-related inequalities of the market have reproduced themselves within the welfare state.

Attacks on the welfare state are not restricted to political economy. Increasingly, the normative principles upon which social policies are, or could be, founded have been challenged. Libertarians and market liberals have been in the van of the moral campaign. Social justice is a mirage; social rights a latter-day version of nonsense on stilts; compulsory taxation a form of theft or, worse still, on a par with forced labour. The welfare state is coercive and through its paternalism systematically undermines the initiative and self-reliance of its citizens. The ideal of state-guaranteed cradle-to-grave security saps the moral fibre of the community. The welfare state has been well named the 'nanny state'.

It is with this kind of assault on the welfare state that this book is primarily concerned. My interest is first and foremost in the moral basis of the public provision of welfare goods. The argument is that an extensive welfare state is a requirement of social justice in any society that wishes to retain the utilitarian and liberal advantages of a market economy. The core of my theory of social justice is not that social justice amounts to the satisfaction of needs *per se*, but that it consists in protecting the status of individuals as full members of the community. The notion of full membership in the community I treat under the rubric of 'citizenship'.

My concern, then, is to defend a particular variety of social democracy; one that revolves around a morally principled commitment to a conception of community. Public power is to be used to achieve moral aims which cannot be reduced to self-interest. The political viability of this ideology depends in the end on the capacity of its adherents to generate a sufficiently widespread consensus on its legitimacy to transform its moral principles into operative elements in the fabric of social, economic and political life. Communitarian social democracy, or citizenship theory, as I dub it, confronts a major political challenge, but one no greater than that facing any of its rivals.

The basis of this book is an approach to the welfare state which became an academic orthodoxy in the 1950s and 1960s. Its principal supporters included R. M. Titmuss, T. H. Marshall, W. A. Robson and P. Townsend, all of whom saw themselves as representatives of the traditional left. For these writers the political and intellectual enemies were always the supporters of free markets; those who have in recent years become known as the 'new right'. This book respects and is organized around the contest between these two ideological perspectives. I begin by examining the essential elements of the thought of the new right in order to set the agenda for what follows. In chapters 2 and 3 I offer an exposition of the moral theory I believe underlies the thought of the 'old left'. Chapters 4 and 5 deal with some questions concerning the ideological unity of the 'citizenship tradition', and I begin my more critical analysis of the adequacy of its fundamental moral principles in the light of the criticisms energetically advanced by the new right. The final part of the book continues the critical analysis and develops a revised version of the principles sustaining a communitarian version of social democracy, in which the value of economic markets is recognized but kept firmly in place. The stark choice between the market and democracy can be avoided. A socially just community determined to treat all of its members as equals is not only morally defensible but politically viable.

1

The 'New Right':
Assailing the Welfare State

Writing in the mid-1950s, Tony Crosland may easily be forgiven for believing that the great laissez-faire dragon had been slain.[1] Mass unemployment, breadlines and the degradation of the means test disgraced the 1930s, but were now banished, never to reappear. So confident was Crosland of this that he could argue that the social system known as capitalism had ceased to exist. The time had come to reinterpret the agenda of socialism in a transfigured world. We know now, of course, that this optimism was misplaced.

Crosland, speaking for a generation on the left, claimed that the combination of the Beveridgean welfare state and Keynesian economic policy had transformed the market economy. The key lay in the commitment to guarantee full employment: a commitment Crosland thought, falsely as it turned out, to be indispensable in a post-war political democracy. Full employment stimulated economic growth, placing purchasing power in the hands of the workers. It had become profitable within the market to supply goods that satisfied the needs of workers and their families. Unmet need was not an ineluctable characteristic of the combination of private property in capital and the market; it was the simple result of a lack of purchasing power.

Full employment required an interventionist state, but the beauty of Keynesian policy lay in the indirect methods by which intervention proceeded. There was no need for a command economy with socialized ownership. Successful regulation required only the manipulation of effective demand, and that could be achieved by influencing budget deficits through tax rates, public spending and the like. The freedom of the market place was respected; liberal freedoms coexisted with social justice. Like the Invisible Hand it replaced, the Keynesian Hand discreetly reconciled private interest and public good.

Economic growth and full employment were indispensable to this scheme of things. Low levels of unemployment translated into economic power for workers. Labour in short supply meant high wages and equalized the bargaining strength of unions and management; thus arbitrary managerial prerogatives could be constrained. High levels of employment also minimized the amount of public provision needed to cope with poverty. Indeed, Crosland believed that through the welfare state absolute poverty at least had been eliminated. Economic growth, moreover, provided resources with which to promote equality. As growth continued, the fiscal dividend accruing automatically to the state permitted redistribution to those worst off without reducing the absolute position of the better off. The intensity of conflict which would accompany attempts to redistribute shares of a pie of a fixed or declining size was dissipated.

Although writing about socialism, Crosland expressed eloquently the principal elements of the post-war consensus characterized as 'Butskellism' after Butler and Gaitskell, who dominated the Conservative and Labour parties respectively for much of the 1950s. Whatever disagreements there may have been about the value of equality as an ideal, and despite controversy over the details of policy, the 1950s were marked by widespread agreement over the structural properties of the political, economic and social systems. Laissez-faire was dead and the welfare state reigned in its place. Keynes and Beveridge had supplanted Smith and Bentham. What was true of political practice and rhetoric was true also of academic debate. This was the era of the 'end of ideology'; political philosophy had expired, the influence of that dinosaur of the right, Hayek, was negligible and the voices of the new left were shrill but largely ignored.

Today, the social democratic consensus appears to have been a mere interregnum. Reductions in the rate of economic growth throughout the West breathed life into the laissez-faire corpse. Poor economic performance was blamed on the welfare state with its rapid increase in the size of government, and its excessive regulation and destruction of the work ethic. Keynesianism was castigated as the root cause of the stagflation for which only monetarism and the restoration of incentives could provide an answer. Whereas only 25 years ago 'market failure' provided sufficient reason to justify state intervention, now a burgeoning literature cites 'state failure' as a complete defence of market provision.

I begin my account of the citizenship view of the welfare state by analysing the recrudescent laissez-faire doctrines of the market liberals or new right, for a number of reasons. Firstly, the type of social policies writers such as Titmuss and Marshall most disapproved of were those which incorporated market principles. Secondly, social policies which continued in the post-war period to reflect market principles were much more common than may be supposed. The Beveridge report, for instance, stated that:

> The state should offer security for service and contribution. The state in organizing security should not stifle incentive, opportunity, responsibility; in establishing a national minimum, it should leave room and encouragement for voluntary action by each individual to provide more than the minimum for himself and his family.[2]

Such principles found their way into the fabric of the welfare state. Security for contribution has led, as Taylor-Gooby points out, to a distinction between a favoured group able to 'insure' itself against the risks of social life through its regular participation in employment, and a stigmatized group of the idle and feckless 'undeserving poor' which depends on a complex structure of means-tested benefits.[3] The level of benefits has also always reflected a concern that no incentive be provided to encourage people to remain dependent rather than become self-supporting in the labour market. A similar worry worked its way into the basis of entitlement for unemployment benefit; to be eligible, one must be available for work.

Thirdly, the writings of Titmuss and others betray a preoccupation with the market liberal version of acceptable social policy. It is beyond doubt that they regarded the market liberals as their major intellectual and political enemies. Finally, in the context of contemporary politics in the West, the new right constitutes the major threat to those institutions of the welfare state that most bear the imprint of the social democratic or democratic socialist vision. If the views of the citizenship school offer a plausible account of the principal contours of a just society, then it is against the challenge of the new right even more than against the marxist left that their claims must be made good.

The new right have benefited from the crumbling of the conditions that succoured social democracy. An era of low economic growth coincided with rapid increases in public spending, a high proportion of which was devoted to the social services. Public expenditure rose both in absolute terms and, perhaps more importantly, as a percentage of national income.[4] The average tax burden increased and new groups hitherto with no taxable income found themselves paying taxes. It was against this background that commentators claimed to detect a welfare backlash. On the face of it, the resurgence of the laissez-faire right was in tune with populist sentiment.

The critique offered by the new right of the social democratic welfare state is not merely directed at the implausibility of Keynesian macro-economic policy, nor at its unresponsiveness to public opinion; it digs much deeper. Social democracy in general, and citizenship theory in particular, stand accused of having misunderstood the nature of liberty and the set of individual rights necessary to protect it. Social rights have been created, even though morally they cannot exist. And theories of social justice have been propounded that rest on fundamentally flawed conceptions of responsibility and presume a capacity, which cannot exist in a complex and free society, to forge consensus on substantive moral ends to be pursued politically. A welfare state is necessarily paternalistic, fails to respect individuals as thinking and choosing agents, and rests upon the use of illegitimate coercion whereby resources are stolen from those entitled to keep them and persons are prevented from realizing their own values in their own way. Quite independently of its practical failings, the welfare state is morally bankrupt.

The rest of this chapter outlines the principal features of the market liberalism of the new right. It would be a mistake, however, to attribute too much homogeneity of opinion to the market liberals. There is deep disagreement within the new right about such fundamental questions, for example, as the proper role of the state in society. There are those who accept that the state may have some part to play in providing welfare services to alleviate destitution as an act of charity;[5] others who assert that the very existence of the state can never be reconciled with respect for individual rights.[6] Some are 'libertarian' only so far as defending the operation of the free market economy is concerned, and are happy to see a strong state actively engaged in preserving and enhancing both social order and the integrity of traditional cultural values.[7] By contrast, others are thoroughgoing libertarians; self-proclaimed defenders of both capitalism and the permissive society.[8] The differences in the structure of argument employed to defend market liberal conclusions are equally profound. At one extreme there is the strict deontological theory of one such as Nozick, who deduces conclusions about the legitimate scope of public power from claims about the natural rights of individuals, and eschews any attempt to incorporate consequentialist reasons in his justification of the minimal state.[9] At the other extreme is Hayek, who draws upon the rational scepticism of Hume to reason in a broadly consequentialist manner.[10] Different yet again are those who employ the techniques of neoclassical welfare economics, which stand within a recognizably utilitarian tradition, to argue for a society based on market echanges.[11]

My analysis reflects these schisms within the new right. I begin with an account of the Hayekian approach to state welfare, proceed to discuss the natural rights approach, and follow with an exposition of the neoclassical foundation of market liberalism. The chapter ends with an examination of various theories of 'state failure'.

Hayek believes that the core weakness of collectivists, socialists and welfare statists is their failure to recognize that there are two entirely different types of social organization which cannot be combined at will. The first of these is the spontaneous order or 'cosmos'; the second, the organization or 'taxis'. A cosmos is a self-generating social order based on abstract, purpose-independent rules. A taxis is not self-generating, it depends on purpose-dependent commands which direct particular outcomes:

> That the two kinds of order regularly coexist in every society of any degree of complexity does not mean . . . that we can combine them in any manner we like . . . It is impossible, not only to replace the spontaneous order by organization and at the same time to utilize as much of the dispersed knowledge of all its members as possible, but also to improve or correct this order by interfering in it by direct commands.[12]

Ultimately, this error can be traced back to a misunderstanding of the nature and limits of reason when applied to the social world. Guilty of the sin of 'constructivist rationalism', opponents of the market order slide from the accurate perception that social institutions are a product of human action to the mistaken assumption that they are therefore the consequence of conscious and purposeful human design. The mistake is to believe that a rational social order is one that is designed to serve particular purposes and that rational social action is based on known facts combined with logical deduction.

The tragedy of social life is that this rationalism, which Hayek believes is rooted in Cartesian doubt, has been insufficiently uprooted by the evolutionary rationalism of the eighteenth century associated with Hume. Social institutions can serve human purposes even though they were not designed to do so. General, abstract rules transmitted by tradition and custom coordinate individual actions. In doing so, use is made of particular bits of knowledge dispersed throughout society – knowledge which could never be centralized and put to productive use within a hierarchically structured command economy.

It follows from this that only decentralized market-oriented societies can be productive and that these best serve the purposes of a representative individual. A 'made order' or taxis necessarily must be simple because the limits of its potential complexity are defined by the ability of the directing mind to process relevant information to achieve the social order's particular goals. By contrast, the cosmos may be more complex than any mind can master. Our knowledge of it is restricted to the general rules which the elements of the order follow, and we cannot know all the elements themselves nor the particular circumstances facing them. At best, we can know enough to influence the general character of the order, not its detail. Over much of the order no effective control is possible. Attempts at control merely impede the forces that produce a spontaneous order.

> Any desire we may have concerning the particular position of individual elements, or the relation between particular individuals or groups, could not be satisfied without upsetting the overall order.[13]

This claim, if true, clearly tells against any social theory which aims to guarantee specific outcomes to particular individuals, or any theory which sees justice as ensuring a definite relation between different people's circumstances. All theories which manifest an impulse to bring the social and economic forces shaping man's destiny under conscious collective control, are victims of the anthropomorphic tendencies of constructivist rationalism. They have failed to realize that the ethics of the tribe have no place in the Great Society of the cosmos.

It turns out that the cosmos, the spontaneous order of the market place, is a universe of freedom. The rules which have evolved to sustain the cosmos also define liberty. As abstract end-independent general prohibitions applying equally to all, the rules command no specific action. They are not coercive because an individual is free to choose from amongst the range of alternatives open to him. He is not compelled to act in any particular way. Coercion requires a threat to inflict harm and an intention to bring about a certain course of action. 'Coercion occurs when one man's actions are made to serve another man's will, not for his own but for the other's purpose.'[14] Liberty is simply the absence of coercion. One great advantage of the market place readily follows this analysis. The market maximizes the opportunity to escape private coercion. If an employer seeks to coerce an employee, the opportunity always exists to walk out and go and work elsewhere.

Liberty is a good in part because it recognizes that individuals are thinking and valuing beings with purposes of their own. In a free society individuals can 'use their knowledge for their purposes, restrained only by rules of just conduct of universal application.'[15] Even though there is no guarantee that a person will be given any particular opportunities, he is left free to make what he will of the circumstances in which he finds himself. In such a world, conditions are provided which maximize the chances of a randomly selected individual satisfying his aims.

At this point there is a genuine meeting of minds between Hayek and others of his market liberal colleagues. Compare, for example, the following comments of Friedman and Hayek:

The heart of the liberal philosophy is a belief in the dignity of the individual, in his freedom to make the most of his capacities and opportunities according to his own lights, subject only to the proviso that he does not interfere with the freedom of other individuals to do the same.[16]

The recognition that each person has his own scale of values which we ought to respect, even if we do not approve of it, is part of the conception of the value of the individual personality. . . . believing in freedom means that we do not regard ourselves as the ultimate judges of another person's values, that we do not feel entitled to prevent him from pursuing ends which we disapprove of so long as he does not infringe the equally protected sphere of others.[17]

Hayek's conception of freedom is somewhat idiosyncratic in that it implies that the general rules defining the market order do not themselves constitute constraints on freedom. It is quite typical, however, in implying that welfare state policies are incompatible with freedom and the rule of law. Most market liberals would accept the following claim, even if it is cast in characteristically Hayekian language:

A government which cannot use coercion except in the enforcement of general rules has no power to achieve particular aims . . . [it] cannot determine the material position of particular people . . . If the government is to determine how particular people ought to be situated, it must be in a position to determine also the direction of individual efforts . . . it requires that people be told what to do and what ends to serve. . . . the decisions as to what the different individuals must be made to do cannot be derived from general rules but must be made in the light of the particular aims and knowledge of the planning authority.[18]

Social policy is necessarily coercive.

This analysis of liberty rules out common arguments which purport to show that state intervention through social policy can be justified in the name of freedom. If freedom is seen as a function of the range of choices facing an individual, then redistribution of income or resources may indeed restrict the freedom of the taxpayer, but only at the same time as it expands the freedom of welfare recipients.[19] What one group loses, the other gains. The argument then shifts to a defence of the justice of different distributions of freedom, although this strategy is excluded if Hayek is right, since the presence or absence of coercion is not related to the variety of potential choice confronting an individual. 'Whether or not I am my own master and can follow my own choice and whether the possibilities from which I must choose are many or few are two entirely different questions.'[20] The claim that welfare policies may contribute to freedom understood as self-development is also excluded. Pithily, Hayek asserts simply that the issue whether a person's choice amongst alternatives is intelligent is quite a different problem from the question of whether others will impose their will upon him.

The traditional socialist claim that individual freedom can be restricted by impersonal economic and social forces, such as those created by the self-generating spontaneous order, fares just as badly. Hayek's response is that coercion exists only where an agent acts with the intention of forcing another to act in line with the plans of the coercer and not in accordance with his own purposes. Coercion, in other words, implies intention and responsibility. But responsibility can be ascribed only for acts whose consequences someone could be expected to foresee; there is no responsibility for the results of actions one neither intended nor foresaw. And since impersonal economic and social forces are inevitably the result of a concatenation of individual acts, the upshot of which no individual could be expected to foresee and certainly did not intend, it follows that no responsibility can be ascribed for their effects. Without responsibility there can be no coercion; without coercion, no loss of freedom. Hayek, like many other market liberals, assimilates the laws of the market place to the laws of nature. One can no more claim that lack of resources reduces one's freedom, than claim that the law of gravity renders one unfree to fly. To assert otherwise is simple nonsense.

At the centre of this account stands a particular notion of responsibility which plays a vital role in Hayek's argument that social justice is a mirage. If he is right, yet another foundation stone of the moral defence of the welfare state will have been removed.

Justice, Responsibility and Freedom

Responsibility can be assigned only for those consequences of individual action which it is in the power of a person to foresee and determine. 'Responsibility to be effective must be individual responsibility'.[21] One is responsible for one's own acts, not the acts of others. Only by being limited in this way can the idea of responsibility fulfil its social function of influencing conduct.

Justice is a moral concept. To describe a state of affairs as just or unjust is to say that someone is responsible for bringing it about. It follows that where there is no responsibility there is no injustice. The consequences of market interactions for the material circumstances of particular people are not intended by the market participants, nor under their individual control. Since no one can be held responsible for such consequences, the resulting market position cannot be assessed as either just or unjust. It is simply a brute fact without moral relevance.

This argument has powerful implications. Much of what critics of market economies object to are precisely the unintended consequences of market exchanges. As tastes or relative costs change, consumption patterns shift and labour is shed. No one intends to create unemployment or drive down wage rates when making purchases in the market place. People are just going about their business, acting rationally in terms of their self-interest and not deliberately interfering with anyone else. Even recognizing that they were part of a mass phenomenon that was putting blacksmiths, for example, out of work, there is nothing that they could do as individuals. Continuing to drive the trap will not work. Probably one will merely wind up with a lame horse. The unemployment of blacksmiths is bad luck for them, but it is part of the price to be paid for the progress of society. Just as it is nonsensical to say that the unemployed blacksmith is unfree to work, so it is meaningless to say he has been treated unjustly by society.

Distributions of wealth, income, employment and security cannot be assessed from the point of view of justice. Again, Hayek expresses the conventional wisdom of the new right. In the face of the clear evidence of the randomness of market distributions, the traditional liberal claim that one's market position reflected one's productivity, contribution or desert has been jettisoned. The new right happily embraces the conclusion that there is no moral basis capable of justifying the distribution of market outcomes. At most it can be said that a particular distribution has emerged without any individual acts of injustice. In that event one can at least say that the position each person finds himself in is not unjust.

Hayek does, however, make one interesting concession. He accepts that if the allocation of the benefits and burdens of market exchanges were the result of design, then the pattern of inequality which characterizes market societies would be unjust. Justice would require much greater equality of material condition. In an economy structured as a taxis, distribution would be subject to control. The question is then whether 'the desire to make something capable of being just is . . . a valid argument for our making it subject to human control.'[22] Predictably, Hayek argues that it is not. Not only would such a society be unproductive and unprogressive, but it could be reached and sustained only by interfering constantly with individual rights and destroying liberty. The final destination of the road to serfdom is a totalitarian nightmare.

As is becoming clear in ever increasing fields of welfare policy, an authority instructed to achieve particular results for the individuals must be given essentially arbitrary powers to make the individuals do what seems necessary to achieve the required result. Full equality for most cannot but mean the equal submission of the great masses under the command of some elite who manages their affairs. While an equality of right under a limited government is a possible and an essential condition of individual freedom, a claim for equality of material position can be met only by a government with totalitarian powers.[23]

To live in a free society is to live under a limited government subject only to general and abstract rules which prohibit interference with the person and property of others. In the Great Society, as Hayek calls his ideal world, the moral obligation to treat all alike has necessarily become attenuated. Morally and practicably, it is impossible to enforce a duty to insure the well-being of our fellows. The only enforceable obligation we have to all human beings, or even to all members of our society, is the duty to avoid harming them by violating their rights to non-interference. Richer moral claims may exist, but these must be voluntarily incurred or arise out of special relationships.

Hayek's vision of the good society is of a market order which is progressive, productive and free. Society-wide relations are primarily economic. But the free market efficiently reconciles the diverse non-economic ends of persons in a manner consistent with freedom, and through a process that benefits all. Exchange relations serve the different and independent purposes of each party to a transaction without requiring that they agree on the values that motivate them to enter it. I do not even need to know why someone wants to trade with me, let alone agree with his reasons for doing so. All that we need to agree on are the terms of our bargain. Consensus on substantive ends is difficult, if not impossible, to attain; agreement on the rules to govern free exchange are much easier to come by. It is precisely this ability to agree on the instrumental rules governing relationships in the face of ineradicable controversy over ultimate ends that underpins a peaceable order and makes freedom possible. Individuals, using knowledge of their circumstances for their own purposes, serve the ends of others without knowing what those ends are. No other form of integration is compatible with peace and freedom, but the price we pay is the lack of a common ordering of ends and the existence of willed social solidarity. On this, as so much else, Friedman agrees with Hayek:

The wider the range of activities covered by the market, the fewer are the issues on which explicitly political decisions are required and hence on which it is necessary to achieve agreement. In turn, the fewer the issues on which agreement is necessary, the greater is the likelihood of getting agreement while maintaining a free society.[24]

The structure of Hayek's moral theory is difficult to specify. Most of the time he seems to argue within a broadly consequentialist framework. The superiority of the cosmos seems to lie in its being the most productive and progressive society available to man. In it, the randomly selected individual has the greatest chance of fulfilling his aims, whatever they might be. Freedom seems to play an instrumental role, valued because of the contribution it makes to progress, and not as something intrinsically valuable. On the other hand, Hayek is no straightforward aggregative utilitarian justifying a market order as a maximizer of social welfare. Indeed, he goes to great lengths to repudiate the utilitarianism of Bentham, and his economics rest on philosophical foundations quite different from those of neoclassical economics, the intellectual descendent of Benthamism. Furthermore, Hayek is not consistent in treating freedom as an instrumental value. He frequently writes as if freedom is intrinsically valuable. What may be the case is that, given his views on the nature of possible social orders, Hayek does not recognize that there ever could be circumstances in which the value of freedom, intrinsically conceived, could ever conflict with the values to which freedom contributes instrumentally. Finally, the role of tradition and evolution in his thought is not always clear. Hayek often writes as if the rules of the cosmos are superior to the rules of a taxis just because they evolved piecemeal through the common law and allegedly withstood some kind of natural selection process. The difficulty this creates, of course, is that the very same selection process seems to have thrown up the centralized and bureaucratic forms of government he dislikes so much.

The Natural Rights Tradition

In contrast to the thought of Hayek with its evolutionary and Humean tenor stands a version of market liberalism rooted more in the natural rights tradition of the seventeenth century. This approach reaches similar conclusions to those of Hayek concerning the unacceptably coercive character of a welfare state and its tendency to violate individual rights. But if the substantive conclusions are similar, the process of reasoning is radically different. For Hayek, the rules defining property rights have evolved through historical processes and at some level owe their superiority to these processes and the beneficial consequences that follow from them. The natural rights tradition, on the other hand, reasons deductively from abstract propositions about the nature of man and the rights he possesses as a presocial being, and denies that there is any essential advantage to be gained from the beneficial consequences of a social order that respects rights. Whereas Hayekian thought is often cast in teleological terms, the thought of the natural rights school is strictly deontological.

Human beings have rights.[25] They possess these rights simply by virtue of being human. The rights of humans include the right not to have one's person interfered with and the right to decide how to use and dispose of all the property one has legitimately acquired. This means that no part of the fruits of one's labour can be taken away without one's consent. To do so is a form of theft.

Most commonly, this set of human rights is defended as an implication of a particular understanding of what it is to be a person. The core idea is that a person is an agent capable of acting deliberately in the world to achieve his purposes. A person has goals and therefore reasons for acting to achieve results which are of value to him. Human dignity resides in the willing, choosing, deliberating nature of man.

Each individual has an interest in preventing others interfering with him as he goes about his business in the world. Prudence alone could be sufficient to lead someone to realize that he cannot expect not to be interfered with himself unless he is prepared not to interfere with others. Alternatively, there may be a direct recognition that morality requires universal rules. Like cases are to be treated alike. One *ought* to treat others as one would wish to be treated. Finally, there may be a straightforward awareness of the moral importance of the generic traits shared by all human beings which the structure of rights must respect.

Saying that human beings act deliberately and have plans and goals of value to them suggests that the intrinsic worth of a person lies in his capacity to act freely. The function of morality is to protect that worth. There are two points here. The first is that it is *individuals* that are of value. The second, that what is to be protected is *freedom*. Taken jointly, these entail that morality is rights based and that the rights of individuals define and guarantee freedom. Property rights are essential because it is only through appropriating and controlling portions of the external world that an individual can act. A right of original acquisition is necessary, as are rights of use and disposition. In thoroughgoing libertarianism rights are essentially property rights. The relationship is almost definitional. Even rights to preserve the integrity of one's person can be seen as an aspect of self-ownership.

Rights are absolute. They define a social space within which each man is sovereign. Interfering with that space for the sake of a greater good is to treat a person as if he were but a tool to be put to the use of others. He is degraded; he becomes merely a means to the realization of the purposes of someone else. He is no longer accorded the respect due to him as a member of Kant's kingdom-of-ends; as an end-in-himself. Taking an individual's property without his consent in order to boost the welfare of someone else is not qualitatively different from forcing him to donate a kidney to save another's life. Both display essentially the same disrespect; taxation is theft. According to Nozick, it is also on a par with forced labour.

Acting on their rights and therefore not infringing the rights of others, individuals can choose how they will live and with whom they will associate. Property rights lead inevitably to a market society. Apart from the obligations imposed by the restraints of fundamental rights, all other obligations are voluntarily incurred through a process of contracting. The free society is one in which involuntary obligations have been reduced to a minimum. An entitlement theory of justice dovetails neatly with this analysis. An individual is entitled to keep full control of whatever property he has, provided only that his possession of it came about without injustice in acquisition or transfer. As in Hayek's theory, there is no suggestion that a person deserves his property as a reward for effort or merit, nor that the distribution of property satisfies any morally sanctioned pattern. What emerges is just, provided that no rights were violated in the process.

A welfare state is morally obnoxious because it almost certainly treats people as means by coercively extracting resources from them in the name of social welfare or 'welfare rights'. To the extent that an argument for the welfare state appeals to utilitarian premises, it neglects the moral importance of those rights which recognize the distinctness and separateness of persons. Appeals to 'welfare rights' misconstrue the notion of a right. The argument can take a variety of forms. At one level it is said that to claim a welfare right is to make a logical error, for conceptually a right necessarily refers to freedom and therefore to nonintervention, not to recipience. Moreover, asserting a right to welfare is incoherent because the very notion of a right entails the existence of a correlative duty, and in the case of a welfare right it is impossible to define those who bear the duty. Claiming a 'right' to welfare may also be a misuse of language. It is alleged that an examination of proper usage indicates that rights-talk properly refers to rights to noninterference and that this is the correct meaning of the notion of rights within our philosophical and legal tradition. Other arguments are substantive. Human rights have to do with freedom because morally speaking freedom is simply the overriding value, and it is dangerously reductive to claim a right to something of much lower moral significance such as welfare. This is particularly so if it is impossible as a practical matter universally to satisfy the claims to welfare, for then we may be tempted to excuse the violations of real human rights which can in fact be universally guaranteed.[26]

Neoclassical Economics

The third major strand of market liberalism is rooted in neoclassical economics.[27] Although this approach makes use of the concepts of freedom and property rights, it is at heart utilitarian. The claim of a free market to greatness resides in its ability to maximize aggregate social welfare. As a form of utilitarianism, it is consequentialist in character: it is not a species of deontology like the natural rights approach. It is worth stressing, however, that in the minds of many market liberals the fundamental rights argument and the utilitarian arguments are complementary. Given certain assumptions about the successful functioning of markets, any potential tension between them is not realized. Productivity and efficiency are forthcoming without compromising individual rights.

In its full-blown glory the neoclassical defence of the market rests upon a number of key assumptions. Individuals are deemed to be the best judges of their own welfare and act so as to maximize it. Markets are assumed to be perfectly competitive so that no firm or individual can exercise power over prices or costs. It is costless to engage in transactions and knowledge is perfect. Finally, there are no externalities – no social costs or benefits arise from a transaction; all costs and benefits are reflected in prices and are therefore paid for.

If these assumptions hold, it can be demonstrated that a series of exchanges between individuals will maximize social welfare. Individuals will trade with each other only when it is mutually beneficial to do so. By definition, individuals will be better off after trading than before. Since individuals are maximizers, transactions are costless and knowledge is perfect, all bargains struck will be mutually advantageous. If I know that you have wheat that you will sell at the market price of £10 per ton and I value wheat at £11 per ton, I will seek you out and contract to buy it from you. This process will continue until there are no more deals to be made. At that point social welfare is maximized and no individual can be made better off without at the same time someone else being made worse off.

Of course, these assumptions do not hold in the real world and standard defences of public intervention rely upon that fact. Externalities exist, and so some say that lump-sum taxes and subsidies should be used to internalize social costs and benefits. Markets are not perfect so producer power over the market needs to be regulated. Knowledge is not perfect so consumers need to be protected from producers prepared to exploit their ignorance, at least where the potential harm to the consumer is serious.

Market liberals have a battery of responses to this. First, the unreality of assumptions is irrelevant because the essential claim is that the free market operates *as if* the assumptions were true.[28] We are not offered an explanation of the functioning of the market to which the truth of the assumptions would be critical, but a description of the results the value of which lies in its predictive power. Thus, even though knowledge isn't perfect and so forth, the market still by and large succeeds in allocating resources to uses which makes the most efficient contribution to social welfare. Secondly, even where market failure genuinely exists, it is quite wrong to assume that state intervention is the most effective antidote. Public intervention carries with it its own inefficiencies. The social welfare implications of relying upon a less than perfect market need to be compared to the implications of relying on an imperfect market 'corrected' by an imperfect state. There is no *a priori* reason to suppose one to be better than the other, but market liberals have in recent years developed theories which cast doubt on the likelihood of the state ever successfully regulating the market. Finally, many market liberals accept that the cost of entering a transaction may be so high that potentially beneficial transactions do not occur. Aggregate welfare will be lower than it need be. This, it is suggested, is the major source of market failure in a complex society. According to the disciples of law and economies, the appropriate solution is to develop laws that mimic the outcomes the market would have achieved were it not for transaction costs. This is done by allocating, through the law, assets to those who value them most and allowing private negotiations to proceed from there. No more state intervention is required than that provided by common law courts developing rules to decide the cases that come before them. Any more intervention is bound to be inefficient.

Given all of this, it is hardly surprising that market liberals have a presumption in favour of market delivery of services. This is true not only for the production and distribution of television sets and bubble gum, but also for those services we think of as satisfying fundamental needs. If needs are backed by purchasing power, the market provides an economically rational and morally acceptable way of satisfying them. Efficiency and freedom are reconciled.

In principle there is no limit to the range of goods a market can supply, with the exception of pure public goods. Housing, medical care, insurance against economic insecurity can all be bought within a free market. Indeed, markets can satisfy a demand for body organs and babies. And why not? If someone wants to buy a kidney or pay a woman to bear a child, on what grounds can we complain? Provided the contract is entered into without duress, both parties are better off for it. To prohibit the agreement not only reduces aggregate social welfare, it is a paternalistic imposition showing lack of respect for both parties as freewilling and autonomous beings.

Market Versus State Welfare Provision

Market delivery of welfare services displays clear advantages over state provision. First and foremost, it is simply that consumers are offered a richer degree of choice than nonmarket services provide. Consumers can choose a service closely tailored to the specificity of a given need. They can put together a package of services covering the range of their needs which correspond to their preferences, not those of a bureaucracy or legislature. By being free to choose, the consumer escapes the forced consumption of a particular type, quantity and quality of a standardized service.

Utilitarian advantages follow from market provision. The state often supplies a service free at the point of consumption. Standard neoclassical economics readily demonstrates that this is inefficient because as the price falls, demand for a service increases and consumers collectively are led to use more of the service than they would have been willing to pay for. This result can be avoided only by requiring consumers to pay for privately enjoyed benefits. Attempts to constrain the supply of a service by the use of rationing techniques apart from price, like queuing for elective (non-essential) surgery or a lottery for body organs, compound the inefficiency by failing to distribute goods to those who value them most, as measured by their willingness to pay. Furthermore, public organizations which operate outside market discipline tend to supply any given level of service less efficiently than a private organization subject to it. In a market setting, management is pressured into acting efficiently by the firm's owners, who have a financial interest in efficiency, and by the fear of takeovers and bankruptcy. A public bureaucracy lacks such effective control.

Secondly, the opportunity freely to make provision for the satisfaction of one's needs encourages the development of individual responsibility and self-reliance. Nothing is more demoralizing than depriving the individual of the right and duty to make provision for himself of those things that are most fundamental to his life. It is a paternalistic slight to express through state policy the perception that although individuals may be competent to buy candy floss they cannot be trusted to educate their children or provide their own unemployment and medical insurance.

The market, on the other hand, recognizes the sovereignty of the individual and minimizes, where state intervention is inevitable, objectionable forms of paternalism.

Most defenders of market liberalism recognize that not all needs are backed by purchasing power. At least sometimes humanity justifies the nonmarket provision of resources to satisfy those needs. But this alone is insufficient to legitimate state intervention. Many needs can and ought to be met through nongovernmental agencies.

In the first place, families owe duties to each other. Aid ought often to be forthcoming through the family. Too many elderly parents who should be cared for at home languish in extended-care wards. Siblings should provide each other with assistance at times of economic distress. Fobbing needy family members off on to public provision is not just an imposition on the community at large, it is a breach of a duty. By making that provision so readily available, the welfare state supplies an incentive for people to shirk their responsibilities.

In addition to the obligations within families, most market liberals accept the existence of an unenforceable obligation to give alms. The duty to act charitably is thought of as an imperfect obligation, that is, one that is owed to no specific individual and one that may be fulfilled on occasions of our choosing. Even if there is no such obligation, it is recognized that some people are altruists. Altruism and imperfect obligation are the basis of charity. To as great a degree as possible private charity should be encouraged to pick up cases of unmet need. A society in which charitable sentiments flourish is attractive, since the moral fabric of the community is enriched and strengthened. Moral approval of the generous and censure of the parsimonious encourages the development of caring and virtuous people. Gifts to the needy elicit appropriate responses of gratitude, and relationships expressing concern and gratitude cement the moral community. But these relationships cannot be enforced; their cultivation is rooted in their voluntarism and spontaneity. Private charity is a delicate plant that needs careful nourishing. Its growth and vitality quickly suffer in a welfare state. Contributions of time, effort and money are less forthcoming if people believe that the government is, or ought to be, dealing with a problem.[29] People are also less willing to give generously if they believe that their disposable income is reduced by an unreasonable or immoral tax burden. To the extent that state provision of welfare goods is inevitable, services should be organized to minimize any deleterious consequences for private charity.

As a practical matter, it has to be accepted that neither family or private charity is likely to catch all cases of unmet need. The need to specify the extent and terms of state intervention is inescapable. One response is simply to say that the implication of private property rights is that there can be no role for the state unless it can be arranged on terms compatible with individual consent. Equally, it may be said, where need results from a failure to insure, there is no reason to step in. Individuals are the best judges of their interests, so if someone does not take out insurance, that merely exhibits a preference to enjoy greater income now while risking low or no income later, rather than lower income now in return for higher income later if the risk insured against materializes. It is inconsistent to argue that an individual is the best judge of his own welfare in advance, and then to interfere with the consequences of his choices afterwards.[30]

In the event however, most market liberals are prepared to sacrifice doctrinal consistency and accept that humanitarianism requires the state to step in. In summary, conventional wisdom holds that a state-funded social safety net is permissible provided it goes no further than meeting cases of absolute or subsistence need and then only on terms compatible with the structure of market incentives.[31] Stripped to its essentials, this means that the terms upon which services are provided must be less attractive than the terms available to those satisfying their needs independently in the market. The principle of lesser eligibility implies that the level of benefits must be lower than those one can earn by selling one's labour or, where it is not possible to adjust the level in this way, as, for example, with medical care to the indigent, strict tests must be used to determine eligibility. If benefits are too generous or too easily available, an incentive is created for individuals to engineer themselves into, and remain in, a condition of dependency. Why work if welfare pays more?

It is worth noting one exception to this principle. There are cases where the needy person is not capable of becoming self-supporting in the market. The generosity of aid could not affect his future behaviour. It may seem therefore that there is no reason to confine the level of benefits to that which market incentives dictate. While this may be true of a limited class of persons, such as the victims of genetic defects where the existence of the need is not the result of alterable human behaviour, it is not generally true. Where the level of benefits can affect the willingness of others to participate in risky activities, market incentives must be respected. If they are not, there will be greater participation in risky activity than is socially optimal. Free medical care will encourage people to drive faster than they would if they had to insure against the medical costs of their accidents. Couples with a predisposition to produce genetically damaged offspring are also likely to overproduce handicapped children if they do not have to bear the cost or insure privately against the risk. The exception is evidently a narrow one.

The constraints of the market impose a second condition on the provision of aid by the state. A monopoly of supply may not be claimed. State services should be organized so as to minimize the barriers inhibiting the entry into the market of other individuals or groups prepared to offer need-satisfying resources.

Furthermore, market imperatives influence the mode of provision. Social policy should depart from market principles to the minimum degree possible. Cash transfers are preferred to aid in kind, thus preserving, to the greatest degree possible, the freedom and independence of the indigent. Leaving it to recipients to decide how to spend their money eliminates any paternalism that could inhere in the relation between the poor and the dispensing authority.

In addition to state provision of resources to alleviate abject need, most adherents of the new right accept that public goods need to be publicly provided or they will not be provided at all. Public goods, as defined by Samuelson, are those for which consumption is both non-rival and non-excludable.[32] This means that the consumption of the goods by one person does not reduce the quantity of the goods available for consumption by others, and that it is not possible to prevent a person consuming the goods if they have been provided. The implication of these conditions is that a self-interested utility maximizer has an incentive to consume the goods but not to pay for them. What is true for one is equally true for all. As a result, the goods will not be produced since everyone will try to take a free ride, and in any case would seek to avoid being taken for a fool as each person would be if he contributed to the cost of goods that no one else would pay for. Public goods therefore must be provided and paid for publicly if they are to be provided at all. Typically, there is no objection to using taxation and the public sector for this, since producing public goods is in the interest of every individual in society (though some market liberals argue that if the goods cannot be produced without individual consent they cannot be produced at all, for to do so is to violate rights, and others dispute the claim that there are *any* goods which are not in principle producible through the market). Standard cases of public goods include law and order and defence, and are not the type of services particularly associated with the welfare state. However, there are some services of the welfare state with a mixed character, partly private and partly public, education is a good example. For such services, the use of vouchers is suggested. The idea is a simple one. Parents would be supplied with vouchers to purchase education from any one of a number of approved suppliers. The combination of the value of the voucher, the licensing of educational institutions to ensure quality, the teaching of a core curriculum and the ability of parents to remove their children from unsatisfactory schools and redeem their vouchers elsewhere, would be sufficient to ensure that the public goods component of education developed and that schools, subjected to market discipline, were efficiently run.

The New Right's Critique of the State

In summary, then, it is apparent that market liberals offer a vigorous and robust defence of the market both as an expression of freedom and as a promoter of efficiency. Coupled with this is a critique of the state, much of which is implicit in what has gone before. The state is inefficient, paternalistic and necessarily relies on coercive techniques to achieve its purposes. It is, moreover, a much cruder instrument for aggregating preferences than the market. The political system necessarily simplifies choice by reducing it to the selection of one of two possibilities, unlike the market which offers multiple choices. And, commonly, democratic decision-making yields policies which a majority opposes, at least where individuals are forced to select between a very limited number of platforms, each containing a number of different planks. The analysis becomes more explicitly political and therefore more of a direct attack upon the presuppositions of social democracy when the new right's theories of pressure group and bureaucratic activity are combined with the interpretation of the nature of electoral competition in a liberal democracy.[33]

The new right's attack on the state goes straight for the jugular. At the heart of all social democratic theories of the state lies the assumption that government is a neutral instrument, capable of being harnessed to promote the public interest. As I have indicated earlier in this chapter, market liberals are sceptical of the claim that there is public interest in anything beyond an interest in the rules underlying a market system. A richer notion of the public interest or, worse still, a conception of the common good, is merely camouflage disguising the imposition of the values of some people on others. But even granted the possibility of a common good, the new right questions whether the state could ever realize it. Bureaucracy, pressure groups and the logic of liberal democracy militate against it.

The first problem lies within the bureaucracy. Bureaucrats are not viewed as disinterested servants of the public interest but as a partisan group intent on pursuing their own interests, which by no means coincide with the interests of their clients. This is a particular danger with welfare professionals having the opportunity to define the 'needs' of those they are supposed to serve. Niskanen, for example, suggests more generally that bureaucrats' behaviour can be explained *as if* they sought to maximise the size of their department's budget.[34] The real motivation may range over power, patronage, reputation, salary or ease of managing the department, but all are treated as a function of budget size. The claim is that political control over the bureaucracy is so ineffective, given the absence of market discipline and the advantages of conferring visible benefits on particular groups when the cost of doing so is spread so widely as to be imperceptible, that the bureaucracy runs free and successfully preempts resources that could be better used in other ways.

Reinforcing this argument, and trading on the same insight, is the belief that pressure groups colonize the state and divert resources away from socially beneficial uses to their own selfish ends. The argument is the same as that which explains bureaucratic behaviour. Pressure groups are well organized and can lobby politicians and bureaucrats to use their power to dispense benefits to them. These benefits tend to be popular, at least with the members of the pressure groups, and their cost is defrayed across the community as a whole. When spread thinly, the cost of any particular benefit is low. The net cost of organizing to resist the dispensation is relatively much greater than the net cost of organizing to procure it, so the political system becomes skewed disproportionately towards interests seeking the expenditure of public funds and against interests seeking to restrain it. The result is a public sector larger than is optimal on efficiency grounds as well as confiscatory taxation.

Electoral politics merely compounds the difficulties. Politicians are assumed to be interested in winning re-election. According to Brittan, in an argument that was popular in the mid to late 1970s, electorates vote as if unhampered by a budget constraint.[35] The reason has already been discussed. To win an election, politicians are forced by the logic of electoral competition to bribe their voters by offering benefits to different groups as the price of their votes. It is in the interests of a voter to vote for the party offering him the best package of policies, since he knows that the cost of those proposals will be spread over all taxpayers who do not share the characteristics of his group. In other words, he does not pay the full price of the benefit he receives. This of course is a generalized phenomenon, and is true for all electors. Even if a particular taxpayer realizes that he is going to be paying for the benefits enjoyed by others but not himself, it is still in his interest to vote for the party offering him the best package of benefits since that is the most likely way to maximize his net position.

Taken together, these processes fuel the growth of public expenditure well beyond that compatible with respect for property rights or that justified by the need to provide pure public goods. The size and composition of public spending is a function of the unprincipled exercise of collective power and electoral bribery. It is an absurdity to claim that state intervention is designed to achieve social justice despite the good intentions of some innocent idealists, or that it could do so.

These processes have further undesirable ramifications which expose social democracy as an emperor bereft of clothes. First, the pressure group-induced interferences in the market destroy the essential conditions for its efficient operation by building institutional rigidities which lead eventually to unemployment, as the price of labour is prevented from falling to a market clearing price. Secondly, by increasing public spending and by politicizing issues of distribution, budget deficits are created and politicians must choose how to finance them. There are only limited choices, each with unpalatable results. Taxes can be increased, but that is electorally unpopular and therefore frequently avoided. Money can be borrowed, but that drives up interest rates in a vicious circle and crowds out investment, thereby reducing economic growth. Finally, politicans can resort to the printing press, but eventually all that does is stimulate inflation. Social democratic politics finds itself in a cleft stick.

It is clear from all that has gone before that the new right offers a systematic and powerful critique of the moral, political and economic presuppositions of collectivists and interventionists in general, and social democrats in particular. If the new right is correct, the pursuit of social justice is indeed a mirage. Continuing the pursuit is costly, both in moral and in economic terms. A careful analysis shows, it seems, that the aspiration to 'social justice' is really fuelled by envy and that the effort to glorify envy in the name of justice is irrational as it erodes the necessary foundations for a successful economy. The destruction of social democracy as a viable political creed is therefore not just accidental; it has fallen apart under the weight of its own contradictions.

The claims of the new right are nothing if not bold. Their radicalism is so striking that the arguments of the social democrats appear defensive and conservative. In the next chapter I begin my analysis of some of the more prominent members of the old left in Britain. My purpose will be to determine whether there is good reason for them to be on the defensive and whether in their moral armoury there are the weapons to show that after all the new right is wrong.

2

Citizenship and the Welfare State: Rejecting the Market

An Overview

A developed and extensive welfare state is an integral element of a morally acceptable society. It is an essential means of promoting social justice, enhancing individual self-development and fostering a sense of community. Without it market societies permit, indeed encourage, the exclusion of individuals from the consumption of benefits generally available to their fellows. Citizens, members of the community, find their membership in the community compromised. They exist at or beyond the margins of their own society: 'in' but not 'of' the community.

This is the basic insight that underlies the work of those writers who constitute what I call the 'citizenship' school. Citizenship theory offers a distinct moral justification of the welfare state. The welfare state is not the practical realization of a simple utilitarian imperative to maximize utility. It does not reflect the enforcement of a *human* right to welfare. No more is it based on institutionalized charity. Rather, the welfare state is rooted in a conception of what it is to be a full member of a community and the social rights that are necessary to protect and reinforce that membership.

The moral identity of the citizenship tradition is moulded, in part, by its critical response to the claims made on behalf of a free market society. Market societies are criticized both for their technical weaknesses and for the morally impoverished character of the relationships they foster. Much influenced by the experience of the interwar years and the loss of capitalism's image as an efficient and rational, let alone just, economic system, citizenship writers looked to the state as an instrument to correct the inadequacies of the market and to realize values which market relations could not exemplify.

In so looking to the state, citizenship writers drew upon standard accounts of market failure. Public intervention is justified as a response to the market's inability to supply public goods, to deal with social costs which are not reflected in price, and to respond to uncertainty. The nonmarket delivery of a wide range of welfare services, including medical care and education, is alleged to be more efficient than leaving the supply of such services to the private market. Public, not private, provision is required by the same criterion used to justify markets; namely, economic efficiency. As we have seen, this claim has been aggressively attacked by proponents of a resurgent economic liberalism.

The economic rationale for public provision is not restricted to efficiency within particular sectors of the economy; it extends to the economy as a whole. Recently it has become fashionable to see the welfare state as a source of the economic difficulties facing Western societies. The right, in particular, regard expenditure on social policy as unproductive and a drag on economic growth. High taxes and large deficits undermine the preconditions for a successful entrepreneurial economy. By contrast, the view of the citizenship school is that the relationship between the welfare state and the economy is as likely to be complementary as competitive. The coincidence, in the thirty years since the end of the second world war, of high rates of growth and the establishment of state welfare systems is not accidental. Free education and medical care contribute to labour productivity. Welfare and unemployment payments help sustain aggregate demand during recessions and thereby counteract the trade cycle. The existence of the welfare state is part of the explanation of the success of post-war economies. The cause of the difficulties of the last decade must be sought elsewhere.

These general economic claims form an important part of the political armoury of the citizenship tradition but they are not exclusive to it. Many of, for example, Titmuss's claims concerning market failure and the relation between social policy and economic growth would be shared by most defenders of a mixed economy, even though they would not agree with his moral philosophy. It is to the moral basis of the citizenship approach that I now turn.

Implicit within citizenship theory is a moral critique of market relationships. This critique will be dealt with fully later and so that discussion will not be pre-empted now. It might be noted, however, that the views of members of this tradition range widely from those who seem to have almost an unmitigated hostility towards the market and who can find in it virtually no morally redeeming feature to those who recognize its acceptability provided there is appropriate regulation and that it operates only within its proper sphere. What is common, however, is a rejection of the belief that a market system is capable of respecting persons and protecting basic rights. At best, the market is concerned with only an aspect of morality, and even then only imperfectly so. Moreover, the market is thought to encourage and reward morally undesirable relationships and, unsupplemented, to provide an inadequate foundation for social integration.

One part of citizenship theory is negative. Its purpose is to criticize the positive claims made on behalf of markets in general and market-based provision of welfare services in particular. A second aspect of this approach is cast in positive terms. Its purpose is to show not only how these moral inadequacies may be compensated for, but also how they may be transcended and positive values be successfully established and sustained. Thus properly constituted social policies are thought of as privileged devices for reflecting, maintaining and promoting a sense of community membership, defined in terms of a set of citizenship rights distributed outside the market according to a principle of socially recognized need. The satisfaction of these socially recognized needs is a matter of justice, not humanitarianism. Therefore, the establishment of the right kind of welfare state is required by justice.

The principles incorporated within morally acceptable social policies are those which protect the status of beneficiaries as full members of the community by defending them against stigma and guaranteeing, on legitimate terms, access to a community way of life. Moreover, the existence of welfare institutions, as an explicit recognition of ' . . . the total ultimate responsibility of the state for the welfare of its people',[1] is rooted in and provides scope for the expression of altruistic sentiments which are regarded as an integrating force within society and a compensation for the divisive selfishness the economic market promotes. As Titmuss, for example, writes, social policy 'manifests . . . society's will to survive as an organic whole',[2] and is 'centred (on) those social institutions that foster integration and discourage alienation'.[3]

> There is nothing permanent about the expression of reciprocity. If the bonds of community giving are broken the result is not a state of value neutralism. The vacuum is likely to be filled by hostility and social conflict.[4]

Social policies, within the welfare state, are crucial to the legitimacy and stability of modern capitalist society.

This brief exposition of the citizenship approach highlights a number of points. First, the summary emphasizes the importance of the notion of citizenship and the related idea of community. As I will show, the concept of community plays an irreducible role within the theory. It provides a goal for social policy. Social policy must create a sense of community that otherwise would not exist, and which is in turn a source of social policy. Both the support for and the content of social policy are rooted in community; it helps provide a framework within which conflicts between principles or about the interpretation of specific principles can be settled. Disputes are to be resolved in the light of a commitment to the community.

Secondly, it clarifies the status and foundation of economic and social rights. These rights are derived from membership in the community and their content can only be explicated by reference to the nature of the community. Social rights confer benefits to which an individual has a claim because he is a member of this community.

Thirdly, the use of the term 'citizenship' to capture the core of this approach to the welfare state is helpful in focusing attention on the moral importance of protecting the status of a person as a full member of the community. Writers such as T. H. Marshall, for example, believe that historically we have witnessed the progressive development and generalization of rights, first in the civil and then in the political sphere. The elaboration of a set of social rights completes the process. The conviction that all members of society are equal in respect of their civil and political rights is extended to the social arena. Social rights are important not only in their own right; they also underpin civil and political rights by creating conditions that make the exercise of those rights worthwhile.

In practical terms, the citizenship approach identifies a number of areas of concern for a properly constituted welfare system. These include, at a minimum, income maintenance programmes, personal social services and social work agencies, housing policy and universal free health care and education. Programmes of these kinds are directed to two types of consumer.

First, are those who are unable to participate independently in the style of life of the society and who are therefore defined as 'in need'. Such people need assistance if they are to be integrated into society. The kind of help required will vary with the facts of the case. For some it will be merely an income supplement; for others, the opportunity to use a publicly provided service as a resource base, while yet others may need the personal help of a social worker to encourage the development of a range of personal and social skills. In each of these cases policy is reactive to perceived shortfalls in the condition of individuals or groups and policy is directed to making good that deficiency through 'curative' policies. Policy might also be preventive, designed to forestall the development of cases of need.

Secondly, there is the beneficiary of welfare policies who is self-sufficient and who could make private provision to meet personal and family needs and insure against future contingencies. This person has the same entitlements as someone actually in need, even though he does not claim them. He does consume benefits, however, where public provision has replaced the market. At some time or other most Britons make use of public education or receive medical care under the National Health Service.

Citizenship writers favour an extensive, elaborate and generous structure of social policies. The benefits of these policies should be freely available to those who need them. For this reason there is disapproval of eligibility tests which discourage take-up or stigmatize the consumer. It is this concern that underlies the argument for universal rather than selective social policy.

Taking all this together it is not surprising that writers within the citizenship tradition enthusiastically endorsed the establishment of the welfare state in post-war Britain. They were and are not, however, mere apologists for the battery of policies that were instituted. Whilst the welfare state was a step in the right direction, it was but a step. In their view, the present system does not go far enough, nor are all of its services organized in accordance with acceptable norms. Too often welfare services are penetrated by market-related criteria, and the principle that policy should satisfy need unrelated to an individual's market position is violated. In practice these scholars have been amongst the most trenchant critics of the realities of the welfare state and were amongst the first to point to its shortcomings. It was they who gave the lie to the complacent assumption that the welfare state had abolished poverty, and who showed how social policies achieved primarily intra-class but not inter-class redistribution of income and wealth.

Hence in citizenship theory we find a perspective which offers a principled defence of the welfare state and the foundations of an immanent critique of its flaws. To a detailed elaboration of that perspective I now turn.

The Rejection of Market-Based Welfare Services

'The social services,' writes T. H. Marshall, are 'not to be regarded as regrettable necessities to be retained only until the capitalist system has been reformed or socialized; they (are) a permanent and even glorious part of the social system itself. They (are) something to be proud of, not apologize for.'[5] Equally enthusiastic is W. A. Robson who sees the welfare state as an instrument providing opportunities for creative individual self-expression. There are, he claims, 'no limits to the positive aims of the welfare state'.[6] The function of the welfare state goes well beyond compensating for the inadequacies of capitalism.

But it is with those inadequacies that it is necessary to start, for the citizenship theory self-consciously reacts to what it takes to be the inherent limitations of capitalism and the market order with which it is associated. Hence in this chapter I elucidate the reasons for the rejection of market-based welfare services. Underlying this repudiation of the market is the belief that, left unsupplemented markets lead to radical insecurity and generate systematic inequality which in turn underwrite morally unacceptable relations of dominance and subservience between groups and individuals in society. An essential part of the function of a properly constituted welfare state is to eliminate these problems.

Citizenship writers display little confidence in the market mechanism as a means of satisfying the needs of those who fall victim of dislocations produced by economic change:

> The market has always failed to provide decent pensions, sickness insurance and other forms of social security, just as it has failed to provide adequate standards and coverage of health care, education, and other social services. Private social security is inequitable and thoroughly inefficient. Pensions decline in value during payment; widows are treated badly; contributors have rights unreasonably withdrawn if they change jobs; and administrative overheads are several times as high as the cost of National Insurance.[7]

Townsend's view is shared by Titmuss who, in a number of studies, concludes that public provision is economically more efficient than private. In *The Gift Relationship* Titmuss analyses the supply of blood under a variety of different delivery systems.[8] His conclusion is that a commercialized market in blood failed in comparison to a voluntary donation system on any efficiency criteria. The use of a price mechanism in the United States leads he argues, to a tremendous waste of blood, to chronic and acute shortages of blood and to much greater bureaucratization and higher administrative overheads than are typical of Britain. Not only are these inefficiencies reflected in the price paid by patients for blood, but commercial markets are also more likely than a nonmarket system to distribute contaminated blood.

Titmuss clearly believes that *The Gift Relationship* is a paradigm for the social services in general; a point of view that is never explicitly defended. But the principal conclusion that the costs of a commercialized system are greater than those associated with a nationalized one have been borne out in the experience of several countries.

It is not my purpose here to assess or review the voluminous social policy literature examining and criticizing the efficiency of market provision to satisfy needs. Suffice it to say that the claims of the market liberals in that respect are not uncontested in any area of welfare provision.[9] The conventional wisdom among students of social policy has historically been that it is more efficient to take a range of welfare policies out of the market, and there is certainly an impressive array of empirical evidence to support that conclusion. The argument for the superior efficiency of nonmarket provision draws on, I think it is fair to say, standard accounts of market failure which stress the difficulties markets have in adequately accounting for social costs and coping with the effects of uncertainty and imperfect information. Moreover, it is not entirely true to say that a blind eye is turned to the problems of 'state failure'. The responsiveness and sensitivity of bureaucracy has been a perennial concern of the left, but rather than look to markets as the instrument for tailoring outcomes more closely to preferences, generally the preferred strategy has been to seek to subject bureaucracies to greater public accountability. The answer to 'state failure' is to be found as a rule in democratization, not privatization.

The claim that markets expand choice has also been the subject of empirical criticism. First, markets structure choice to eliminate or significantly reduce the eligibility of certain types of options. A conclusion of *The Gift Relationship* is that commercial markets in blood operate by way of a Gresham's law in which bad motives drive out good as selfishly motivated actors crowd out those who would act altruistically. Secondly, specific options are eliminated. An example is the way in which private power in the market can affect the range of choice. Studies of the private pension market show the beneficiaries' lack of choice and control. Workers have no choice whether or not to participate in the schemes offered; no choice over the type of scheme operated; and no choice with respect to the terms of transferability and preservation of pension rights.

In sum, Titmuss, as a typical representative of the citizenship school, rejects both the efficiency claim and the argument that private markets offer more choice to consumers. He also expressly repudiates what he takes to be an essential element of the economic liberal's argument, namely that economic growth without the support of a deliberately redistributive welfare state could eradicate poverty. Titmuss marshalls evidence designed to show the persistence of poverty in both Britain and the United States in the face of historically rapid economic growth. He writes:

> Had private markets in education, medical care and social security been substituted for public policies during the past twenty years of economic growth (the) conclusions, in both absolute and relative terms, as to the extent of poverty in Britain today would, I suggest, have been even more striking.[10]

Finally, and very briefly, citizenship writers share the social democratic view that the structure of social policies in the welfare state has not been a burden on economic growth; rather, it has been a handmaiden of economic success.[11] State welfare institutions have helped sustain high levels of aggregate demand and have assisted in countering the effects of the trade cycle. It is unclear that taxation has been a disincentive to investment. If anything, sustaining demand has stimulated investment by ensuring the availability of markets. Moreover, the presence of a reasonably adequate welfare system has made it easier to introduce modern technologies because workers are more willing to accept technical change in an economy with relatively low unemployment and where the costs to them of a period of unemployment are minimized. In sum, there are several reasons to suppose that the welfare state has contributed to economic growth and next to no statistical evidence to show that economies tied to well-developed welfare systems fare relatively badly.

Citizenship Theory and the Compensation Principle

Citizenship theory rejects the moral theory underlying a means-testing selective welfare safety-net. There are two principal grounds for this. First, economic liberals fail to recognize the extent to which more generous policies are required as compensation to individuals for bearing the cost of economic and social change. And, secondly, delivery of welfare policies in accordance with market principles stigmatizes recipients and thereby fails to satisfy a principle of respect for persons.

The compensation argument is most clearly suggested by Titmuss, who argues that many social welfare policies must be understood as compensation to individuals and families who have suffered the consequences of industrial change, but where the causally responsible agents cannot be identified and charged with the costs. Hence, many benefits or services:

> are not essentially benefits or increments to welfare at all; they represent partial compensations for disservices, for social costs and for social insecurities which are the product of a rapidly changing industrial society.[12]

These responses to 'socially caused diswelfares (are) part of the price we pay to some people for bearing part of the costs of other people's progress'.[13] Social policies are an expression of an unwillingness to allow costs to lie where they fall.

Implicitly, the compensation principle invokes a notion of fairness. It also assumes that responsibility for the costs of progress can be ascribed within a society, even where the individual behaviour generating those costs is itself not blameworthy. This is a clear break from the very narrow conception of responsibility put forward by market liberals. Typically, for them, responsibility is ascribable only if one can point to individual conduct that is itself blameworthy. In the paradigm case, one may be held responsible for what one intended to produce or ought to have foreseen as the consequence of one's act.

As we have seen, on this view social outcomes are nobody's fault. No individual could foresee that the upshot of an act when conjoined with the acts of many others would result in unemployment, the decline of an industry, the death of a town. Yet it may well be that the acts of all those persons taken together led to that result.

If social outcomes are no one's fault and no individually unjust conduct can be pointed to as their cause, then social outcomes are simply not assessable from a moral point of view. They are neither just nor unjust, moral nor immoral. Their moral character is analogous to the consequences of the laws of nature. And frequently it is to those laws, especially to their immutable and amoral properties, that the upshot of market interactions are assimilated.

To the market liberal it is clearly simply an error to assert that those who suffer losses as the result of the operation of the market have any entitlement to be compensated or to have their position in any way protected. While it may be unfortunate that certain people sustain heavy losses, there can be no social duty to respond, except in accordance with the principles discussed in the first chapter.

This view is anathema to the citizenship theorist. Even if it is true that damaging social consequences succeed individually legitimate activity, it does not follow that there is no duty to respond. There is nothing logically contradictory about the idea that a person may have a duty to alleviate or remedy a situation even though he personally bears no responsibility for having brought it about. Consider, to take an extreme example, the case of an individual who finds another lying face down in a puddle and in danger of drowning. All that is necessary to save him is to turn him over. There is absolutely no risk to the rescuer. Surely most of us would agree that there is indeed a moral, although not a legal, duty so to respond.

This example goes further than Titmuss needs, for the duty to compensate those bearing the social costs of the progress of others is not straightforwardly analogous to a rescuer straying across an accident victim. In that case the victim has not conferred any benefit, however indirectly, upon his rescuer. Titmuss's compensation principle is stronger than this. His claim is that those who are to be compensated are members of a class or group who are making a contribution to the well-being of a class or group who are thereby under a duty to compensate. At the minimum this contribution is made simply by participating in a system which permits heavy localized costs to fall on specific groups. The contribution is made simply by bearing the risk of incurring heavy losses in a system that flourishes on risk-taking. More typically, it is possible to trace patterns of advantage and disadvantage arising out of market relationships. In the aggregate, at least, flows of benefit and cost can be spotted, winners and losers identified. To disclaim any duty to aid losers on the ground that no unjust individual actions can be found, or that patterns of contribution cannot be individuated, is unacceptable.

As I have stated it the foundation of the compensation principle is ambiguous. Commonly the assumption seems to be that compensation is required in the light of a contribution that loss-bearers make. I am entitled to recompense from you because if I had not borne these losses you would not be better off. My losses are a necessary condition of your gain. Alternatively, the foundation of the principle seems to trade on a right not to be harmed, without any suggestion that the harm suffered constitutes a contribution to the welfare of others. There is no textual evidence upon which decisively to choose one basis in preference to the other, though the practical advantage of the latter is clear. To justify compensation it is necessary to demonstrate only the relevant harm. There is no need to satisfy the further requirement that by incurring the loss a contribution was made. Morally, however, the claim by way of contribution has a definite appeal. Not only is there responsibility for the harm caused, but one is claiming that it is repugnant to profit at someone else's expense. So stated the principle captures intuitions of the injustice of exploitation.

The compensation principle based on contribution is clearly too broadly stated. It is one thing to invoke a conception of responsibility wider than that relied on by market liberals; it is quite another to suggest, as seems to be the case here, that any contribution, however indirect, can give rise to a duty to compensate. If that were so, could any benefit enjoyed by X arising by virtue of Y's actions be retained by X without the consent of Y? Just one example is sufficient to expose the implausibility of that view. Susan and Sally are neighbours. Both enjoy gardens. Only Sally likes to garden. From her bedroom window Susan has an uninterrupted view of Sally's garden and spends many hours admiring it. Sally notices this and asks Susan to pay her some part of the cost of the garden. The external benefit of the garden is surely not one for which Susan is under any duty to pay, even if there is nothing to stop Sally building a wall, blocking the view and then charging a price to remove it.

The compensation principle is overly broad. It catches cases that a citizenship writer would have no interest in protecting. Imagine a wealthy entrepreneur whose investments have yielded employment in the past but who suffers heavy losses as the result of market changes. His contribution to the progress of others is every bit as real as that of his employees. His contribution is direct both in terms of jobs and wealth created, and exists by virtue of his participation in the market system. Let us say that despite these losses the entrepreneur remains moderately affluent. His workers meanwhile have incurred losses which individually are much smaller than his, though they have been left unemployed. It would be very surprising if any citizenship writer argued that the compensation principle required that he be protected against those losses even though they would not 'represent a benefit at all but a compensation for disservices caused by society'.

One way of narrowing the compensation principle is strictly utilitarian. Any requirement to compensate for bearing social costs has to recognize that individuals enjoy social benefits too. For any randomly selected individual, external benefits probably cancel out external costs over the long term. To the extent that this is likely, no compensation is justified. The need for compensation arises only where particularly heavy and concentrated losses occur which are unlikely to be swamped either by a few major external benefits or a myriad of small ones. Moreover, a scheme of compensation for major losses makes its own contribution to welfare by underwriting a sense of security and eliminating the anxiety that people would have realizing that they face potential calamity alone.[14]

This type of argument makes a case for policies designed to protect individuals against major losses. The utilitarian can also explain why it is proper not to compensate the businessman even where his monetary loss is many times greater than that of the workers. The key to the argument is that it is frequently assumed that income is subject to the principle of diminishing marginal utility so that each additional pound contributes less to utility than the previous one. Hence the welfare loss incurred by a relatively poor person whose income is reduced by £10 a week is much greater than that suffered by a wealthy man who loses a fortune.

Even if the principle of the diminishing marginal utility of income does not hold for all individuals, or where, despite its operation, a rich man's loss outweighs the losses of the poor, the utilitarian can still defend not compensating the wealthy if it is expensive to develop a policy sufficiently discriminating to identify accurately these unusual cases. In other words, although such losses ought to be compensated in principle, a utilitarian calculation of the costs of establishing a policy to do so suggests that the net benefit is negative.

The utilitarian rationale of limited compensation is not, however, the basis of citizenship theory. In the next chapter I will deal more fully with the non-utilitarian foundations of the school. Here it is necessary only to point out that an assumption of diminishing marginal utility is not the key to the compensation aspect of social policy. Rather, what is essential is that certain types of social disservices are peculiarly likely to compromise the status of individuals as full and participating members of the community.

A good example is loss of employment in a society in which work is a prized activity and in which the sentiment still prevails that failure to hold or find a job is a reflection of personal failure. Not only does unemployment mean loss of income in the absence of income maintenance programmes, it also is apt to entail loss of face, a loss of self-respect.

Employment is a good because it is a source of the wherewithal to participate in a community way of life; to engage in the consumption activities of one's society. A lack of resources leads to exclusion. But so too does a lack of self-respect, and there is considerable sociological evidence cataloguing the consequences of long-term unemployment: the unemployed lose a sense of self-esteem, become withdrawn and apathetic, and live at the margin of society. In a society in which what you are is bound up closely with what you do, work is source of self-definition. To be effectively deprived of an opportunity to work is to be cruelly handicapped.

Compensation therefore is required where social processes operate in ways which prejudice one's standing as a full member of the community. This is true whether the foundation of the principle is contribution or simply a right not to be harmed. Although the claim to be compensated for bearing the costs of the progress of others is free–standing, it must be satisfied only where not to do so undercuts one's community membership. Thus the argument presupposes a theory of rights radically different from the property rights theory of market liberals. It suggests the existence of a right to have one's status as a full member of the community protected by social rights in the name of citizenship. The suggestion that property rights and private trading on the basis of those rights is sufficient to protect that status is rejected.

The Limitations of Compensation

There is no doubt that writers within the citizenship tradition regard a considerable part of the welfare apparatus as justified by a compensation principle. It is equally certain that this principle is not considered sufficient to justify all social policy. Many welfare policies neither can nor should be explained as providing compensation. Often it is simply not possible to point to anyone who requires compensation. Equally, it is frequently the case that resources to finance welfare policies are taken from taxpayers who are neither the cause of the harm nor beneficiaries of it. Consider, for example, unemployment caused by foreign competition.

Compensating someone suggests that he has been harmed by treatment which has made him worse off than he would otherwise have been. It is necessary to be able to identify, at least in general terms, the social process which causes the harm, as well as the agents who bear responsibility for its rectification and those who are to benefit. Some social policies are not, however, responses to harm. Much medical care is required for illnesses which simply have natural causes. Of course, it is true that many diseases are related to occupational hazards, and for these a compensation approach may be suitable, but many health risks are just facts of life. There simply is no one against whom compensation could be demanded, no one upon whom to impose a duty as a beneficiary of a process causing harm to others. Indeed, frequently, if anyone can be held responsible for the medical risks being run by an individual, it is himself. Life-style diseases caused by alcohol, tobacco and poor diet are major killers in modern society.

The same point could be made of other welfare policies. Social workers are often concerned with cases which are genuinely the product of individual pathology or simply bad luck. Assistance to a family to cope with a congenitally handicapped child is not compensation, nor is counselling a teenage single mother who knew and understood the risks but took them all the same. Not all of education is compensation; a good deal of it is simply preparation. And, finally, it would be unreasonable to regard child allowances as compensation to parents for having children.

In cases like this, citizenship theorists implicitly draw upon an even broader conception of responsibility than that which underlies the compensation argument. There, the duty to compensate was imposed in the light of benefits consumed by some at the expense of others, or alternatively to protect people against socially generated harms for which responsibility could only broadly be ascribed. Here the analogy with the man in the puddle *is* apt. Even though one stands in no causal relation to the facts requiring alleviation, nor does one derive any advantage from them, it is asserted that nevertheless there is a duty to respond and provide aid. Moreover, the duty is a perfect obligation (in that morally one has no choice whether or when to fulfil it), not just a duty to be charitable, or something which although good is supererogatory.

Intuitively, it is much more difficult to justify a duty in this case than where one is a member of a class deriving benefits from a practice which imposes costs on others. While most of us would agree that we have a duty to turn the man in the puddle over and to revive him or call for help, we might hesitate to accept that we must dive into the ocean to save him. Certainly, the line would have to be drawn somewhere. Rescuers have legitimate interests of their own, and at some point the risks and the burden of rescue become so great that the duty to aid vanishes.

Citizenship theory cannot avoid drawing upon the analogy of the rescuer. It must assert a general duty to aid. Unlike market liberalism, it cannot rest content to limit general non-consensual duties to the duty of non-interference in cases where there is no special relationship. The basis of the duty to aid is the right of each individual to have his status as a full member of the community protected. Yet, having said that, it must be the case that the effect of that right in the rescue case is constrained by the moral interests of the rescuer. These interests are of more weight than when we are concerned with compensation. We can demand less of a rescuer than of someone who owes an obligation. What can be expected of the rescuer must be morally of less significance than what is gained by the victim, perhaps much less. There may be an absolute limit to the burden that can be imposed on a rescuer beyond which it is impermissible to go, no matter what the gain to the victim. Where a debt is owed, however, it is proper to extract it even if the gain by the 'creditor' is less than the loss to the 'debtor'.

Given this, it follows that the moral foundation for interfering with market outcomes is most secure where citizenship theorists can press the argument that intervention is required by a contribution-based compensation principle. In defending compensation, a satisfactory account of the social processes that benefit some by imposing costs on others is required. If that is provided, it is easier to argue that by accepting these benefits one assumes an obligation to compensate the victim, even though one has not acted unjustly toward any specific person. The injustice inheres in the social process itself and in the failure to recognize the unfairness of any claim to keep full control of the use and disposition of resources so derived. It is not simply that one is not entitled to everything one earns because one does not deserve it on the grounds of effort or desert; one's lack of entitlement is a consequence of the price which some must pay to make those earnings possible.

The argument is also relatively strong when compensation is founded upon a right not to be harmed. In that case, it is necessary to show the nature of the social process causing harm, but again the duty to respond is rooted in the identification of agents responsible (even if not individually) for the outcomes. In practice, it may seem that treating welfare policy in this way reduces it to a form of collective social insurance in which the basic risk insured against is the risk to one's standing as a full member of the community. This is not correct, however, because the foundation of the obligation to contribute does not reflect actuarial principles but one's responsibility for causing harm. Social policy is redistributive not only towards those who actually suffer harm, as is insurance, but also from those who are socially responsible for such harm. Empirically, citizenship writers believe that neither the responsibility for putting others at risk, nor the bearing of that risk, is randomly or equally distributed. The risk of harm to status is disproportionally caused by the activities of the better-off and borne by the worse-off. Hence, even a compensation principle that extends a right to be protected against harm can be expected to be sharply redistributive.

Finally, the argument is least secure where no responsibility to compensate can be grounded, but where instead reliance is placed on a duty to rescue. At bottom, the citizenship view depends on a defence of the proposition that the moral importance of sustaining community membership so outweighs the costs of imposing an obligation to respond that the relevant duty may properly be seen as a requirement of justice.

Freedom and Self-Respect: Stigma Versus Universal Welfare Provision

My discussion so far has been concerned to show why the market liberal view is seen to rely first upon an unacceptably narrow theory of responsibility and an implausible account of the consistency of market arrangements and individual rights. The second principal reason for rejecting a system of market-related social policy is that selective, means-tested policies stigmatize the recipients. The two arguments are related. It is clearly wrong to provide policies designed to satisfy justice on terms that generate stigmas among the recipients.

Stigma, according to Titmuss, involves a 'spoiled identity'. It occurs where discrimination by society is adopted as a subjective reality by an individual. Crucially, it results in a loss of self-respect and personal dignity. An acceptance of inferiority and a sense of social failure are taken over from the values expressed by and incorporated within social institutions. The use of private markets in the supply of basic needs are, in Titmuss's view, particularly effective in undermining the self-respect of significant sections of the community.

Stigma is generated in a number of ways; it is not simply the product of the level of public provision. First, it is created by the inevitable tendency of the market to exclude the individual. For many, private welfare is not available due to the absence of a willing seller:

> Private enterprise social service institutions operate on the principle
> of excluding the 'bad risks' and the social casualties of change.
> Thus, private occupational schemes exclude the chronically sick,
> the disabled, the elderly, the mentally handicapped, new entrants,
> most categories of women . . . and so on . . .[15]

Secondly, it is not simply the fact of exclusion that is damaging, but also the *process* of exclusion. The way in which those who will be excluded are commonly treated violates the principle of respect for persons.

Thirdly, means-testing stigmatizes. The process of ensuring that only those who are entitled to a free service use it, and not those who have private means, involves identifying and separating out a group of the poor. Titmuss argues that:

> The fundamental objective of all (means) tests is to keep people out; not to let them in. They must, therefore, be treated as applicants or supplicants; not beneficiaries or consumers.[16]

Identifying oneself as poor is 'to declare, in effect, "I am an unequal person" '.[17] Since 'money (and the lack of it) is linked to personal and family self-respect,'[18] such a declaration results in a 'humiliating loss of status, dignity or self-respect.'[19] 'There should be no sense of inferiority, pauperism, shame or stigma in the use of a publicly provided service; no attribution that one was being or becoming a "public burden" '.[20] So runs conventional wisdom.

Stigmatization is avoidable provided that services are made universally available. Universal services make it more difficult to identify those who do not have the means to support themselves independently. They also promote a sense of common experience.

Fourthly, stigma is created in any mixed public/private system. 'If (welfare) services (are) not provided for everybody by everybody they (will) either not be available at all, or only for those who (can) afford them, and for others on such terms as (will) involve the infliction of a sense of inferiority and stigma.'[21] In a mixed system, the very existence of a separate sector for the indigent creates a sense that public provision is for failures. Small wonder, then, that a means-test acts as a barrier, so that individuals fail to avail themselves of a service even when they need, and have a right to, it. Moreover, the public component of the system would probably provide only a second-class service. Incapable of attracting the quality of staff from the private sector necessary to supply an adequate standard of service, 'separate discriminatory services for poor people have always tended to be poor quality services'.[22]

The need for welfare policies is created in large part by the insecurities associated with the economy. The nature of appropriate policy should be influenced by the imperative not to stigmatize and thereby damage the self-respect of welfare recipients. At first sight it seems that citizenship theory is prepared simply to sacrifice the interests of one section of the community by restricting their freedom to participate in the market place for welfare services, whether it be for education, medical or unemployment insurance or pensions, to protect the self-respect of another section.

If that were the nature of the choice, it would be draconian indeed.

Not only would it be morally difficult to justify the sacrifice of the interests of so many to protect the relatively few, but it would be difficult to defend the means adopted. After all, if the major problems of stigma stem from public branding as a failure, that in turn derives from a lack of resources, then these problems can largely be avoided by an anonymous and impersonal redistribution of income, either through the tax system or by way of a guaranteed income. In this way, the resources necessary both to satisfy any compensation-based principle of justice, and to facilitate participation in the market, could be assured.

This suggests that there is more to the claim for universality than merely defending against stigma. What more there is will be discussed in the next chapter. It also suggests that the nature of the choice is not as stark as it first appears. First, the upshot of the empirical scepticism towards the claims made for markets indicates that non-market provision may well be in the interests of those who could buy for themselves. Not only may it be cheaper, but it also may not compromise the value of freedom as seriously as might be assumed. As has already been indicated, citizenship writers have little confidence in private markets to reflect or enlarge choice, even for those who are apparently well served by them.

Secondly, non-market provision is consistent with freedom in other ways too. Survey data from developed countries indicate a continuing high level of support for most of the basic elements of the welfare system notwithstanding the apparently fierce reaction against the welfare state seen in recent years.[23] It is not unreasonable to regard the establishment of the welfare state as a collective act of free choice with the purpose of imposing a certain structure upon society that simply could not be created by a multitude of discrete actions occuring within a market. In other words, opting politically for a welfare state is freely to choose to be one kind of society rather than another. Through collective action society has overcome what Hirsch calls the 'tyranny of small choices'. As he describes it:

> The core of the problem is that the market provides a full range of choice between alternative piecemal, discrete, marginal adjustments, but no facility for selection between alternative states. Since the piecemeal choices between the opportunities that are available through market transactions at any given time involve unintended and at times undesired repercussions, choice in the small does not provide choice in the large. . . . The choice is posed at each stage in a dynamic process; there is no chance of selection between the states at either end of the process.[24]

The citizenship theorist would find it most congenial to regard the erection of the welfare state as just such a selection, even if the architectural design chosen displays significant flaws.

In this way, the apparent sacrifice of individual freedom by non-market provision is partially dissipated. Many citizens are taken to have consented politically to a constraint upon their economic freedom. It is clear that to several citizenship writers this consent is the result of a widespread sense of altruism which is channelled through the political system. In this way politics and state intervention provide opportunities for the exercise of altruistic choices that would not exist, or exist only in an attenuated form, in the market.

Finally, the choice of freedom for some versus self-respect for others poses the issue incorrectly, in that the argument for non-market provision does not presuppose that self-respect and freedom are unrelated. The main point here is just that policies which have the effect of protecting the self-respect of the indigent also make a contribution to autonomy. This happens not simply by making resources available which can be used in the course of acting freely, or which open up choices that would otherwise not exist for lack of means, for this would be true of any redistributive policy, even one resulting in stigmatization; rather, they support autonomy by underwriting the social and psychological conditions that make acting freely and exercising choice worthwhile to that person. It is this that Titmuss, for example, has in mind when he argues that social policy is about participation, freedom, and integration. Unless self-respect is protected, individuals are unlikely to make good use of opportunities that are available to them. They are unlikely to act in ways that exemplify the ideal of self-development.

Viewed in this light, the values of freedom and autonomy appear on both sides of the ledger. It is inappropriate to see the moral dilemma posed by non-market provision of welfare services as a simple choice that trades off freedom for preservation of self-respect. Instead the values are cross-cutting. The moral issue is blurred. It cannot be resolved simply by asserting the rigid priority of freedom. If the basic insight that private markets in welfare inflict heavy damage on the self-respect of the indigent is correct, and if a loss of self-respect does undermine the effective ability to act autonomously, then the only satisfactory resolution of this question will be one that contains a developed account of the just distribution of the conditions of autonomy in an industrialized society.

Redistribution in the Welfare State

At the beginning of this chapter, I stated that underlying the arguments of the citizenship school was the belief that unsupplemented markets generated radical insecurity and stimulated economic inequality that led to unacceptable relations of domination. My discussion has presupposed the validity of these claims. Certainly, the notion that social policies are required to compensate individuals for bearing the costs of the progress of others rests upon both of them. The imperative to introduce nonstigmatizing universal policies is also related to the theme of domination. By underwriting self-respect, the tendency to subservient behaviour is inhibited.

But this does not exhaust the theme of domination. Free markets, as is well known, foster economic inequality. Talented or lucky people can amass fortune. Fortunes can be passed on. In the market systems we know, inequality is self-reproducing. Capitalist systems are less open to talent than at first appears, since class origins have a profound affect upon social destination. Structurally, the middle and upper class benefit more from present legal, social and economic arrangements than the working class.

The welfare state mitigates these tendencies. To the limited extent that it is redistributive, it compensates as justice requires. It is also a source of power. Insofar as domination in a capitalist society is rooted in unequal bargaining power, the welfare state helps correct the balance. Social rights underwrite the influence of trade unions by reducing the costs of unemployment and strikes. The countervailing power of unions limits the scope of management to act arbitrarily and permits more effective bargaining over pay and conditions.

Income maintenance programmes also assist the ability of the nonunionized to resist domination. The opportunity to fall back on public support makes it easier for workers to refuse to enter the labour market on exploitative terms. It has often been argued that the fundamental source of inequality in society can be traced to the fact that workers have no choice but to offer their labour for sale, whereas capitalists are free, and able, to refuse to offer to buy it. The welfare state goes some way in redressing that imbalance.

Finally, the welfare state addresses the theme of domination by offering itself as an instrument capable of breaking down class-related barriers that benefit the better off. Education, in particular, is seen as the major area capable of opening up opportunities to individual and social advancement that otherwise would not exist. Through education and other policies, the welfare state works on a structure that yields an unequal distribution of life chances and, ideally, equalizes them. Welfare policy is seen then as a tool for reshaping the distribution of the benefits of communal living in such a way that society is seen to exist for and belong to everybody, not just the lucky, the talented, the rich and the well-born.

In this chapter I have tried to give some idea of the reasons why citizenship writers reject the market as a mechanism for delivering social policy. My purpose has been to bring into focus the type of political theory upon which the judgements of the school are based. In the next chapter the theory is discussed more fully.

My account raises many questions and answers only a few. In later chapters, I deal with some of its more obvious difficulties. At a practical level, it is clear that the presently existing welfare state fails satisfactorily to incorporate the principles upon which the repudiation of the market rests. The welfare state, in fact, is not noticeably redistributive across class lines. Most redistribution is intra-class and across an individual's life-time. Welfare policy operates more as a scheme of compulsory insurance than as compensation. Similarly, the evidence suggests that the welfare state has failed to secure a more equal distribution of life chances. Even though absolute rates of social mobility have improved in the post-war period, relative rates have changed little, with the upshot being an increasingly homogenous and marginalized unskilled working class.

Of course, it is clear that citizenship writers have never claimed that the welfare state actually corresponds to the ideal. The purpose of much of their writing has been to expose its inadequacies and promote reform. But this is inconclusive. It seems that the disappointments are not caused by remediable faults, but must be traced to systemic roots. Moreover, there is some cause to be sceptical concerning the appropriateness of the policy responses associated with the citizenship school. Stigma certainly is a problem. But how much of stigma is in fact rooted in the conditions which create dependency, for example, the lack of capacity to perform in the market, rather than the responses to that dependency? Is there not a case to be made that universal free social policies, like the health services or education, have become institutions through which systemic inequality has reproduced itself, thereby frustrating the goal of redistribution? Can it not plausibly be argued that an almost theological antipathy to market relations has led to a gross undervaluing of the contribution markets could make to citizenship goals; that markets and social democratic objectives are not necessarily in tension but may even be complementary? In later chapters I will return to these themes.

3

Citizenship and the Welfare State: Needs, Rights and Community

T. H. Marshall provides one of the clearest statements of the primary objectives of social policy within the welfare state. Social policy has, he alleges, three possible aims: the elimination of poverty, the maximization of welfare and the pursuit of equality.[1] Marshall opts for the second of these and suggests that welfare policy so grounded is concerned with achieving optimum welfare for all and not simply with guaranteeing a minimum for the poor.

Two points emerge from this. First, Marshall seems to distance himself from the philosophy of other citizenship writers by not adopting equality as a key value to be promoted by the welfare state. While there is certainly a difference of emphasis here, I shall argue later that there is nevertheless sufficient common ground to justify treating Marshall as a member of a common tradition.

Secondly, Marshall has apparently adopted a simple utilitarian moral theory. If this were so, his defence of the welfare state could be reduced to the claim that state intervention is necessary because it is relatively the most efficient way of ensuring general well-being. In that event the argument would turn entirely on the plausibility of the claim that comparative advantage favours public rather than private provision. The essential elements in the defence of the welfare state would be simply a theory of market failure coupled probably with an assumption of the diminishing marginal utility of income. Assuming that the empirical and psychological propositions hold water, everything would turn on the acceptability of utilitarianism as a moral theory.

In my view, it is wrong to regard Marshall or any other citizenship theorist as nothing more than a utilitarian. As I will show, and as the last chapter has intimated, the goods that the welfare system exists to promote cannot be reduced to the subjective experience of well-being, even though experiences of ill-being inflicted by unregulated markets are to be reduced, compensated for, and, better still, prevented. Rather, social policy ought to promote a range of values that stand independent of utility. Social rights, based on needs defined in relation to conditions necessary to preserve an individual's status as a full member of the community, for example, are not reducible to utility.

It is clear that Marshall himself accepts that a principle of satisfying needs is free-standing and, therefore, not to be subsumed under a simple aggregative principle of maximizing welfare. Social policy is to be directed to satisfying real human needs and cannot be based upon a simple and direct reaction to individual subjective desires. At the minimum, it is accepted that revealed preferences in the market are an inadequate foundation for identifying needs. But it is not going too far to suggest that Marshall would agree that to some extent needs can be ascribed to persons independently of their subjective preferences, whether revealed through market exchanges or based upon statements about their own desires.[2]

Treating need as having an independent and objectively identifiable existence has important implications. Injecting objective elements into its identification captures some common perceptions about need. First, it indicates some kind of significant difference between needs and preferences. We often think, for example, that someone may want something they do not need (champagne possibly), and consider that a reason not to provide it. Or, alternatively, that they may need what they do not want, for instance, medical attention, and consider that the need alone is a reason to respond. Furthermore, we commonly regard individuals simply to be mistaken about their needs or to be ignorant of them and, therefore, worry about relying just on revealed subjective preferences as a means of satisfying needs.

Secondly, the argument that welfare policies should be aimed at the satisfaction of particular needs does not depend simply upon a contingent relationship between satisfying needs and maximizing welfare. So, although it may often be true that the best way of promoting the general welfare is by satisfying needs, nothing is lost if it turned out that the aggregative imperative prescribed a distribution in favour of the wealthy at the expense of the poor. Justice alone is sufficient to rule that policy out.

The need principle plays a key role in defining the distinctiveness of the citizenship approach. George and Wilding, for example, indicate that the 'fundamental principle of radical social policy is that resources, whether in the field of health, education, housing or income, should be distributed according to need'.[3] Need satisfaction is also at the core of Titmuss's 'institutional redistributive model' of welfare, which sees 'social welfare as a major integrated institution in society, providing universalist services outside the market on the principle of need'.[4]

Several functions of the need principle can be identified. First, it operates as a principle of distribution, a notion that will be fully analyzed in chapter 7. Secondly, since needs can be identified independently of their articulation in the market, a principle of need satisfaction serves as a criterion for assessing the justice of market outcomes. Thirdly, the needs principle identifies an area of concern that is especially the province of welfare policy. The principle thereby defines the boundary between those matters properly falling within the sphere of the market and those reserved for welfare policy. Fourthly, basing the defence of welfare policy on need trades on the sense that the moral imperative to satisfy unmet need is stronger than any prescription to facilitate the satisfaction of wants. In this way, the priority of policies directed to need as distinct from wants is established. And, given the comparatively stable and constant character of needs, a morally sturdy foundation for the welfare state is assured. Finally, the need principle provides the foundation for the immanent critique of the existing welfare system, particularly of the extent to which social policy is penetrated by market-related criteria, for example, in the form of earnings-related pensions and unemployment insurance.

The role of 'need' in citizenship theory is essential to the theory's ideological identity. Three claims related to need are presupposed within this ideology: first, that needs are the foundation of welfare rights; secondly, that the needs relevant to claiming welfare rights are those connected with sustaining a person as a full member of the community; and thirdly, that satisfying the range of morally required welfare rights involves establishing a framework of universal social policies.

A central theme unifying the citizenship school, therefore, is that the provision of welfare services to meet need is required to honour the social rights of citizens. Titmuss writes of 'services provided, as social rights, on criteria of the needs of specific categories'.[5] Marshall devotes an essay to 'The Right to Welfare', and in 'Citizenship and Social Class' details, with evident satisfaction, the rise to prominence of social rights as a vital ingredient of an enriched status of citizenship.[6] Robson in *Welfare State and Welfare Society* stresses the importance of social rights in a socially just society, at the same time as he warns of the danger of their abuse.[7] One could go on and on. Even the most cursory examination of the vast body of literature produced by the citizenship school demonstrates the overriding importance of social rights as a category of claim a just society must meet.

In Marshall's classic article, 'Citizenship and Social Class', social rights are contrasted with political and civil rights. Political rights guarantee opportunities to participate in the political process. Civil rights define areas of non-interference which create opportunities for private action. Social rights, on the other hand, refer to a wide spectrum of claims:

> From the right to a modicum of economic welfare and security to the right to share to the full in the social heritage and to live the life of a civilized being according to the standards prevailing in the society.[8]

Social Rights and the Community

Social rights enrich the 'concrete substance of civilized life' by establishing individuated claims on the common patrimony.[9] 'The components of a civilized and cultured life' are brought 'within the reach of the many' by 'creating a universal right to real income which is not proportionate to the market value of the claimant'.[10] In attempting to guarantee a range of outcomes and not merely a set of opportunities, 'social rights in their modern form imply an invasion of contract by status, the subordination of market price to social justice, the replacement of the free bargain by the declaration of rights'.[11] This view is echoed by Robson, who writes that:

> There is ... a vast difference between a society based on the assumption that free competition and individual enterprise are the highest goods and that the right to possess whatever can be acquired by these means is morally, legally and politically justified, and a society based on the principle that social justice is essential to the concept of legitimacy.[12]

For Robson, as for other citizenship writers, the recognition and protection of social rights is the essence of achieving social justice. The establishment of the right kind of welfare state is, therefore, a matter of justice, morally required to respect rights; it is not a collective act of charity motivated by humanitarianism.

Merely to say, however, that the welfare system is based on a set of social rights is not enough. In principle, social rights might confer rights only to a narrow range of benefits; for example, a right to have subsistence needs met, or a right to a place in the workhouse. It is necessary to show why the range of benefits which social rights entitle one to should be both broad and generous. The key to the citizenship approach to defining the substance of social rights is simply that these rights are created to protect one's standing as a full and participating member of the community. In other words, social rights are rooted in a conception of need which takes its bearing from what is necessary to grant an individual fair access to his society's way of life.

One obvious implication of this is that the concept of absolute need is not a sufficient foundation upon which to build a defence of the welfare system. Rather, need is to be defined in relation to standards prevailing in the society as a whole. One is in need to the extent that one cannot 'share to the full in the social heritage'.[13] The notion that need exists if an individual falls far short of average standards and is, therefore, excluded from the way of life of the society, is a crucial element of social policy.

David Donnison puts this well in his discussion of poverty:

People are 'poor' because they are deprived of opportunities, comforts, and self-respect regarded as normal in the community to which they belong. It is therefore the continually moving average standards of that community that are the starting points for an assessment of its poverty, and the poor are those who fall sufficiently far below these average standards.[14]

The same point is made by Peter Townsend:

Poverty can be defined objectively and applied consistently only in terms of the concept of relative deprivation. . . . Individuals, families and groups in the population can be said to be in poverty when they lack the resources to obtain the types of diet, participate in the activities and have the living conditions and amenities which are customary, or at least widely encouraged or approved, in the societies to which they belong. Their resources are so seriously below those commanded by the average individual or family that they are, in effect, excluded from ordinary living patterns, customs and activities.[15]

Inequality, and poverty are not equivalent concepts, however. Townsend believes that 'as resources for any individual or family are diminished there is a point at which there occurs a sudden withdrawal from participation in the customs and activities sanctioned by the culture'.[16] Beyond a certain point, lack of resources entails exclusion; individuals are 'in' but not 'of' the community. Although they are members of the community, they are in no position to enjoy its fruits.

Needs, then, are socially constructed. 'Needs arise by virtue of the kind of society to which individuals belong. Society imposes expectations, through its occupational, educational, economic and other systems, and it also creates wants, through its organization and customs'.[17] Needs can be identified by examining prevailing expectations and 'styles of living' in the community.

Citizenship theory picks out as the needs to be satisfied those which can be identified by reference to what it is necessary to have in order to gain access to the community's way of life. It is because the inequality and insecurity associated with the free play of economic forces are thought to be especially likely to alienate people from the community, that social policy is seen as having the function of restoring, guaranteeing or promoting the status of individuals as full members of the community. Hence, writes Titmuss, the focus of social policy is on:

> Integrative institutions: on processes, transactions and institutions which promote an individual's sense of identity, participation and community and . . . discourage a sense of individual alienation.[18]

Marshall adopts the same view, suggesting that, for example, the 'modern rights to education and health are . . . part of the mechanism by which the individual is absorbed into society (not isolated from it).'[19]

It is clear that citizenship theory is concerned with more than absolute deprivation. Social rights exist to protect a person's membership in the community. They help create the conditions necessary for any individual to sustain himself as a self-respecting, equal and fully paid-up member of the club.

According to Marshall, social rights are rights 'created by the community itself and attached to the status of its citizenship'.[20] Elsewhere, he defines citizenship as:

> a status bestowed on those who are full members of a community. All who possess the status are equal with respect to the rights and duties with which the status is endowed. There is no universal principle that determines what these rights and duties shall be, but societies in which citizenship is a developing institution create an image of an ideal citizenship against which achievement can be measured and towards which aspiration can be directed.[21]

Social rights are rights to be distributed according to a principle of citizenship rooted in a 'conception of equal social worth, not merely of equal natural rights'.[22] The definition of these rights is accomplished within the political process. Ideally, it is an act of collective self-definition, drawing on altruism and a 'direct sense of community membership based on loyalty to a civilization which is a common possession'.[23] The political articulation of social rights aspires to rise above the narrow pursuit of individual and group self-interest. The very act of politically declaring the existence of social rights is morally educative. By drawing upon sentiments of altruism and social responsibility, a community is forged.

Freedom and Life Chances in Social Policy

My exposition has indicated why social policy must go beyond the mere relief of distress in order to provide the material basis for participation in the way of life of the society. This explains the generosity of provision within the citizenship schema. It does not explain why services should be provided universally and outside the market. After all, it might be possible to satisfy the demands of citizenship writers by allowing a mixed public/private system in which the public safety-net escaped the discipline of the market to provide high quality services capable of meeting a wide range of needs. Indeed, it is by no means obvious that services need, in general, to be in kind. Cash transfers might be just as effective and, perhaps, administratively more efficient.

A critical part of the argument in favour of non-market universalist policy has already been canvassed. In the last chapter I showed how the need to preserve self-respect and self-esteem is taken to rule out selective means-tested services operating within a mixed system. Universalist welfare policies are required to avoid damaging the self-respect of the indigent by protecting them from the humiliation of 'exclusionary' means testing and the process of being branded a public burden. Furthermore, the need to preserve the secure status and the continuing respect by others which underlies self-respect becomes more important as economic progress continues. Universalism is necessary also to promote integration. Universal social services are a mechanism for integrating all members of a society into the community, not merely the indigent. Social policies are the most important institutions capable of giving expression to principles of common citizenship. They do so because they identify a set of common needs. Relying on common needs draws attention to vital characteristics that all members of a society share, and thus social services constitute a foundation for a sense of social solidarity. In a manner of speaking, universal social services are an objectification of that sense of community. Invoking common citizenship picks out a principle which 'permeates the whole life of the society and penetrates the consciousness of its members'.[24] That sense of common citizenship should 'be strengthened, not weakened, by being universalized'.[25]

Universal social policies are linked, therefore, to the concept of the community in several ways. First, they are an institutional recognition of what individual members of society hold in common. Secondly, they elicit a recognition of that fact from the individuals who participate in the schemes. In this way universal social policies are thought to be morally educative. Thirdly, they draw upon sentiments of altruism and fellowship both for their existence and their functioning. Finally, much individual need is the consequence of the operation of impersonal economic and social mechanisms which can best be dealt with through a framework of universal policies on efficiency grounds alone. Underlying this claim is the thesis that individual pathology does not account for the genesis of need to anything like the extent commonly assumed by market liberals.

My discussion in this chapter has concentrated on the interrelationship between needs and social rights and to a lesser degree citizenship and community. As has been seen, the welfare state is charged with the responsibility of defending, through a structure of social rights, the needs linked to full membership of the community. The identity of citizenship theory lies both in its communitarian character and the claim that social rights are part of the definition of citizenship. The right of an individual to have his needs met is derived from his membership in the community, not directly from his human attributes as it would be in a human rights theory. Later in this chapter the role of community will be fleshed out more fully.

Social policies, generally, seek to guarantee certain outcomes to people. They might ensure access to education up to a certain standard, or the availability of health care or shelter and so forth. Their object is to secure the satisfaction of the needs of community members. Within citizenship theory social policies operate in two ways. First, each citizen is guaranteed access to certain resource bases which permit participation in the community's way of life on terms which protect self-respect. Here I have in mind income maintenance programmes and personal social services which are resorted to only where individuals are incapable of otherwise participating in the way of life. Other social policies are used by all community members even though some, or perhaps most, could provide themselves with those resources. Education and medical care are two obvious examples. Policies of this kind are centred on a core of common needs; needs which are integral to society's definition of its essential nature. The needs to be met are specific and it is this fact, together with a concern to encourage a common participation in the delivery of services to meet those needs, that accounts for a tendency to rely on services in kind, rather than cash grants. Universal in kind services are seen as building blocks in the fabric of an enriched sense of community. Private provision running parallel to public services are acceptable only in so far as they do not threaten either the quality of public provision or fracture the sense that our community is one dedicated to meeting the needs of its members. Typically, citizenship writers believe that the threat is posed by private provision and, especially in the case of education, that it underlies many inequalities which fundamentally compromise equality of status.

The defence of the welfare state is not just a matter of ensuring that a certain set of needs are met in acceptable ways. Needs are instrumental to the realization of other values and I have already stressed the importance of social policy as an instrument to promote participation in a community's way of life. This suggests that underneath the concern with needs lie the values of freedom and the worth of freedom. Very little is said in the citizenship tradition about the nature of freedom but it is clear enough that freedom is seen as a function of the range of choice facing an individual. Restrictions on the number of worthwhile options have implications for freedom and, as impersonal economic and social forces affect the range of viable choices, social policy is a vehicle of enlarging the freedom of some by creating opportunities for meaningful participation in the community.

Here there is a clear break with the very narrow conception of freedom supported by the market liberals. Unlike the new right, citizenship theory presupposes that where the range of valuable choices facing a person is restricted by remediable impersonal forces, those forces may be interfered with either in the name of freedom itself or of the worth of freedom. The circumstances which justify interference are, as David Miller has argued, to be related to a theory of obligations.[26] Hence, a person may be regarded as unfree to work, for example, if his unemployment is the result of the failure by government to adopt employment creating policies which it has a duty to implement. The duties owed to persons require an independent defence of which a theory of responsibility must be part, but it is clear, as I have indicated in chapter 2, that citizenship theory rejects the very restrictive interpretation of occasions when responsibility may properly be ascribed, argued for by Hayek amongst others.

Social policies intervene to produce results that would not otherwise occur. They have the effect of redistributing the pattern of freedom which markets would generate. The effect is not simply a reduction in the freedom of some by depriving them of resources to meet the needs of others.[27] Markets are themselves structures defined by a pattern of freedoms and unfreedoms correlated with property rights.[28] The inevitable issue when assessing social policy from the point of view of freedom is not simply freedom itself but the justice of different distributions of freedom.

The concern to promote freedom is only part of the interest citizenship theorists have in choice and opportunities. Individuals may be unable to act in certain ways or take advantage of opportunities, not because they are unfree to do so but because they lack the ability. Being unfree to do something and being unable to do it are not the same thing. Before someone's freedom is infringed there must be an interference with or constraint upon that person's opportunities, for which an agent can be held responsible either for bringing it about or for failing to remove it. But there may be barriers to action for which nobody can be held accountable. I am unable to jump twenty feet in the air because my physical strength is insufficient to overcome the force of gravity. It makes no sense to say that my freedom has been constrained. Equally, there are circumstances where a person's failure to participate in the community owes more to personal inability than to restrictions on freedom. Some people are simply very poor decision-makers or lack the strength of character required to take advantage of opportunities, assuming that they desire to do so. Clearly some misfortune is to be brought home to the incapacity of individuals and not shuffled off as an interference with freedom. For this reason freedom is not sufficient to account for the interest in choice and opportunities, and it is necessary to consider the concept of life chances.

Life chances encompass both freedom and ability. The reference is to the effective opportunities facing a person. The concern, therefore, is not only with the opportunities a person theoretically enjoys, but also with the probability of his being able to act upon them if he chooses to do so. At the heart of the notion of life chances are those chances which are fundamental to participation in the way of life of the society, in particular those life chances which are the key to gaining access to the rich variety of the benefits of social cooperation. This explains much of the preoccupation of citizenship writers with health care and education. Being a full member of society depends on the resource base that make life chances practicable possibilities and also on the possession of the skills, knowledge and rationality required to be an effective chooser. Social policies have to be concerned with buttressing these skills through personal social services, compensatory education and the encouragement of active client participation in the delivery of community-based services, as well as ensuring that the distribution of basic material resources is fair.

Viewed in this light, the concept of life chances is much wider than the market liberal understanding of freedom. There the concern was primarily with intentional coercion. The range and value of a set of choices fell outside the interest in freedom. So too did any assessment of how likely it was that a person should avail himself successfully of his opportunities. Life chances notice these concerns and reflect them. It is a much richer and morally more appealing idea than the market liberal's freedom because it describes more accurately the reasons why we think that choice is a good thing. It builds on but transcends the restrictive definition of freedom and makes it possible to bypass the somewhat sterile debate about the exact circumstances in which freedom rather than mere inability is at issue, without requiring us to jettison a concern with the reasons why someone is unable to take advantage of his opportunities.

The Role of Altruism

I have emphasized the importance of community several times in my exposition of citizenship theory. I have stressed that social policies should aim at sustaining the status of individuals as full members of the community and should seek to reintegrate those who have been pushed to its margins or beyond. But the importance of community does not end with the integration of recipients. Donors are to be integrated too. Social policies are thought of as resting an altruistic sentiments which are institutionalized into a scheme of mutual aid. In *The Gift Relationship*, Titmuss argues that social policies can be seen as 'agents of altruistic opportunities'.[29] Titmuss believes that expressions of mutual concern need to be nurtured. He fears that if 'the bonds of community giving are broken the result is not a state of value neutralism. The vacuum is likely to be filled by hostility and social conflict.[30] It is this anxiety which accounts for the focus of *The Gift Relationship* on 'the extent to which specific instruments of public policy encourage or discourage, foster or destroy the individual expression of altruism and regard for the needs of others'.[31]

Marshall, too, treats welfare policies as rooted in altruism. 'Welfare decisions', he writes:

> are generally altruistic, and they must draw on standards of value embodied in an autonomous ethical system which, though an intrinsic part of the contemporary civilization, is not the product of the summation of individual preferences (as in a market) or of a hypothetical majority vote.[32]

Altruism has a significant role to play, therefore, in creating a sense of community. As Marshall avers, 'welfare policy would be of little use if it did not actively help to create standards of value in its field and promote consensus on them. It is by nature educational.'[33] For both Marshall and Titmuss a genuinely integrated society is one in which its members are directly concerned about the welfare of their fellows and establish welfare institutions to reflect that concern. This is in marked contrast to the Hayekian view that peaceful integration is possible only where the sole society-wide relationships are economic and where the only general obligations are ones of noninterference.

In the previous chapter I suggested that it is a mistake to see citizenship theory as a defence of a certain kind of insurance scheme based on a collective pooling of risks which is in the long-term self-interest of each member of society as it is cheaper than insuring privately. Even if the contingencies covered by a properly constituted welfare state were the same as those which individuals would insure against, the role of altruism would make the institution qualitatively different from an insurance scheme. Enlightened self-interest may play a role, but here the reasons for supporting the policies are also directly founded on a moral concern for the condition of one's fellow-beings. The welfare state cannot be reduced to a marriage of convenience.

A properly constituted welfare system is communitarian in a strong sense. As Raymond Plant has shown, community 'is not just a matter of particular outcomes, but of right intentional relationships, relationships that involve benevolence, altruism, fraternity'.[34] In other words, for a community to exist there must be 'an intention among the members of the group to act in certain ways toward one another, to respond to each other in particular ways, and to value each person as a member of the group'.[35] Insurance models of welfare do not capture this sense of right intentional relations, though citizenship theory manifestly does.

The Gift Relationship is an extended examination of right intentional relationships in one area of social policy: blood donation. Titmuss analyses different methods of supplying blood in order to identify the moral principles they rest upon. His conclusion is that a non-market system of voluntary blood donation enlists sufficient altruistic behaviour from the community to ensure that the demand for blood is satisfied more efficiently than by any alternative market-oriented system. For Titmuss, voluntary blood donation is a paradigm for the social services generally. By defining a distinctive principle as underlying welfare provision, Titmuss hopes to describe the moral boundaries of the nonmarket welfare system. Polemically, he writes:

> If blood is morally sanctioned as something to be bought and sold what ultimately is the justification for not promoting individualistic private markets in other component areas of medical care, and in education, social security, welfare service, child foster care, social work skills . . . and other 'social service' institutions and processes.[36]

There is little doubt that Titmuss and Marshall overstate the case for treating altruism as a major causal element in the genesis of welfare institutions. Self-interest in the form of pressure group or class politics has certainly been a far more significant element than altruism. But be that as it may, altruism still has an important role to play in the moral defence of the welfare state; a properly constituted welfare system may be one which draws on and institutionalizes altruism. For that reason it is necessary to consider the nature of altruism according to Titmuss.

The principal feature of altruism is that it is a concern for the well-being of other people which does nothing to stigmatize them for their dependency. Some forms of altruism threaten the self-respect of the recipient. Titmuss is especially concerned with the way that, historically, charity had been associated with relations of dominance and subservience as the poor were compelled to express grovelling gratitude for the receipt of alms when they bore no responsibility for their indigency. Titmuss is deeply impressed by studies of the way gift-giving can be used as an instrument to reinforce status differences and exercise social control. The humiliation and branding of the subjects of the good works of the Charity Organization Society was an experience not to be repeated in an acceptable welfare state.

As I will show more fully in chapter 4, Titmuss seeks to avoid the risks of 'the gratitude imperative' by imposing conditions of anonymity and impersonality on the gift. The gift of blood is a gift to the unnamed, universal stranger. There are to be no 'personal expressions of gratitude or of other sentiments'.[37] Equally, the gift cannot be made contingent upon the recipient's characteristics, such as his race, religion or class. Gifts of this kind are quite unlike gifts given in the normal setting, where knowledge of the recipient is intimate and personal relations are richly textured.

Titmuss believes that anonymous and impersonal gifts to the 'universal stranger' could play a vital part in overcoming 'the explicit or implicit institutionalization of separateness, whether categorized in terms of income, class, race, colour or religion, rather than the recognition of the similarities between people and their needs which causes much of the world's suffering'.[38] Altruistic sentiments, focused on commonness, provide the cement to forge an integrated community. Altruism opposes the divisive and 'possessive egoism of the market'.

Altruism is at the heart of right intentional relations. It takes as its object the common needs of the members of society. It concerns itself, therefore, with the status of those whose standing in the community is most threatened. Without altruism, capitalist societies are condemned to conflict and intolerable levels of alienation. Altruism is, however, a delicate flower, which withers rapidly in the arid and polluted air of self-interest and market relations. When certain things become commodities to be bought and sold their nature changes and the incentive to give is removed. As Singer has noted, in defence of Titmuss, if blood is donated freely its significance as a gift is tied directly to the need of the recipient, but if it can be bought and sold the gift merely saves someone money – its significance is a function of the wealth of the recipient.[39] For Titmuss:

> it is the responsibility of the state ... to reduce or eliminate or
> control the forces of market coercions which place men in

situations in which they have less freedom or little freedom to make moral choices and to behave altruistically if they so will.[40]

The centrality of altruism is clear. First, it is a source capable of generating a flow of resources to satisfy needs. The case study of blood is designed to show that altruism is not in inherently short supply. Secondly, altruistic behaviour is an expression of fellowship; it binds the community together. Thirdly, it permits the identification of a proper domain for social policy. Unilateral gifts characterize welfare policies; bilateral transfers, the market. The distinction helps ground a principled division of functions between the welfare state and the private market.

The issue of how to define the proper scope of the welfare state can therefore be approached from two different directions. It can be approached either from the point of view of needs, as I suggested at the beginning of the chapter, or from the perspective of altruism. The starting point may be different but in either case the destination is the same. It would be an error, however, to expect either a definition of needs or an account of altruism to yield very precise prescriptions for the detailed nature and character of welfare policies. Need is largely a socially constituted notion, at least when we get beyond abject destitution. It has to be identified by reference to the way of life of the community, and that way of life is itself something which emerges through history, evolves incrementally and can be subject to articulation and redefinition through the political system. As Marshall has indicated, 'societies . . . create an image of an ideal citizenship', and so there is no universal principle to determine what the social rights and duties are.[41] To some considerable extent, the definition and structure of a society's welfare system falls within political discretion; it is an act of political will. This discretion encompasses, within limits, the decision that certain needs are to be included within the welfare orbit and, more importantly, the details of the methods to be used to satisfy them. The discretion is limited, however, because a large measure of a society's way of life is a given at any time, and certain types of delivery mechanism are clearly ruled out as incompatible with treating someone as a full member of the community however that community is defined.

There is, then, a measure of political freedom associated with settling the scope and terms of welfare. Here community plays an important role once again. Welfare institutions are expected to be educative and to instill a sense of wider social responsibility to those who are harmed by forces beyond their control. The expectation is that involvement in the welfare state will lead to a reorientation of attitudes in the populace generally. Political conflict is inescapable but more easily resolved if citizens bring to the process a commitment to the community and a recognition of their social obligations. Admittedly, present-day conflicts reflect the unprincipled pursuit of private advantage thinly veiled by laissez-faire doctrine, but the goal of citizenship theory is to create a community in which legitimate self-interest is constrained and balanced by a recognition of social duty. An object of citizenship theory is the establishment of a society which belongs to all its members in place of one belonging to the well-off, the talented, the lucky and the well-born. It is to create a community in which everyone is at home, in which everyone belongs, in place of one in which many are excluded. It is to make the fruits of a common heritage accessible to all and to provide hope to those who see society as alien and existing for others. In a properly constituted welfare state democratically determined policies would reflect these sentiments as self-interest becomes modified by duty. The political task is to make moral duty an operative element in the politics of large societies.

The Relation of the Welfare System to the Market

Before closing my exposition of citizenship theory, it is necessary to say something more about the relationship between the welfare system and the economic market. Although needs and altruism, mediated within the political system, provide some guidance to the terms of that relationship, it remains unclear what the role of the private economy is expected to be. With the exception of Marshall, citizenship writers seem to have rarely risen above a generally hostile disposition to the private market. The possibility that it might manifest desirable attributes is scarcely acknowledged. At best, some writers, including Townsend, seem to do little more than take for granted the hypothesis that an acceptable welfare system must be married to a socialist, planned economy. Titmuss, too, often creates the impression that the market exists to be abolished and that private market relationships have no morally redeeming virtues. On this view, 'welfare values' can be expected to displace 'market values' in a just society.

There is, of course, another way of examining the problem, especially given the powerful case that can be made for markets. In the light of the actual experience of attempts to plan economies, the argument that markets are relatively good at achieving allocative efficiency cannot be lightly dismissed. Furthermore, economic freedom is not only a type of freedom, it is one that experience suggests is highly valued and properly so by members of advanced societies. Also, notwithstanding tendencies to concentration, markets do achieve a dispersal of power and there is much merit in the argument that thereby the conditions of political freedom are supported. Finally, the productivity of economies which are orientated towards markets, without being exclusively laissez-faire, in comparison to primarily planned economies, makes it difficult to resist the claim that the connection is not accidental.

For these reasons it is worthwhile to posit another characterization of the relationship between the welfare system and the market. Here there is no suggestion of a moral hegemony for welfare, rather, a properly constituted welfare system is but a part of society which confers legitimacy upon a suitably constrained market. The welfare state civilizes market relations; it compensates for their inadequacies and promotes goals they could never achieve alone. It does not, however, seek totally to replace the market. Some such understanding of citizenship theory is not only viable, it is necessary if it is to command the allegiance of the citizenry. To interpret citizenship theory as requiring the transcendence of the market in a socialist utopia, or as entailing extensive central planning through public ownership of the 'commanding heights' of the economy, is to doom it to political sterility and to permit the political agenda to be dominated by thoroughly uncongenial ideological competitors.

It is clear from what has gone before the citizenship theory is hostile to the delivery of certain welfare services through reliance on private markets. I have spent some time detailing the moral objections to markets in these goods and, more generally, the moral costs of laissez-faire economic arrangements, especially in so far as they lead to insecurity and unfairly burden certain groups. From the discussion of altruism it is also clear that markets which rely on self-interest are seen to be corrosive of community. In a society in which market relationships are extensive, most people, most of the time, act out of self-interest. This colours personal relationships, and ensures that other individuals are regarded instrumentally. The tendency is to be coldly calculating in one's treatment of others. Economic relationships are characterized by mutual indifference. By legitimating the competitive pursuit of self-interest a society encourages not merely indifference towards others but selfishness and acquisitiveness. Individuals think of themselves first and others not at all. In this game, if you are a success, your personal virtues have been properly rewarded. If you fail, it is because of your personal inadequacies. The successful are encouraged to believe that they have received only what they deserve to keep. Acquisitiveness and egoism lead individuals to neglect their social obligations; self-interest corrodes social and moral bonds. An unwillingness to put the public interest before the private leads to hostility and social conflict. The acid of self-interest rots the foundations of the social order.

But taken jointly, these arguments do not provide a reason to reject the market wholesale. They do no more than point to reasons to constrain its operation and compensate for its failures. What is needed is a more principled account of what is intrinsically wrong with markets. David Watson is one of the few writers within the tradition to attempt an explicit and systematic account of the thoroughgoing moral inadequacies of markets. For Watson, the market offers relationships which are economic only, and which lack therefore any moral dimension. Market relationships are instrumental, non-tuistic and impersonal:

> This gives us . . . insight into the reasons why economic policy, motivated by egoism or perhaps non-tuism, is non-moral. It asks us not to conceive of the relationships it governs as relationships between human beings. It asks us not to regard the individuals participating in economic exchange, to use Kantian language, as ends-in-themselves. It disregards even their basic social relationships founded on their common humanity. The participants are, literally, alien.[42]

Watson argues that economic markets display a moral weakness because the relationships within them are amoral in failing to exemplify a principle that persons are to be respected as ends and not just as means.

The foundation of Watson's argument is as follows. First, for individuals involved in an exchange the interests of the other are not ends to be promoted. Individuals participate in economic relations to further their own interests or the interests of others not party to them. In the former case the motivation is egoistic, in the latter non-tuistic. Neither of these is a moral attitude. They are amoral because they are not universalizable, and universalizability is a necessary condition of morality. Parties to economic exchanges treat each other instrumentally, as means to the fulfilment of some goal or other, and not also as ends-in-themselves. The justification of economic relationships, avers Watson, must be of an amoral kind.[43]

There are a number of problems with this argument. Watson offers no defence of his claim that non-tuistic reasons for entering economic exchanges cannot be universalized. I can see no reason why they cannot be. Moreover, entering exchanges with third parties may often be the best way of fulfilling one's moral obligations. Parents, for example, earn money to feed their children. Some may sell assets to give to charities. Why is the justification of economic relationships of these kinds not a moral one? Watson seems to want to deny that it can be just because the motivation to engage in the exchange is not to further the interests of the other party.

Further, the fact that two persons do not enter an exchange expressly to promote each other's interests does not entail that the relationship is amoral. The way in which the relationship is conducted may involve an explicit or implicit recognition of the moral status of the other participant as an end-in-himself. Concretely, the relationship may involve, through a process of contracting, a recognition of the other as a free human being, bearing rights and with interests of his own. Indeed, the relationship can create moral claims where these did not exist before. Watson seems to assume that the question whether a particular relationship is moral or not turns solely on the reasons why it has been entered into. But this is not acceptable. A relationship may be moral because of the manner in which it is conducted if that shows that a person is not a means only but also an end.

'It is clear', Watson writes, 'that in all cases of economic exchange the individuals do not regard the interests of each other as ends to be promoted.[44] But is it so clear? It is certainly not a necessary truth. What if I buy from the Oxfam shop to support Oxfam? What if governments deliberately place contracts with domestic industry to protect it from foreign competition, or if a party to a continuing relationship decides to sacrifice his own short-term interests to foster those of the other party in order to preserve the relationship over the long haul? Economic relationships allow for greater awareness of mutual benefit, and a sense that each person's self-interest is bound up with that of the other, than is commonly allowed. If these arguments are correct then Watson's account of the moral failure of market relations must be rejected, and with it his defence of the distinction between the proper function of the market and a social policy which is premised on the assumption that a clear line can be drawn between policy that is justified by an appeal to moral status and identity, and policy that is not.

I return to the point that whatever the failures of markets there are powerful reasons to recognize both moral and practical advantages to making use of them in a just community. There should be scope for the legitimate pursuit of self-interest in any acceptable society. But, equally, markets cannot run everywhere. The arguments of the citizenship school powerfully suggest the limits of the moral appeal of markets. It is worth stressing, however, that it is *limits* which they suggest. Even the arguments of Titmuss, rather than his dispositions, will not bear the weight of a conclusion that markets should be transcended.

That the moral reasons underlying an extensive welfare state imply only a circumscribed rejection of the market is seen most clearly by Marshall. Marshall develops his view in 'Value Problems of Welfare Capitalism', in which he discusses the notion of a 'hyphenated society'. He writes:

The hyphen links two (or can it be three) different and contrasted elements together to create a new entity whose character is a product of the combination, but not the fusion, of the components, whose separate identities are preserved intact and are of equal contributory status. . . . the differences strengthen the structure because they are complementary rather than divisive. . . . The parts are meaningless except in their relationship with one another.[45]

What we are offered here is a model of society in which different sectors, organized on different principles, coexist in a stable form. For Marshall, there are three key sectors in society: the private market; the welfare system; and political democracy. Each sector is of 'equal contributory status'. In summing up his position he says:

I am one of those who believe that it is hardly possible to maintain democratic freedom in a society which does not contain a large area of economic freedom and that the incentives provided by and expressed in competitive markets make a contribution to efficiency and to progress in the production and distribution of wealth which cannot, in a large and complex society, be derived from any other source.[46]

However, Marshall goes on to criticize those who believe that 'the inability of the market to meet its social obligations' can be compensated for 'by attaching a framework or scaffolding of welfare services alongside the market economy, matching its operations and engaged to patch cracks, fill holes, dress wounds' and so forth. 'Already', he states, 'there is too much of this, and to put still greater reliance upon it would lead to the gradual degradation of the welfare principle.'[47]

Marshall's analysis contains, therefore, a relatively enthusiastic endorsement of private markets tempered by a sensitivity to their practical and moral weaknesses. There is no question but that he is at odds with other members of the citizenship tradition on this point, and to that extent it may be a little artificial to treat them as members of the same school, despite the common agreement on the values which infuse the welfare system itself. There is, however, some justice in the commonplace criticism that citizenship writers have given little thought to the production of the resources they are so anxious to distribute justly. In my view, Marshall's awareness of the importance of the private economic market is to be preferred to the emotional hostility of Titmuss. In the struggle for the hearts and minds of the citizenry, proper attention will have to be paid to the foundations of economic prosperity and Marshall is correct to stress the importance of markets in this connection.

In this chapter, as in the previous one, I have sought to articulate the type of moral theory which underlies citizenship theory. This moral theory is clearly attractive. Few deny the allure of community and nobody admits to not caring about the reality of life for those who fare relatively badly in capitalist societies. The objection to citizenship theory is not with its aspirations so much as with its muddled thinking about the nature and content of rights, the moral acceptability of market outcomes, the relation between moral notions such as rights and altruism, equality and freedom and so forth. Citizenship theory, it is objected, bears out the old maxim about the road to hell. In the next chapters I turn to some of these issues in an effort to see whether this tradition can withstand and respond to its critics.

4

Altruism, Rights and Integration

Two elements play a crucial role within citizenship theory. Welfare policy is viewed as a response to the social rights of citizens. It is also an expression of altruism. Jointly, rights and altruism are the moral bedrock upon which a defence of the welfare state is founded. But can they operate in tandem in this way? Or does drawing upon a rights-based justification of social policy preclude the invocation of the merits of altruistically-motivated relationships? Are not citizenship writers attempting to have the best of two fundamentally different and utterly irreconcilable moral worlds? Even supposing that their moral universe is not scarred by a fatal *philosophical* incoherence, what of its sociological plausibility? A good case can be made out that the citizenship school has too quickly assumed that altruism and the recognition of social rights will combine to achieve social integration and eradicate the stigmatization of the poor and the dependent. If that is so, what then? Is citizenship theory doomed to the sterility of arm-waving utopianism?

The philosophical problem is quickly stated. To focus on altruistic giving, embodied in a voluntary 'gift relationship', ignores the fact that the only secure moral foundation for justifying social welfare is the recognition that certain basic needs ground rights to welfare. Such rights entail that those who possess sufficient resources have a strict obligation to allow them to be made available to those in need. The provision of these resources is not a matter of choice for the donor. Involving rather the recognition of a duty, it cannot be classified as voluntary altruism because altruism presupposes the freedom to decide whether or not to give. The idea of social or welfare rights deprives donors of exactly that freedom. Integrating both altruism and rights into the foundations of a theory must be incoherent. If one cannot have a right to a gift, and if one has a right to welfare, then welfare cannot be a gift. A choice must be made. Either one opts for a gift-based altruism or for social rights, but one cannot successfully integrate both into the same account.

Are we forced to accept this incoherence? Choosing between rights and altruism is damaging to the integrity of the citizenship tradition. On the face of it, giving up altruism is tantamount to jettisoning communitarian aspirations. After all, gift-giving relationships are the key to creating a sense of fellowship; a necessary condition of integrating a community around the explicit recognition and protection of those things we share. It is not just the protection of needs that matters; it is that they are protected in ways which elicit an affectionate sense of communality. Equally, if the notion of rights were removed, much that protects the status of the needy would be lost. Not only may needs be satisfied in ways which humiliate the needy, but the sense of security that needs *will* be satisfied will be eroded. Claiming rights to welfare offers the best guarantee that needs will be met, because the enforcement of rights is properly a matter for government, and the existence of rights-based claims goes some way to establish the priority of those claims against rival considerations. The establishment of a moral right to welfare serves to protect the basic interests of those in need.

It also affects the nature of the moral relationships between persons. Claiming a right to a benefit avoids the need to supplicate for it. Satisfying a right as a right is an essential part of what it is to respect a person. Rights to welfare are an intrinsic element in guaranteeing a recognition of equality of status. Given these moral advantages it is hardly surprising that there is a desire to cling onto both altruism and rights. But can this be done?

Titmuss: Welfare Rights and Altruism

The book which raises the issue most clearly is *The Gift Relationship*, for there Titmuss wrote most glowingly about the virtues of an altruistic welfare society, without paying attention to the tension that this created for his conception of welfare rights.[1] In many respects, Titmuss's use of blood donation as a paradigm for social policy is extremely unfortunate. In the first place he failed to articulate a defence of the proposition that blood donation can stand as a symbol of the social services in general, or that the moral relationships found in a voluntary donation system could be, or were, replicated elsewhere. Moreover, in selecting blood he chose something which it is difficult, though by no means impossible, to argue that anyone has a right to. Claiming a right to some of the food on the rich man's table is one thing; claiming that there is an *enforceable* obligation to donate blood is quite another. Many who readily accept that welfare rights do ground enforceable claims on the material resources of citizens, balk at the idea that similar claims could be made out against the living tissues of their bodies. Titmuss's concern in *The Gift Relationship* is with the contrast between two different reasons for donating blood: altruism and profit. Perhaps for this reason he nowhere discusses the possibility that those in need of blood have an enforceable right to receive it, but equally he nowhere rejects it. The issue should have been dealt with if only to clarify the relationship between this work and the rest of his corpus. Unless we are to say that Titmuss's philosophy underwent an unacknowledged radical change in his last book, we are left with the result that rights and altruism both have a key role to play in justifying welfare policy and that no real inconsistency between them is perceived.

There are two obvious and different ways of relating rights and altruism. The first asserts that the domain of welfare is bifurcated. One part of the domain is identified by its concern with rights-based claims, the other by its concern with altruism. Hence, welfare rights which ground strict obligations and which protect basic interests do not exhaust the sphere of welfare. Altruism, therefore, can have a legitimate role to play in 'topping up' welfare provision. Alternatively, altruistic giving might provide a degree of 'fine tuning' in social policy, given that rights-based claims typically invoke rather blunt categories which leave the particularity of certain needs unprotected. Raymond Plant takes a view like this when he writes that:

> State-provided welfare as a matter of right is never likely to be able to tailor exactly resources to detailed need among the deprived just because the amount of detailed information required is not likely to be available, and it is at the interstices of felt need and state provision that the ultra obligations of altruism and gift-giving are always going to have a place in a welfare society.[2]

Viewed in this way it is possible to interpret *The Gift Relationship* not as a direct argument for the welfare state, but rather as one that asserts the value of practices of direct giving which are not mediated by institutional structures. These practices could well exist alongside the formal welfare state, independent of it, but contributing to it by creating a sense of community. Julia Parker suggests something like this in pointing out that in *The Gift Relationship* Titmuss:

> was expressing his faith not in the activities of governments but in particular kinds of relationships between the governed as pointing the way to the welfare society.[3]

Adopting this suggestion leads to the conclusion that the role of altruism is to fuel non-governmental relationships in the welfare society, whereas rights underpin a battery of governmental organizations in the welfare state. It is a philosophy for the mixed economy of welfare. Although no doubt plausible in its own right, this understanding of the relationship of altruism to the basic need-satisfying institutions in society does not attribute to altruism the foundational importance it had for Titmuss as a way to satisfying the essential needs of 'unknown strangers'. The value of altruistic relationships is retained, but at the expense of displacing them from centre stage. Altruism is marginalized; it has been reduced to the role of a bit player. Moreover, the altruism incorporated within this suggestion differs radically from the account proposed by Titmuss. Imposed upon the account of altruism in *The Gift Relationship* are conditions of impersonality, not the particularity of needs. Resources are given to unnamed strangers of whom nothing is known by the donor (except of course the existence of needs of a certain kind), and are received by individuals from unknown sources. Plant's argument implies a much more personal and richly textured set of relationships than Titmuss had in mind. Finally, the conditions of impersonality and anonymity seem to imply that public institutions have a key role to play in the delivery of welfare services, particularly where these institutions constitute the core of the welfare state and are focused on the most basic and fundamental needs. In other words, public institutional structures are necessary not only as a concrete embodiment of the expression of community, but also because they are the only structures capable of maintaining the anonymity and impersonality which are the key elements defining the nature of the gift relationship.

A second way of holding on to both rights and altruism is simply to deny the incompatibility of rights and gifts. David Watson in *Caring for Strangers* adopts this view.[4] His argument is that the gift of welfare aid is something the needy have a right to claim. In other words, he denies that the provision of resources to fulfil a strict obligation is incompatible with the provision of resources as a gift.

Certainly this claim is not totally implausible, for there are, indeed, some types of gift-giving where the recipient has a kind of entitlement to receive. The giving of gifts at Christmas to one's children, for example, is not an entirely voluntary affair. Children and other relatives have a legitimate expectation that they will receive some presents; an expectation which it is offensive to deny. But, nevertheless, this resolution of the problem is not entirely convincing. In *The Gift Relationship*, Titmuss is quite clear that the giving of blood is voluntary. He discusses at length institutionalized forms of gift-giving in primitive societies which occur within a web of obligations to give and rights to receive. The point of these discussions is not to assimilate the gift of blood (and hence other social policy gifts) to this mode; rather, it is to distinguish between altruistic, voluntary gift-giving and traditional forms of gift ceremony. In several places in his account of the British blood-donation system, Titmuss recurs to the voluntary character of the blood gift. He points out that 'there are no personal, predictable penalties for not giving; no socially enforced sanctions of remorse, shame or guilt',[5] that altruism and gift-giving of this kind presupposes 'the freedom to give or not to give',[6] and that if there is an obligation of any kind to give, then it should be thought of as an 'ultra-obligation',[7] that is, as involving only supererogatory acts. It is clear that Titmuss's intention is to establish the view that to act altruistically is to act freely; to do what one ought to do (at least on occasions), but not what one is under a strict obligation to do. To act altruistically is to choose to do something morally worthwhile; but one has the choice whether or not so to act. If one were under a strict obligation, there would be no such freedom, and one *would be* under such an obligation if there were a right to welfare. Watson's resolution of the problem is satisfactory, therefore, only if the voluntary character of altruism is ignored. But it is precisely its voluntarism that Titmuss regards as one of its most important characteristics.

Neither of the proposals discussed so far dispels the incoherence that seems to lurk at the heart of the citizenship approach. Altruism and rights appear to be competitive ideals. There is, however, a way in which both ideas can be coherently reconciled. The basis of this reconciliation is to regard altruism as overlying rights in well-constituted relationships. Both Altruism and rights exist simultaneously, but while relationships are founded on altruism, rights are not invoked, since they are not needed. Rights lie dormant, though they do not cease to exist. Only when altruism fades, and the interests that rights are created to protect are threatened, does it become necessary to claim and act on rights. Only at that moment do rights come into competition with altruism and where necessary displace it.

An example may clarify the argument. Imagine a contented family. Husband and wife owe each other a series of obligations. At one level, viewed both from a moral and a legal perspective, marriage is an agreement under which a couple assume mutual duties. Added to these are rights in matrimonial property which become effective only in the event of marital breakdown. Moreover, duties are owed to children. A child has an enforceable claim to be provided with the necessaries of life and not to be abused. Equally, moral obligations are owed to parents and to siblings. Yet despite the existence of these moral and legal rights it would be highly unusual to refer to those rights as part of an explanation of the nature of relationships within the family. In a happy family, members act on the basis of affection, love, concern and respect; not because of a duty to respect each other's rights. If they were reminded of the fact that their actions fulfilled their mutual obligations, the most likely response would be some kind of disclaimer, coupled with the assertion that to see their relationships in that way misunderstands their essential character. Most of the time, relationships within a loving family would not be characterized by a recognition of duty. Indeed, any assessment of the quality of relationships with a family need not make any explicit reference to the fact that their actions were in accordance with some pattern of rights and obligations.

As I have indicated above, this is not to say that these rights cease to exist when individuals are engaged in familial relationships. It is nearer the truth to regard them as being overlaid or as lying inactive. Rights and obligations become morally significant only if individuals one would expect normally to act in ways which do not conflict with these dormant rights, begin to act in ways which do flout them. In these circumstances, rights can be invoked and enforced. Indeed, it is in just those cases where loving relationships are absent or have broken down that individuals within the family may begin to act out of a sense of duty, or where members may claim to have their rights enforced. Rights, therefore, continue to exist even where their presence does not colour or affect family relationships under normal circumstances. They continue to exist as protective devices which can be asserted if circumstances warrant.

Relationships within the family can stand as an analogue of the connection between voluntary altruism and welfare rights in a properly constituted welfare state. So, if altruistic behaviour generates a sufficient flow of resources to meet needs, it would not be necessary to invoke rights-based claims. Rights to welfare would continue to exist just as a child's rights against his parents continue to exist, though the recognition of a strict obligation would not itself be the reason why individuals made resources available, any more than it is the reason why most parents care for the needs of their children. Rights are devices created to protect basic individual interests, which need to be invoked only if those basic interests are being threatened. If basic interests are not under threat, rights lie dormant, though they do not cease to exist. Thus rights take over in conditions marked by the absence of altruism, but are overlaid or displaced in its presence.

There is nothing particularly quirky about thinking of rights in this way, nor is it a feature exclusively of family-like relationships. After all, you have a right to life, but the reason why I don't kill you could have more to do with my squeamishness at the sight of blood than with my awareness of your rights. The same is true in contractual relationships. We may act so as to fulfil the terms of our agreement not because doing so is to respect those terms, but more mundanely because it is our respective self-interest to do so. Moreover, while our relationship subsists we will each hold against the other a complex of rights, created by the agreement, which await only the breakdown of our agreement to be invoked. If you fail to deliver the car to me, you will owe me damages.

If you deliver the wrong car, I can send it back. The existence of a right, therefore, does not depend on whether it is invoked on every occasion that a relationship corresponds to its requirements, any more than it is necessary for a relationship to conform to those requirements that the actors entering it are motivated by a desire to respect the right.

Altruism, Rights and Community

Given this it can be seen that the citizenship approach need not be taken to be asserting philosophically incompatible principles. Rather the principles may be complementary. A properly constituted welfare state in which there existed a strong sense of community would depend, first, on altruistic behaviour to supply need-satisfying resources and, second, if necessary, on a backup system of enforceable rights if ever there were a shortfall of resources. If altruism fails, rights take over; if altruism works, rights do not need to be invoked. In this way both rights and altruism can be integrated into the foundations of a defence of the welfare state.

But how plausible is this? The immediate objection is that the original incoherence remains. The type of altruism that Titmuss defends describes altruistic giving as an ultra-obligation. Being a voluntary act, one has a choice whether or not to give. My resolution of the problem apparently denies this choice by arguing that, if one does not give for altruistic reasons, one will be forced to give on the grounds that a strict obligation has to be enforced. The tension between the enforceable obligation and voluntary altruism is not dispelled because one is not free not to give.

There are two rejoinders to this. First, being free to give or not to give may be interpreted as meaning that one is free to decide whether or not to give *altruistically*. If one does not freely decide to give, then the necessary resources will be extracted. The choice one has is not the choice to decide whether or not some resources presently under one's control will be transferred to a third party. It is the choice to decide on what terms they will be transferred. In other words, one is free to decide whether to give them up for altruistic reasons, transfer them because one recognized one's duty, or have them extracted because the state enforces strict obligations. Of course, if it is a necessary condition for altruistic giving that the disposition of one's resources is under one's control, in the strong sense that one can determine whether or not they are to be transferred, then this response fails and the incoherence remains.

The second rejoinder is more persuasive and more consistent with the tenor of *The Gift Relationship*. The point is that the opportunity for any individual freely to make available some of his resources to meet others' needs depends on the actions of other individuals. If a sufficient number of individuals are giving altruistically, and the supply of resources produced is enough to satisfy demand, then any particular individual, taken randomly, is free to choose whether or not to transfer resources. Problems are created only if all or a certain critical number of donors decide not to give. In that event the apparatus of rights and obligations has to come into effect. The total supply of resources available for meeting need has to be topped up by enforcing obligations against some individuals. The freedom of some citizens not to give has to be curtailed.

Resolving the problem in this way fits easily with Titmuss's account because it assumes that a sufficient flow of resources could be generated spontaneously. Titmuss suggests that altruistic behaviour is not in inherently scarce supply. His evidence is that increasing demand for blood produces an adequate supply. Beyond this it is by no means clear what the mechanisms are.[8] Certainly, he and others within the tradition think of a welfare state that incorporates or rests on a bedrock of altruism as a morally educative set of institutions, capable of bonding people through an increased awareness of common need and common frailty before the overwhelming contingencies of social life. Titmuss seems to believe passionately that participation in institutions which meet common needs and which create a sense of common experience help break down barriers that divide people and encourage an over-widening sense of social responsibility by generalizing compassion. Like so many of his generation, Titmuss is profoundly influenced by the Second World War when the effects of evacuation, war work and, above all, air raids combined to dislodge the barriers of social class. Bombs knew no class, and the forced commonality of nights in tube stations and days spent in war work forged a transcendent communitarian ardour. Claiming that the institutions of the welfare state were the post-war mechanism by which the Dunkirk spirit could be kept alive may be an exaggeration. But for Titmuss and many others on the left, it is only a slight one.

A second objection to this interpretation of the relationship between rights-based claims and altruistic giving is that it ignores the importance that rights have as devices designed to protect self-respect.[9] Allowing voluntary altruistic giving to overlay rights exposes individuals to the dangers of stigmatization and risks reinforcing inherently unequal relationships. Welfare founded on altruism seems extremely close to charity. And charity smacks of grovelling gratitude on the part of recipients and the imposition of social control at the behest of the donors. If self-respect is to be protected, constant reliance on rights-based principles is necessary.

Titmuss's response to this criticism is clear. He denies that the impersonal, voluntary gift to the unnamed stranger would be open to this kind of abuse. In several places in *The Gift Relationship* he characterizes altruism in a way which avoids this problem. For example:

> Unlike gift exchange in traditional societies, there is in the free gift of blood to unnamed strangers no contract of custom, no legal bond, no functional determinism, no situations of disciplinary power, domination, constraint or compulsion, no sense of shame or guilt, no gratitude imperative and no need for the penitence of a Chrysostom.[10]

Titmuss believes that the account he offers of altruistic giving to strangers avoids the dangers of stigmatization. Gifts to strangers are anonymous and impersonal. Because donor and recipient are not personally known to each other there can 'be no personal expressions of gratitude or of other sentiments'.[11] Under these conditions the gift cannot function as a form of deliberate social control. Anonymity, by abstracting from particular differences between people (e.g. race, religion, politics), transcends factors which serve to set people apart and identifies and reinforces aspects which they hold in common. In this way bonds are created which encourage integration without threatening self-respect.

Earlier on I suggested that we could model the relationship of rights and altruism in citizenship theory on the relationship of rights to love and affection within a contented family. Treating the moral society as a happy family writ large captures much of what is attractive about citizenship theory. But on further examination it is clear that the analogy breaks down, even if it is not hopelessly utopian. Desiring to avoid the risk that the provision of aid to the needy would result in stigmitization, Titmuss stresses that altruistic behaviour expressing 'affection' for the needy must be channelled through impersonal and anonymous institutions. But the price of avoiding stigma is high.

Normally, as Plant observes, one associates altruistic and fraternal relationships with detailed personal knowledge and intimacy. Much of the value of these relationships stems from their warmth and intensity, predicated as they are upon mutual recognition of each person's specialness or uniqueness. Fraternal relationships of this kind typically serve to bond relatively small numbers of people and the fraternal glue is to be found in just those things which mark the group off from other groups. The basis of fraternity is in what *we* share, but others lack. We may share common membership of a family, circle of friends, college, rugby club or trade union. Characteristically, such fraternal relationships are characterized by intensity, warmth and a sense of common identity, originating, in part, in the existence of insiders and outsiders.

Titmuss's analysis of impersonal altruism differs substantially from altruistic fraternity in small-scale situations. First, the focus is not a small group, but the society as a whole. Second, it is characterized not by intimacy and personal knowledge but by impersonality and anonymity. Titmuss eliminates from his account of altruism and fraternity the conditions which usually characterize it. In their place are conditions which deprive the Titmussian fraternity of the opportunity to embody genuine warmth; we are offered a rather cold, not to say austere, basis upon which to build a sense of community. In establishing conditions of impersonality and anonymity, Titmuss deprives his variety of altruistic behaviour of much that normally gives altruism its value.

This is indeed a high price to pay. Titmuss wants a defence of the welfare state which sees it as embodying a sense of fellowship. He offers an account of altruistic behaviour/fellowship which lacks the warmth, intimacy, affection of the standard case. Yet the fact that fraternal relationships embody these characteristics is the reason why they are offered as more humanly satisfying than ones founded on the mutual recognition of rights and duties. If this is so, how can Titmuss's account of altruism hold out more humanly satisfying relationships than those created by recognizing rights and duties? Certainly, Titmuss's account of altruistic behaviour does not offer any opportunities to engage in more 'meaningful' intimate relationships. The practices of giving and receiving are mediated by institutions which preserve impersonality and anonymity. The recipient is not assured of a greater quantity of resources just because of the gift relationship. All that he is assured of is that the resources have been made available willingly by others who cared that cases like his existed and who felt that they would like to help. The contrast is with a society in which resources are extracted from resentful citizens who pay their taxes just because it is their duty or for fear of the consequences of hiding income. In these circumstances, a recipient may feel that society is doing its duty by him with bad grace and consequently feel 'alienated' or a 'public burden'. But here the critical distinction is not between altruism and duty. The recipient may feel himself a burden if he believes that society is doing its duty just for duty's sake. If, on the other hand, he felt that society (and individuals within it) was doing its duty with alacrity, with a positive commitment to the reasons why that duty was a duty, then he might feel quite differently. The critical distinction really is between actions which embody a positive and enthusiastic commitment to the purposes of duty and ones which embody at best a reluctant compliance because duty is duty. It is doubtful that a welfare recipient would feel greatly more at home just because he knew that the resources he was consuming originated in altruistic behaviour rather than in the enthusiastic endorsement of duty.

Perhaps, by contrast, voluntary altruism may make more of a

difference to the donor. If sufficient resources were forthcoming through altruistic behaviour, a randomly selected donor could well consider himself free to decide whether or not to give. Possibly, he might take some not unworthy satisfaction from helping others in need, and his example might encourage others to display similar virtues. So on the donation side there may be some moral advantage to altruism, but even so it is doubtful whether the satisfaction available to the altruistic gift-giver is significantly different from that to be derived by enthusiastically endorsing his duties, or whether a more worthy example is set in the former than the latter case.

The problem with building a defence of state welfare on altruism, therefore, lies in taking a value with a distinct moral flavour and then imposing conditions upon its exercise that do much to dissipate its attractiveness. As I have suggested, there is little significant difference, in terms of the nature of human relationships, between a society in which behaviour is predominantly altruistic (as this is understood by Titmuss) and one in which there is an enthusiastic recognition of duty. The critical distinction is not between the recognition of rights and altruism, but between reluctant commitments to duty or their endorsement with alacrity. The fundamental problem, then, is not so much one of encouraging altruistic behaviour in a properly constituted welfare state, as finding ways of stimulating a positive confirmation of those duties it is 'proper' to recognize.

Integration and Conflict within Welfare

The attempt to combine rights and altruism into the defence of the welfare state goes beyond a discussion of moral principle. Altruism and rights play a crucial role in achieving social integration. Recipients are integrated through a structure of universalist services meeting needs outside the market as of right and donors are integrated via their free decisions to give. Implicitly, a major element of welfare is thought of as redistributive. From the independent to the dependent, from those not in need to the needy, redistribution transcends the class inequalities and divisions of the capitalist market, as well as redistributing within classes and across lifetimes as the risks of social contingency unpredictably materialize. But whether integration is an ideal to be aimed at or a fact successfully achieved is not always clear. Certainly, many policies of the welfare state, particularly those employing means-tested selectivity, are considered to be divisive. In respect of these, integration is a goal to be striven for through the transition to greater universality. But in other respects, the integrative effects of welfare state policies are taken for granted. It seems to be assumed that rights do protect self-respect and avoid stigmatization and that the policies do draw upon widespread sentiments of altruism. Taken as a whole, the welfare state draws upon and embodies a large amount of altruism, and is a major integrative force within society,

But how plausible is this? There is certainly a sense in which integration is achieved. The provision of resources to those in need makes it possible for them to engage in consumption patterns which otherwise they could not. On the other hand, universal services for most people merely make available to them outside the market resources they could provide for themselves within it. Universal services provide nothing extra by way of integration for such people. Thus, although the capacity to participate in forms of consumption that are widely approved of within a society is an important element in defining what it is to be an integrated member of the community, integration is not to be reduced to mere consumption. Instead, integration describes a set of moral relationships.

What then is the evidence of integration welded in the crucible of rights and altruism in the contemporary welfare state? In recent years it has become almost trite to argue that the welfare state is more a source of social conflict than of integration. Spurious social rights in particular are credited with sowing the seeds of dissension. The views of the new right on this have already been briefly canvassed in chapter 1. Making the government responsible for material social outcomes forces into the political arena issues which previously fell to the market. Political issues require explicit agreement, and the greater the number of issues, the harder it is to reach agreement on any one. Moreover, governmental responsibility for distributional outcomes presupposes the capacity to build consensus on the criteria to which a distribution must conform. But, given the variety and incompatibility of the possible candidates for the preferred theory of social justice and the multiplicity of interests with reason to support one version rather than another, it is extremely unlikely that the necessary consensus could be reached. The welfare state and the 'social rights' it spawns provide, in Enoch Powell's words, 'unlimited fuel for dissatisfaction'.[12] Pressure groups and welfare professionals coalesce around the institutions of state clamouring for recognition of their 'special needs' and 'rights'. 'Politics', claims Powell, speaking for the new right:

> is thus caught in a vicious circle. Violence feeds on 'social grievances' which derive from unfulfillable 'rights'. The result is that ever wider and deeper state intervention is demanded while the State has itself become the source, as well as the focus, of social grievances.[13]

That social conflict is generated by guaranteeing social rights is not the contention of just the market liberals or new right. John Goldthorpe, for example, a democratic socialist of a non-communitarian stripe, argues in several places that citizenship rights have promoted social conflict.[14] Briefly, social rights give power resources to the working class by guaranteeing that individual life chances and industrial bargaining power are not determined exclusively by market position. In particular, social rights have indirectly strengthened the bargaining power of trade unions by ensuring that the basic needs of strikers' families will be met during periods of industrial conflict, and by reducing the costs of unemployment. At the same time, the traditional status order has decayed. Derived from feudal principles that legitimated inequality of status as a reflection of a divinely ordered and morally sanctioned universe, the status order served capitalism well by restraining the pursuit of collective self-interest within the market.[15] As the plausibility of the belief that the structured inequality of market outcomes corresponded to moral criteria faded, to be replaced by the extension of the ideology of self-interest, so the use of unconstrained collective power developed. Trade unions, partly under-written by the welfare state, acted to force resources in the direction of their members, and to a greater or lesser extent sought to capture state institutions to co-opt political power for the same purposes. For Goldthorpe, the welfare state supports the class conflict required to force a redistribution of social and economic benefits within capitalism, and is an institutional structure through which that conflict can be conducted, provided that the collective power of the working class is marshalled rigorously enough.[16] For others on the left also the welfare state is a forum for conflict rather than integration.[17] Traditionally, marxists have ascribed to the welfare state Janus-like qualities. As an instrument of capitalism, the welfare state suppresses the revolutionary potential of the working class, and serves the interests of capital by maintaining workers in thrall to an economic system that conflicts with their true interests in building socialism. But because of its recognition of need as a criterion of distribution, the welfare state can be used as an instrument of socialism. Welfare professionals in particular are in an excellent position to carry on the struggle for the overthrow of capitalism within the institutions of the state, by first educating and then enlisting the workers for the call to arms. To the extent that welfare institutions appear to have achieved social peace and headed off revolution or popular discontent, as some of the welfare reforms of the late nineteenth century, especially in Germany, were clearly intended to do, and as the post-war reforms have had the effect of doing, the radical left argues that only a false integration has been produced. Masking the contradictions of a capitalist economy is at best a temporary expedient. Eventually, the tensions will resurface, as they appeared to do in the 1970s, and the stark reality of the conflict of class interests will be fully exposed.

Whatever their differences, these approaches hold in common a rejection of the claim that the welfare state can foster legitimate integration. Insofar as they have implications for a descriptive account of the genesis of the welfare state, they suggest a relatively minor role for altruism or any other form of disinterested humanitarianism. Much more significant are the political forces of competitive self-interest, whether they are rooted in the pluralistic pressure group activity of recipients, state employees, pension funds, and so forth; in the clash of antagonistic classes; or in the corporatist adjustment of unions, business and government. No doubt these factors have all to a greater or lesser extent played a part in shaping the welfare state, though I suspect that to stress only self-interest is to distort the historical record by downplaying the humanitarian impulse behind welfare reform in general, and in particular the pervasive sense in the immediate post-war years that the welfare state was being established in the name of social justice. At the very least this is true for the support given to the sick, disabled and elderly.

Be that as it may, in the late 1970s it was quite plausible to regard the welfare state as a source of conflict. Throughout the West, we seemed to be witnessing a welfare backlash as the public reacted to declining real income, rapidly increasing welfare costs and a rise in the tax burden. The backlash appeared to be strongest, in Britain, among the poorly paid and unskilled who increasingly found themselves paying taxes which reduced their real income to levels barely higher than welfare recipients enjoying benefits of increased real value. Fanned by sensationalist media reports, 'scroungerphobia' led, say Golding and Middleton, to 'a shrill and mounting antagonism to the welfare system and its clients'.[18] 'The crisis in the British economy', they write, 'has become the occasion for a social derision of the poor so punitive as to threaten the very props of the welfare state.'[19] Support for the redistributive elements of the welfare state, in the form of social security payments and unemployment benefit, has always seemed to be fragile. The anti-collectivist mood of the times seemed to suggest that it had effectively vanished. Studies in Britain and elsewhere showed a remarkably high disposition to blame the victim for his poverty or unemployment. In an EEC survey in 1976, 43 per cent of Britons attributed living in need to 'laziness and lack of willpower', compared with an average of 25 per cent for the EEC as a whole.[20] As Klein commented in 1974:

> The nineteenth century division between the deserving and undeserving poor seems to be alive and kicking – despite the effort of social reformers to abolish it over the past 70 years – in the minds of a majority of the people.[21]

As one might expect, this phenomenon is discouraging for those who believe that welfare institutions can and do integrate all citizens into the community. But there are two comments to be made on this account. The first is that if there was indeed a welfare backlash, it seems to have waned, at least in Britain. The survey results and other data published in *Poor Britain* indicate that in the 1980s as unemployment has climbed inexorably higher the tendency to blame the victim has diminished and the tendency to ascribe the existence of poverty to injustice, or at any rate structural factors, correspondingly increased.[22] Moreover, the authors of *Poor Britain* claim, there is evidence of much greater dissatisfaction with the level of benefits. A majority of the population believe that supplementary benefit is too low, and 40 per cent think that unemployment benefit is too low.[23] According to a Gallup poll in 1976, only 9 per cent thought that unemployment benefit was too low. For an 'integrationist', these trends offer a glimmer of hope, suggesting as they do greater support for what have historically been the least popular pillars of the welfare state.

The second comment is that the reports of a welfare backlash were almost certainly exaggerated. Peter Taylor-Gooby's work on public attitudes to the welfare state, based on surveys conducted in 1981, shows that, as Klein suggested, nineteenth-century attitudes towards the 'deserving and undeserving' poor have been a feature of the welfare state since its inception.[24] There was no sudden falling away of support for the welfare state as such. Rather, support for those aspects of the welfare state dealing with the dependency of the able-bodied has always been relatively low. This is to be contrasted with high levels of commitment to state provision in the fields of health, education, pensions and aid to the disabled. Support for these policies is uniformly high across all social classes. Approval of these services did not noticeably diminish during the 'welfare backlash'. One other major strand of public opinion is worthy of note here. Taylor-Gooby found overwhelming commitment to the principle that individuals ought to have the right to contract out of state provision, to provide for their own health, pension and education requirements.[25]

On more specific issues Taylor-Gooby found little support for the proposition that the welfare state encourages community support or altruism.[26] Majorities disagreed with the statements that the welfare state makes people more ready to help each other (70 per cent) and makes for a more caring society (60 per cent), while 49 per cent denied that it gives people the satisfaction of helping others they don't know (33 per cent agreed that it did). The welfare state is not seen as efficient, unobtrusive or egalitarian: 70 per cent agreed that the welfare state had too many rules and regulations, 60 per cent that it interfered too much in peoples' lives, and 64 per cent disagreed that it made people more equal. Moreover, 68 per cent agreed that the welfare state is a source of bad feeling between taxpayers and recipients and a small plurality agreed that welfare services tend to foster stigma by making people who get benefits and services feel like second class citizens (48 per cent agreed with that proposition while 42 per cent did not). The welfare state is also seen as eroding the work ethic (60 per cent), undermining self-help (61 per cent) and aiding the undeserving (70 per cent). (For most of these questions roughly 12 per cent had neutral attitudes.)

These results offer little confirmation for the notion that the welfare state promotes integration by stimulating altruism. As Taylor-Gooby suggests, the structure of opinion on social welfare is probably best explained as 'a matter of self-interest defined by the dominant ideology of a society in which desired goods are bought and sold'.[27] The most highly favoured services are those used by the masses (with the exception of child benefit, which is universally available but not especially popular), and the most disfavoured are those which serve the needs of the minority and which most people are unlikely to need (with the exception of very popular benefits for the sick and the disabled). The self-interest derives not only from the roles of the individuals as consumers, but also as suppliers of the service in their capacity as employees of state agencies of one kind or another. Clearly, people have an interest in the provision of services they will need and are more willing to pay for such a service than one they will probably not need. There is little evidence that altruism has stepped in to fill the gap here, except in the case of sickness and disabled benefits. Taylor-Gooby speculates that popular attitudes to these benefits may reflect a value judgement. He cites 'desert' as the relevant value, but it is unclear what he means by that. If it means in effect that people believe that the sick and disabled deserve to be helped because they are not to blame for their need, then something is given to the citizenship school to work with. It is exactly this type of claim that citizenship writers want to make in respect of the great mass of the poor. They are poor through no fault of their own, they therefore 'deserve' to be helped. If the conclusions of the 'Breadline Britain' survey published in *Poor Britain* are accurate, a shift in popular attitudes of this kind has occurred in the face of mass unemployment. Whether the trend could be prevented from reversing itself if full employment ever returned to the economy is an open question. The risk must be that with jobs freely available, the temptation to castigate the dependent as idle and feckless would return.

Taylor-Gooby's study offers some crumbs of comfort to a citizenship theorist. Nearly 40 per cent of those asked in the survey thought that the welfare state makes for a just society compared with 41 per cent who disagreed, and 47 per cent thought it more or less fair. General support for the welfare state is also very high. Over 90 per cent believe it to be good in principle even if in need of reform, 84 per cent regard it as necessary in modern society and 68 per cent accept that it gives people a greater sense of security. All of this clearly does not add up to a massive and enthusiastic endorsement of a welfare state organized in accordance with citizenship principles, but at least there is something to work with.

If altruism plays second fiddle to self-interest in the modern welfare state and integration is not noticeably enhanced on that score, what of the claim that welfare rights integrate recipients by protecting their self-respect through the use of non-stigmatizing delivery mechanisms? Once again the evidence is discouraging. Pinker has suggested that:

> As we grow up the most authentic rights we acquire are those we use in the roles of buyers and sellers in the market place. We do not have to be persuaded that we have rights to what we buy. The idea of paying through taxes or holding authentic claims by virtue of citizenship remains largely an intellectual conceit of the social scientist and the socialist. For the majority the idea of participant citizenship in distributive processes outside the market place has very little meaning. Consequently, most applicants for social services remain paupers at heart.[28]

For Pinker, unilateral transfers have the effect of reinforcing a lack of self-worth in a society in which self-respect is generally encouraged by participation in reciprocal transfers where something of equal value is exchanged.

The weakness of the citizenship approach was to place too much faith in the power of rights to dispel stigma. Probably this is because of a narrow focus on the processes and characteristics of welfare services. While it is undoubtedly true that denial of access to services and degrading treatment within them reinforces stigma, and leads, as Hilary Rose has graphically written, to 'an exchange of public cash for personal humiliation' so that before a Supplementary Benefit Appeal Tribunal the 'applicant must adopt a suppliant role, like a medieval leper exhibiting his sores',[29] it is improbable that merely to change the institutional structure in the light of social rights is sufficient. The existence of social rights may help in ensuring minimum levels of treatment and in reducing the abuse of discretion by welfare officials, but standing alone they cannot go to the roots of stigmatization.

At bottom, stigma stems, as Paul Spicker argues, primarily from the characteristics of the users of welfare services, rather than from the character of the services. Being poor, dependent, a failure in a competitive society, is stigmatizing in itself, and the poor and dependent bring that stigma with them to the services that offer support. Stigmatization involves a process of public branding, and, as Spicker suggests, the contribution made by the social services themselves to the generation of stigma is the result of identifying a dependent group:

> Because the group is stigmatized before it becomes dependent, the main determinant of rejection is not whether they have rights, but whether the service draws attention to them.[30]

Universal services can mitigate this to a limited degree by concealing the existence of dependent groups, and it is in this, rather than in the invocation of rights, that their principal advantage lies. But it must be doubted that the mere existence of universal services contributes greatly to a sense that certain kinds of dependency are legitimate. The fact that some universal services are widely appreciated and their use generally not associated with stigma is not a consequence of the services' universality, but of popular attitudes towards the legitimacy of the dependencies to which these services cater. The challenge facing citizenship theory is to find ways to spread those attitudes over to other forms of dependency that are not at present widely deemed to be legitimate. In other words, it is to break the grip of an ideology which makes it easy to blame the victim. Erecting universal structures are alone not enough.

Stigma is real. The problem is to eradicate it. Policies to deal with it pull in different directions and create their own difficulties. Dependency can be reduced somewhat by social work agencies teaching individuals to cope, but rehabilitation cannot work for all and reinforces the stigma of those who fail. Poverty can be alleviated by redistribution, but redistribution extends and deepens dependency. Opportunities can be created to establish reciprocity by offering recipients the chance to contribute through work, participation in community projects, or by basing entitlements to welfare benefits on insurance principles. But not all are capable of working or participating and certainly not all can make insurance contributions. A wedge is driven between those who come under the umbrella of the scheme and those who stand exposed without. As Spicker argues:

> It is contradictory to encourage participation and attempt to conceal a stigmatized group. It is contradictory to assert that both a minimum standard of living and a 'right to fail' are necessary for respect. And, although it happens throughout the social services, it is contradictory to give a person rights and status and then tell him that his condition is not legitimate and that he must be rehabilitated.[31]

Underlying the arguments of citizenship writers is the assumption that full membership of society is a matter of guaranteeing equality of status as a necessary condition of preserving self-respect. Being a full member of society is defined in terms of status, which in turn is defined in terms of citizenship rights, of which social rights are one part. Status is seen in relational terms. Social rights exist in order to compensate for inequalities of status created by individuals acting on the basis of their civil and political rights. The first thing to note is that citizenship writers tend to see *equality* of status as a necessary condition for integration. Noteworthy too is the fact, discussed in chapter 3, that the self-respect of individuals is seen to be threatened by the structure of inequality in a society and by the opportunities it creates or destroys for individuals to participate in the life of the community. Social policies, therefore, are engaged in a process of redistributing social outcomes and opportunities in ways required to underwrite equality of status.

Focusing on redistribution draws attention to a third important characteristic: the relationship between integration and social justice. Unfortunately, the nature of this relationship is not clearly spelled out in citizenship theory. Is the integrated society, that is, one in which altruistic behaviour produces the resources necessary to confirm full community membership to all, socially just? That is, is social justice defined in terms of the achievement of integration? Or is social justice a basis of integration, in the sense that a society's possession of a just distribution of opportunities, outcomes, and so in, is one reason why citizens are committed to it, in ways which achieve an integrated community? Often, as David Donnison has noted, these two ways of looking at the relationship drift together; no potential conflict is recognized.[32] This, however, is an important oversight, for if social justice is to count as the basis of integration, an independent analysis of what is socially just must be put forward, coupled with an explanation of the link between social justice and its recognition by citizens as a basis of community. On the other hand, if the former interpretation is adopted, no independent account of social justice would be required. Social justice would be defined in terms of whatever pattern of opportunities and so forth happened to be associated with an integrated community.

Material Inequality and Redistribution

For most citizenship writers the integration of welfare recipients is seen as depending on meeting needs and guaranteeing access to a community kind of life in ways which respect their status as equal and full members of society. Being a full member of society is inextricably connected to equality. Even though a precise account of equality is lacking, it is clear that equality of status, for citizenship writers, requires equality in respect of a range of material conditions, for example, equal satisfaction of basic needs or substantive equality in respect of certain opportunities. It follows that a definite relationship exists between material equality and social justice. A citizenship approach should adopt, therefore, an independent notion of social justice. In consequence it confronts the problem of spelling out the relationship between social justice and integration.

The reasons why the existence of material inequalities is associated with a divided society are well known. Material inequalities lead to a segmented society in which social ties are restricted to persons with a similar social status to oneself; persons who engage in similar activities, patterns of consumption and so on. Few social ties exist across social strata:

> Within each social stratum relationships may of course be as fraternal as one would like, but between strata there is likely to be incomprehension and hostility. Lacking direct personal connections, people in one class form stereotypes of those in others. They find themselves unable to sympathize with the predicament of people whose circumstances are markedly different from their own.[33]

Society is, thus, characterized by division and lack of a sense of community. Greater material equality is thought of as a precondition of establishing both a sense of fraternity and, most importantly, a sense of self-respect amongst the deprived.

Attractive though this seems, the connection between equality and integration is far from straightforward. As has already been suggested, non-stigmatizing universalist policies may do little to promote the self-respect of the indigent. Equally, those who pay high taxes to finance redistribution may well resent the burden on their disposable income, and in truly Nozickian manner regard the government as a coercive and alien force that is stealing what is theirs and reducing them to the status of mere means for the purposes of others. Any compression of the scale of inequality in society could lead to more social conflict than peace as groups mobilize to try to protect their differential advantages. In Britain, for example, precisely such a phenomenon seems to have occurred in the 'winter of discontent' of 1978–9 when a period of several years of erosion of pay differentials spawned intense industrial conflict as trade unions sought to recoup lost ground. Tawney may well have underestimated the vitality of both amoral self-interest and the disagreement on principles of justice when he wrote:

Peace comes ... when everyone recognizes that the material, objective, external arrangements of society are based on principles which they feel correspond with their subjective ideas of justice.[34]

The problem faced by citizenship writers is not merely that the attempt to achieve integration must face the difficulties posed by self-interest and dissension on principles of justice, but that there may be other and more effective ways of fostering integration which do not presuppose egalitarianism.

Equality of status need not figure prominently in, for example, an integrated nationalist society or one united by particular religion. Yet it is not perhaps unreasonable to regard a sense of nation, commitments to a militant religion or appeals to traditional values, as potentially effective integrative forces, and ones which in achieving integration would succeed in bolstering the self-respect of the relatively deprived.

Moreover, it is possible to give an interpretation of equality of status as a full member of society which does not presuppose material equality in respect of certain life chances. For example, consider a hierarchically structured society in which individuals are born into certain positions. Some are born to leadership positions, others to become tradesmen, yet others to become peasants. At first sight this would appear a clear and obvious example of a society in which inequality of status was the norm, and, of course, in an immediate sense this would be true. But, if one looks deeper one can detect a principle of equality at work even here. Suppose this society was indeed integrated and individuals viewed the different ranks, and the rights and duties corresponding to them, as interlocking and justified by reference to the purposes of the community. It would, indeed, be true that the different ranks could be characterized in terms of different statuses, perhaps as higher and lower in a rank ordering. But despite this it would be possible to argue that these differences were not inconsistent with an underlying notion of equality. Each individual, high or low, could be thought of as just as much a member of the community as any other, providing that he was discharging his functions properly. Each part of the society might be thought of as just as much a part of the whole as any other. Each individual would be equal in his status as a full member of the community, even though the functions of different individuals differed, and no necessary reference to an egalitarian distribution of a specifiable range of life chances had been made.

Even if this is not accepted, the problem can be put in another way. It is by no means clear that equality of status is a necessary condition of self-respect. Self-respect can flourish in an hierarchical society. Notwithstanding our disposition to dismiss as false consciousness examples of a subjective self-worth under conditions of inequality, the sense of self-respect is genuine all the same. Individual blacksmiths may find meaning for their lives in an appreciation that they are part of a divinely ordered universe, for example. And, although a Burkean society of this kind may be rejected, it is still possible that self-respect and equality of status are not closely related. The self-respect of individuals may be primarily a function of the quality of their relationships with their friends, work-mates, colleagues and families. If this is so, the self-respect of individuals is likely little affected by wider (say, society-wide) inequalities of status.

Taken all in all it is apparent that citizenship theory has rather too quickly assumed that universal welfare institutions will foster integration and preserve and enhance the self-respect of welfare clients. But this alone serves only to define the nature of the moral and political challenge the theory faces. Whatever the tensions within welfare policy, there is no doubt that services as currently constituted serve to reinforce unjustified stigma. Attempting to develop institutions which so far as possible eradicate that stigma is morally legitimate. Whatever the theoretical possibilities of preserving self-respect in the presence of systematic and gross inequalities, the reality is that these inequalities do compromise self-respect in a society founded largely on the belief that material and social success reflects personal virtue. While it is no doubt true that in modern capitalist societies patriotism supplies an integrative force which cuts across class, and many individuals live primarily private lives, this alone is insufficient to create a morally acceptable community. A manifestly unjust society is not, from a moral point of view, a properly integrated one. The political challenge, for the challenge is ultimately political, facing citizenship theory is to win over the population to the view that social justice is a necessary condition of legitimate society, and having done so to build institutions founded on those principles which, because of their legitimacy, contribute to integration. Historically, citizenship writers may have been too sanguine in expecting universal services to promote self-respect and integration. It has not happened. The political task is to make it happen.

5

Equality

If anything distinguishes the beliefs of both the new right and citizenship writers, it is their attitude to equality. Left wing thought in general is peculiarly preoccupied with the importance of promoting greater equality, while the right, when not celebrating the glories of inequality, disdainfully treats the fascination with pursuing equality as at best leading to a mediocre and boring uniformity and at worst as an invitation to totalitarianism. There is much evidence to confirm the centrality of equality in both the thought of the left and the competition between left and right. Tawney, for example, the great apostle of British egalitarianism, urged that the political programme of the left cohere around a strategy of equality.[1] Crosland, in *The Future of Socialism*, identified a political interest in promoting greater social equality as the distinctive concern of socialism in the world of post-war capitalism.[2] And Durbin, in his little read but fine treatise, *The Politics of Democratic Socialism*, focused on the problems of reconciling liberty and equality in a political democracy.[3] Within the citizenship school, equality also bulks large. Abel-Smith notes that social services 'are needed because there is a problem of inequality',[4] and Titmuss wrote that, 'socialist social policies are (or should be) preeminently about equality, freedom and social integration'.[5] On the right, one doesn't need to go very far to sense that the need to avoid the siren calls of egalitarianism is at the root of moral and political regeneration. The writings of Joseph and Sumption,[6] Hayek,[7] Nozick,[8] and the authors in the compilation by Letwin[9] are the small tip of a large iceberg.

Equality appears therefore to be a critical element in defining the integrity and identity of ideologies. This poses a dilemma for my account of the citizenship school, for I have described the existence of a single school with a relatively cohesive ideological foundation. Yet when the tradition is examined more closely the unity dissolves. Included within the school are writers who apparently do not value equality. T. H. Marshall, for example, expressly repudiates the pursuit of equality as an objective of social policy. His concern is the satisfaction of particular needs without requiring either that beneficiaries be poor or that the effect reduces social inequality.[10] Even though successful social policies will often lead to a reduction of social inequality, that is merely a consequence of satisfying needs and is not valuable in its own right. Robson joins Marshall in adopting a sceptical attitude towards pursuing equality as an end of social policy.[11] Like Marshall, he sees the implications for equality of implementing socially just social policies as secondary. Social policies designed to promote a just distribution of welfare in society will affect the structure of inequality but this is not their direct object.

In this chapter I examine the principle of equality and ask how it might lend support to the substantive conclusions of the citizenship school. I address also the issue whether there is, within the school, a schism which divides moral egalitarians from non-egalitarians. My conclusion is that, as a matter of moral theory, there is no major difference of principle dividing, say, Marshall and Titmuss. Finally, having questioned whether much of the moral theory underpinning the citizenship approach is genuinely egalitarian, I consider the appropriate role of equality within it.

Equity in Social Policy

Equality enters into an evaluation of social policy first in the guise of equity, which trades heavily upon the requirements imposed on argument by the standards of rationality and consistency. Equity boils down to the proposition that like cases should be treated alike, and unlike cases unlike: a principle which is often seen to follow from, or restate, the presumption in favour of equality. According to a popular argument, equal treatment needs no special justification, whereas unequal does. It follows therefore that in order to treat one individual or group differently from another, some good reason based on relevant grounds must be provided.

Equity can have egalitarian implications for social policy. As Albert Weale has pointed out, much social administration is concerned to draw attention to the fact that two or more groups which are treated differently are, from the point of view of the ends served by a policy, in all relevant respects, identical. From this it is argued that differences in treatment should be eliminated and that benefits received by the most favoured group should be distributed to all others similarly placed.

Weale himself considers two cases where the application of an equity principle yields conclusions which would be suitable for citizenship purposes; child endowment schemes and housing subsidies. In both cases he argues that the schemes existing in the 1970s violate the equity principle. The child endowment scheme violates equity because payments are made through a system of child tax allowances and child benefit. The effect is that families with higher incomes are better off than those with lower, because 'the benefits of the child tax allowance increase with income within certain tax ranges and . . . many people too poor to pay the full standard rate do not receive any benefit or only small benefits from the allowance'.[12] Weale argues that if the objective of family benefits is to act as a subsidy to assist parents in meeting the economic costs of child-rearing, then an equity argument supports the replacement of the present system with a scheme of flat rate payments, provided that it is safe to assume that the economic cost of raising a child is not a function of parental income.

A similar argument is made out in the case of housing subsidies. House buying is subsidized by a number of different schemes administered by category of tenure group. Weale notes five methods of subsidy in effect in Britain in 1978. They are:

1 tax relief given to owner occupiers for the interest paid on their mortgage;
2 direct subsidies to local authorities and some housing associations;
3 the indirect aid given to private tenants in controlled properties;
4 tax relief to housing authorities and on the profits of local authorities;
5 rebates on rent given to tenants in the public and private sector on test of means.[13]

As he argues, 'the structure of housing subsidies is haphazard, and often unrelated to the true economic cost borne by the consumer'.[14] In particular, owners of expensive homes receive a relatively greater subsidy than those on low incomes or renting from the private sector:

> If we say that what is being subsidized is housing consumption, then equity considerations begin to get a foothold as an argument for changing the structure of benefits between tenure groups, and not just within them. From the overall point of view therefore equity considerations can be used as an argument for altering the structure in favour of a more even balance of resources between different tenure-groups.[15]

The difficulty with equity arguments is that they are crucially dependent upon the definition of a policy objective. Once a policy has been defined, equity requires the consistent application of the policy to all individuals or groups to whom the policy properly applies. Hence, if the policy objective is to subsidize the costs of child rearing, equity can get a grip upon the way a policy is administered, and it is clearly inequitable that greater benefits be received by some groups than others where the differences in treatment is not rationally related to the policy objective. But what this really shows is that equity is not a substantive egalitarian principle at all; it is nothing more than a requirement of reason or consistency. Its impact upon the structure of inequality in a society is entirely contingent upon the definition of the policy objective and equity has nothing to say about that. Equity is merely a reason for the consistent application of a policy. Standing alone, equity provides no reason to prefer a levelling up of groups receiving poor treatment to a levelling down of groups receiving preferential treatment. Equity has no implications for deciding what quality of service is appropriate. Inferior services can be equitably administered just as readily as superior ones.

Questions about what quality of a service should be provided and whether upgrading is preferable to downgrading can be answered only by a consideration of the purposes served by a policy. One advantage of equity arguments, however, is that they are difficult to dissent from. Disagreement reflects inconsistency and irrationality, not a genuine and perhaps irresolvable conflict over the weight to be given the value of equality in shaping policy. Hence, equity could have an important role to play in building consensus on the terms of social policy.

But these advantages are not easily captured. The major difficulty is that an equity argument can be deployed successfully only where there is a prior agreement on the objectives of the policy itself. Disagreement may concern both the definition of the policy objective and its justification. It may also range over the criteria to be employed to identify groups as being relevantly similar and therefore candidates for equitable treatment. Take housing subsidies, for example. It is by no means clear what equity requires in terms of the distribution of subsidies, if only because it is not obvious what the policy objective is. Subsidies may be intended to reduce the costs of housing consumption but not necessarily or exclusively on a per consumer basis. Relatively greater subsidies may accrue to certain tenure groups precisely to encourage the holding of those types of tenure. A bias in favour of a property-owning democracy could well result in extra subsidization of those individuals likely to buy houses. Or, alternatively, if there were concern that higher income families were smaller than lower income families and it was thought desirable to encourage the better-off to have more children, then, relative to that policy objective, the greater tax subsidies to the rich would not contravene any principle of equity. This is not to say that equity considerations will never be affective, for often a haphazard set of policies will be little more than the result of incremental responses to political pressure, and attempts to defend inequities as the consequences of a 'consistent' application of policy will be specious reasoning in bad faith; nothing more than a cloak to protect special interests. The point remains, though, that only where there is agreement about a policy goal can equity be effective, for equity alone can, in principle, make no contribution to the assessment of the objectives of policy. Thus in general, if equity is to have egalitarian implications it will be because it is handmaiden to an egalitarian policy; it will be because a prior agreement that egalitarian objectives should be pursued will have been forged.

There are a number of other reasons for believing that a presumptivist argument for equality is not capable of doing the work required of it by the egalitarian citizenship writers. The argument assumes that in the absence of considerations to the contrary, equal distribution is justified. Berlin's example of the division of a cake is well known:

> If I have a cake and there are ten persons among whom I wish to divide it, then if I give exactly one tenth to each, this will not, at any rate automatically, call for justification; whereas if I depart from this principle of equal division I am expected to produce a special reason.[16]

The problem with this argument is that it trades upon the presence of special, indeed unusual, conditions. Equal distribution requires no justification, only unequal distribution does; but that is not to say that justification cannot be provided. Moreover, the reasons for unequal distribution do not have to be morally persuasive to override the equality imperative. All that is necessary is to adduce reasons which are relative or non-arbitrarily related to the proposal for unequal distribution. In other words, the presumptivist argument for equality will yield the substantive conclusion that goods should be equally distributed only if there is a complete absence of considerations which would suggest that they should be unequally distributed.

This reveals the presumption of the presumptivist argument, namely that there will be circumstances when it will have some bearing on the world; that there will be circumstances when there will indeed be a complete absence of considerations to the contrary. But this is surely unrealistic. Even in the case of a cake there are commonplace circumstances which justify unequal distribution. George may have eaten so many sweets that one tenth of the cake will make him ill; Billy is malnourished and needs more; Little Mary is the leader of the gang and a larger slice is required to protect her status.

The important point to note here is that *any* consideration in favour of inequality will defeat the presumptivist view, providing that it can be stated in terms which amount to a reason for unequal distribution.

Weale's own formulation of the presumptivist view makes the mistake of assuming that the reason has to be a good one. It does not. It just has to be relevant to the case in question. Therefore, a bad reason will defeat the presumptivist position just as readily as a good one. The presumptivist view is not a positive entitlement to equality. It cannot enter into the moral fray with arguments justifying inequality. It is nothing more than an empty formal claim which could have substantive implications only if there were a vacuum of competing considerations with distributional implications. And, of course, this vacuum does not exist. As Nozick has noted, cakes and other candidates for (re)distribution do not appear as if by magic.[17] They come into the world with claims already attached to them, normally as a result of entitlements generated within the productive process. If equality in the distribution of certain goods is to be achieved, then it needs to be justified by reference to a positive entitlement to equality. A presumptivist view has next to no substantive implications for distribution. Any utility it does have will be in the area of equity arguments.

Rationalizing Equality

Two alternative ways of extracting a defence of equality by relying upon non-evaluative principles of rationality and relevance should be noted. Both have a bearing upon citizenship theory. Both capture, I believe, some part of the case for equality presupposed by writers within the citizenship tradition. The first has been characterized as 'negative egalitarianism'. The second belongs to Bernard Williams and has been aptly dubbed 'relevant-reason egalitarianism'. In each case, the belief is that the requirement that a distribution be justified by relevant reasons yields substantive egalitarian results.

Negative egalitarianism amounts to the claim that inequalities should be eradicated if they are based on irrelevant reasons. This is a weaker notion than the principle that a distribution of a good be made on relevant grounds, where it is thought that, at least for some goods, there is a unique and unambiguous ground for distribution which stands in a necessary relation to the good itself. If arguments of this kind can be successfully established, they have the happy result of producing substantive moral conclusions about principles of distribution which upon their face appear controversial, but which on closer examination turn out to be required by reason itself. To deny the appropriateness of the principle of distribution in a particular case is not therefore to express a moral disagreement but to expose oneself to the charge of irrationality.

Negative egalitarianism presupposes only that it is possible to identify certain reasons as irrelevant; it does not assume any agreement about what is a relevant reason in some positive sense. It may well be easier to be confident that a particular reason for distribution is irrelevant than to know what would be a relevant reason. Hence we may well be perplexed when considering how job opportunities ought to be distributed, while at the same time we know that, generally speaking, the sex of the applicant is irrelevant. The same could be true for other distributions. It may well turn out that presently existing inequalities in the distribution of the benefits and burdens of social cooperation correlate with factors such as race, sex, status or class and that these factors are irrelevant to goods so distributed. At this point a presumption in favour of equality revives to justify the elimination of the irrational distribution and its replacement by a non-irrational equal one.

There are several difficulties with this suggestion for egalitarians. The first is that the argument is only contingently egalitarian. If only irrelevant reasons support presently existing inequalities then their removal will indeed have egalitarian implications. However, it might well be that actual inequalities can be supported by reasons which are not irrelevant, in which case the structure of inequality is unaffected, or that presently existing equalities are supported by irrelevant reasons, in which case a move to inequality is required. Secondly, the concept of irrelevance when viewed as a requirement of logic and therefore as not concealing question-begging moral values, is incapable of distinguishing good from bad reasons. One possible way to escape this conclusion is the suggestion that matters of distribution necessarily require reference to 'justice' and 'justification', and therefore necessarily also to rules and that the notion of a rule eliminates bad 'reasons'. But this is an unsuccessful gambit because the most that the concept of a rule requires is that a rule be formulated suitably in general and abstract terms. So although this eliminates, 'I get all the chocolates because I am me' as a possible rule justifying a distribution, it does so not on the ground of irrelevance but because it is not a rule. On the other hand, 'All chocolates are to be given to anyone who is bearded, five foot eleven, weighs eleven stone, has an extremely high instep and prehensile toes, etc.' is a rule of distribution that cannot be eliminated by the concept of a rule, even though in the end it applies only to me. If this rule is not to count as a rule of distribution of chocolates it must be because the idea of irrelevance is not purely formal but conceals evaluation. The truth is that the proposed principle of distribution is to be ruled out because it is a *bad* reason not because it is 'irrelevant'. Or, to put it another way, if the reason it depends upon is an irrelevant reason, it is because it is a bad reason given the moral beliefs that cluster around the production and consumption of chocolate.

The same problem bedevils Williams's analysis of the idea of equality.[18] Williams believes that it is possible to identify a single necessary and sufficient principle of distribution of some goods which necessarily follows from a consideration of the nature of the social practice with which those goods are associated. Hence:

> Leaving aside preventative medicine, the proper ground of distribution of medical care is ill health: this is a necessary truth. Now in very many societies, while ill health may work as a necessary condition of receiving treatment, it does not work as a sufficient condition, since treatment costs money and not all who are ill have money; hence the possession of money becomes in fact an additional necessary condition of actually receiving treatment . . . When we have the situation in which . . . wealth is a further necessary condition of the receipt of medical treatment, we can once more apply the notions of equality and inequality . . . since we have straight-forwardly the situation of those whose needs are the same not receiving the same treatment, though the needs are the ground of the treatment.[19]

It is simply irrational for equally ill people to receive unequal medical treatment. The same argument could be made out in respect of the distribution of any other good of which it could be said that need is similarly the proper ground of the distribution. But, if this argument works, it does so not because of any formal, logical or conceptual analysis of relevance derived from an examination of the nature of a particular activity or the way we talk about it. It succeeds only if there is sufficiently wide agreement about the moral values that shape and sustain an activity. Hence it is only because we believe that, morally speaking, medical care is the practice of catering to need, that we can say that medical need is the sole principle of distributing medical care.[20] But if that is true then we are not offered an argument *for* equality of need satisfaction, but a description of what follows from the consensus on the role of medical care in our society. The justification of the principle of distribution is inseperable from the justification of the ends served by the practice itself. If that practice is justified, independently of the fact of the consensus, then so too is the principle of distribution, but not otherwise.

But, on the face of it, there is not, even in our societies, consensus on the moral ends of medical practice sufficient to establish need as a sufficient basis for distribution of medical care. Nozick has a telling point when he questions whether the internal goal (meeting needs) of an activity automatically takes precedence over the reasons why someone participates in the practice. Barbers, he rightly argues, do not have to distribute their services according to need even though people need barbering services. In wielding their scissors, barbers legitimately take into account their own interests, in earning money or enjoying witty conversation.[21] Why should doctors be treated any differently? If need is to be the proper principle of distribution of medical care, direct moral reasons must be produced to yield that result. A non-evaluative account of relevance will not work.

The difficulty with these strategies to justify equality do not end here. Equality is a relational value. Equality exists, for example, when between two persons or groups an identity in respect of some property exists. Hence, A and B may be equal in respect of their age, meaning that A and B have an identical age. Or, if Bill and Ben both earn £10,000 a year, then they have equal salaries. To value equality is to value the identity relation that exists. If it is valuable that Bill and Ben have equal income then what is valued is the fact that both have the same income, not that the income is £10,000. The fact that the income is £10,000 may also be a good thing, a better thing, for example, than if the income were £5,000, but valuing the income level itself is quite different from valuing the fact that the income is the same.

With this in mind, consider the following case. Bill searches for a job and accepts an offer training lions for Ben, who performs death-defying tricks in the ring. The arrangement is that the circus pays Ben £20,000 for his trouble, and Bill and Ben agree that Bill will receive £10,000. The circus pays up and Ben hands on £10,000. At the end of the year they have both received the same income and all is well in the world. But all is well not because they have been paid the *same* but because each of them has received what he is independently entitled to. The equality relation is not of any value in itself. If Bill is not paid his salary he may sue Ben, who has tried to hang onto the full £20,000, and recover his income. There will have been a redistribution from Ben to Bill and greater equality will result.

Greater equality in the distribution of benefits may occur, therefore, on occasions where the fact that equality would be the result plays no part in justifying the redistribution. The reason is, of course, that greater equality may be a by-product of policies justified by other considerations. As Raz has noted, '(a)ll principles of entitlement generate equality (in some respect) as an incidental by-product since all who have equal qualification under them have an equal entitlement.'[22] But it is the fact that one possesses a property, in this case a contractual obligation, that grounds one's entitlement to the benefit, not the fact that that property is possessed equally.

This point is important because it draws attention to the fact that the reason why someone is entitled to something, and the question of how much of that thing he should have relative to someone else, may be separate questions. Another example reinforces the point: all human beings possess an intrinsic human capacity, the capacity to read Shakespeare. There are one hundred human beings and one hundred copies of the *Complete Works*. A principle exists which says that resources should be distributed to respect human capacities. Consider two possible worlds. In the first, each person has a copy of Shakespeare. In the second, half of the population has two copies each, the others none. What is wrong with the second world is not that the copies of the *Works* are unequally distributed. This can be seen if we consider one possible solution to the inequality problem: the destruction of all the copies of present owners. Everyone would be equal in being without the *Complete Works*. Consider also a variation on world two in which everybody had one copy and half the population a second. In this case the reaction would probably be, so what: What is wrong, it seems, is that there are people in the second world whose individual entitlements to have their capacities respected have not been protected. What is satisfying about the first world is not that a relation of equality has been satisfied, but that each human being, taken individually, has had his personal entitlement to have his human capacities respected satisfied.

What this suggests is that whenever individual entitlements are satiable the equality of those entitled to a certain benefit is an incidental by-product of satisfying each individual entitlement. A concern with the relationship of equality between the individual actors in respect of the good to be distributed contributes nothing of independent moral value. But this argument also points to those conditions where equality does have implications. Equality may matter if the capacity to satisfy entitlements is less than that required to satisfy all entitlements fully. Suppose, for example, that in a third world there are only fifty copies of Shakespeare and no ability to produce more. Here there is a clear shortfall of resources relative to entitlements and the question of how they should be distributed cannot be avoided. This would be true anyway, but is all the more pressing if we were to assert that it is the fact that one possessed the capacity to read Shakespeare that qualifies one for a copy, not one's ability to appreciate it, and so on. It follows, therefore, that questions of distribution (to which equality would be one answer) arise whenever conditions of scarcity exist. As Raz argues, a theory is genuinely egalitarian whenever equality dominates other considerations in settling how entitlement-satisfying resources should be fulfilled under conditions of scarcity.[23] Equality may also be implicated whenever it is impossible to identify what an individual is entitled to without making a comparison of the position of others. In such a case, relational factors are incorporated within the definition of entitlement. Let us suppose, for the sake of argument, that need exists whenever a person possesses less than the average quantity of resources prevailing in a society. If distribution is according to need, what a person's entitlement is can be understood only by reference to the relation of an individual's resource holding compared to the resource holding of others. In this case the relational element and the entitlement are inextricably connected; it makes little sense to separate an evaluation of the relation and the entitlement. Finally, it is plausible to argue, as David Miller has done, that there are cases where although equality is instrumental to further ends, or perhaps a by-product of the achievement of those ends, that nevertheless 'certain of these ends have so close a connection to equality itself that they are properly and usefully seen as part of an egalitarian package'.[24]

Equality in Citizenship Theory

Given this framework, what kind of equality principles are relied upon by the citizenship tradition? The nearest that Titmuss comes to putting forward a positive argument for equality comes in his enthusiastic endorsement of Tawney's analysis in the introduction Titmuss contributed to an edition of *Equality*. One passage is worth quoting at length:

> The social and moral case for equality, as stated by Tawney cannot be more persuasively argued. . . . He did not write of it in the naive sense of equality of talent or merit or personality. His concern was with fundamental equalities before the law; the removal of collectively imposed social and economic inequalities; the equalizing of opportunities for all to secure certain goods and services; the education of all children to make them capable of freedom and more capable of fulfilling their personal differences; the enlargement of personal liberties through the discovery by each individual of his own and his neighbour's endowment. Hence he stressed the critical role of education and of equality in communication between human beings. The supreme consideration was everyman's uniqueness 'without regard to the vulgar irrelevancies of class and income'. In spite of their varying characters and capacities 'men possess in their common humanity a quality which is worth cultivating . . .'[25]

Elsewhere, in a passage not quoted by Titmuss, Tawney suggests that the notion of equality expresses an ethical judgement which asserts that although men many:

> differ profoundly as individuals in capacity and character, they are equally entitled as human beings to consideration and respect, and

that the well-being of a society is likely to be increased if it so plans its organization that, whether their powers are great or small, all its members may be equally enabled to make the best of such powers as they possess.[26]

The first thing to notice about these quotations is that they repeatedly draw attention to inequality; the second is that they establish a relationship between inequality and the failure to realize other valued objectives; the third is that they do indeed contain the kernel of a theory justifying a positive entitlement to equality.

This suggests one way to approach the place of equality within citizenship theory. The egalitarians should be thought of as often not so much offering a moral evaluation of equality as such, but as demanding that certain inequalities be offered a rational justification. The argument is a species of negative egalitarianism of the kind canvassed above. Thus, in the absence of a convincing rational justification, and on the assumption that inequalities are remediable, a *prima facie* case exists for removing them. This case is strengthened if it can be shown that presently existing inequalities are a barrier to the realization of other valued states of affairs. In this way, equality is an instrumental value. It is valued only because greater equality is a necessary condition of achieving other goals which are valued as ends in themselves. At least some part of the citizenship argument is best regarded as 'quasi-egalitarian' in this sense.

Much of the role played by equality in egalitarian citizenship theory is to be interpreted in this way. Equality, therefore, is largely an instrumental value. Citizenship writers have been guilty of misidentifying the structure of their moral theory. They have made a false move in implying that, because values such as freedom, for example, have been undercut by the structure of inequality, then equality is a central value within their schema. If this is correct, then I find no significant difference in the normative basis of, for example, Marshall in comparison with Titmuss. Rather, Marshall's understanding of the relation of equality to the ends of a citizenship approach is more perspicacious than that of Titmuss. Correspondingly, it leads to less confusion. This is not to say, however, that differences might not exist in empirical judgements concerning (1) the relationship between the structure of inequality and the failure to see an end realized, or (2) the relationship between the removal of the inequality and the achievement of that end. In practice, there might well be a difference in judgements concerning the structure of legitimate inequality, but this difference does not vary systematically with the fact that one side of the tradition is egalitarian whereas the other is not.

In practice it is rather difficult to tell whether greater (or what kinds of) inequality would exist in an ideal Tawney or Titmuss world compared to an ideal Marshall world. Marshall is quite explicit that a measure of economic inequality is required to maintain an incentive structure for the economy and reward effort and responsibility.[27] But Tawney accepted this too, and noted the need to give greater rewards in recognition of the acceptance of responsibility.[28] One difference, however, is that Marshall is probably more willing to accept that pecuniary rewards are required to elicit work effort, whereas Tawney hoped to replace, to some degree, the economic pursuit of personal gain by the cooperative engagement in providing 'professional' services.

Of course, the connection between the presence of inequality and the failure to realize a value, or conversely between achieving a value and the reduction of inequality, is not always accidental. For writers within the citizenship school the existence of social and economic inequality is intrinsically associated with damaging moral consequences. And these consequences can be overcome only by reducing inequality. Hence, it is no accident that self-respect is compromised in a highly unequal society if the effect of the inequality is to raise the level of income required to earn a decent living and if earning a decent living is a precondition of respectability and respectability of self-respect. As inequality increases so does the minimum required for a decent life and with it the numbers of people unable to meet the standard. Where this is the case, the preservation of self-respect will require that limits be set to permissible inequalities. Much the same is true of other characteristic citizenship arguments. Social integration through the encouragement of altruistic relations is a case in point if it is accepted that in our types of society economic inequality correlates with segmented social relations which inhibit the flourishing of fraternity. As Tawney argues, a community requires a common culture which in turn rests upon economic foundations; without 'a large measure of economic equality' a true community cannot maintain itself.[29]

Beyond this, however, there is a stronger sense in which equality is implicated in citizenship theory, and it is clear that Marshall is as much an egalitarian in this respect as Titmuss. As we have seen, social policies should be directed towards guaranteeing a range of life chances to the citizens of a society. The relevant life chances are those required to protect the status of individuals as full members of the community. Their purpose is to offer material opportunities to participate in the way of life of the society. Needs, by implication, are defined as whatever is necessary to that end. An individual is 'in need' for the purposes of social policy to the extent that he lacks the resources to participate as a full member of society in its way of life.

It should be noted that this kind of analysis presupposes a relatively affluent society, one in which having the necessary resource basis to be a full participating member is in addition to the meeting of basic needs. It would be an unacceptable paradox to argue that need did not exist in an extremely poor but egalitarian society in which all could participate in its 'way of life' despite extensive malnutrition.

The question this raises is whether individual entitlements to have a status as a full member of the community respected and protected presuppose a context in which relational questions are of independent moral relevance? The answer to this question is yes, as a matter of principle, if it is not possible to identify any individual's entitlement to a resource independently of an explicit consideration of the relevant resources possessed by others. It is also yes if, for purely practical reasons, the resource to be distributed is scarce relative to total aggregated entitlement. The problem, therefore, is in determining whether each individual's entitlement can be satisfied only if a certain pattern between individuals exists, or if needs are insatiable at given levels of entitlement-meeting capacity.

Distributional concerns do enter the argument in relevant or appropriate ways on occasions. Some part of the notion of need is accounted for by what some individuals lack in comparison with what is possessed by others. The need of some is created just by the difference between themselves and others – remove that difference and the need is abolished. This much at least is implied by the analysis of relative deprivation discussed in chapter 3. Distributional concerns enter the picture in other ways too. Consider health needs, for example. It seems reasonably clear that the health needs of individuals are insatiable – as certain killer diseases are eradicated or cures for them discovered, other illnesses become more pressing and, it appears, more expensive to treat. Difficult decisions concerning how resources should be distributed relative to medical needs cannot be avoided.

The implication of this is that there are occasions where distributional questions are of unavoidable and direct moral relevance. It follows therefore that the connection between inequality and the failure to fulfill some individual entitlements may not just be accidental in the sense that one could imagine a world in which all individual entitlements were satisfied by moving the whole structure of inequality several notches up the scale.

Entitlement to Equality

What is still required therefore is some account of the reasons why there can be said to be a positive entitlement to equality. Most of the principles commonly put forward as a statement of this entitlement are unhelpful. As Raz has shown, statements incorporating a principle of 'common humanity' or equal concern and respect are little more than statements of humanism which draw attention to the fact that those qualities which justify showing respect to a human being are qualities possessed by all human beings. 'It is clear', he writes, 'that universality is not by itself sufficient to make a principle into an egalitarian one'.[30] Raz continues:

> Statements to the effect that all are entitled to equal concern and respect or care or to equal treatment or equal protection, etc., by their common interpretations mean little more than that every person should count and that benefits and advantages should not be distributed on grounds excluding the well-being of some people.[31]

At the very least, therefore, it is necessary to go beyond what has been said so far in order to substantiate the claim that there is a positive entitlement to equality. It must be shown not just that there is an entitlement to, let's say, consideration and respect, but that independent moral weight attaches to equality in satisfying that entitlement.

If a positive entitlement to equality does exist within citizenship theory, it appears that it is captured by a principle which asserts that the way in which each person's entitlement to be considered and respected within a given society is best established if each person's status as an *equal* member of the community is publicly recognized and honoured. For this principle to work as a genuinely egalitarian one it must be the case that what matters is the relation of *equal* status. That status so far as individuals *qua* recipients are concerned is defined in terms of a range of citizenship rights which includes civil and political along with social rights. The argument has to be that these rights, governing basic life chances, ought to be *equally* distributed – just because each is to be thought of as just as much a member of the community as any other. In other words, a direct intention of the citizenship school is to offer a persuasive definition of what it is to be a member of a community, and publicly to institutionalize a recognition of the equality of all members of the society with respect to the status of citizenship.

What this seems to suggest is something like the following. It may be hypothesized that, for any given society, there exists a range of goods (including need-satisfying resources, opportunities, etc.) which are a prerequisite both for action as, and recognition by others as, a full member of the society. If a society ascribes rights to an individual which guarantee access to this range of goods, then it recognizes that person as possessing the status of a full member of the society. The issue of which rights are required to recognize full membership raises the distributional question in a number of ways. First, the description of the relevant range of goods is partly a function of standards prevailing in a society; second, the potential entitlements to the kinds of goods in question (at least sometimes) exceed the capacity of any society fully to meet them (e.g., medical needs). So the question of how rights should be distributed cannot be avoided.

My suggestion is that we should understand the positive entitlement to equality within the citizenship school as an entitlement to an equal distribution of those rights pertaining to the recognition of the status as a member of a society. Being a full member of the society is not to be assessed entirely in a non-comparative context; rather, it is something which admits of degree. Thus there are a number of distinct elements at work here. First, an identification of categories of goods which pertain to one's inclusion in or exclusion from the way of life of the community. These categories may refer to medical, housing, financial need; to opportunities to gain access to valued forms of life, jobs, education; and to the possession of skills required to act on the basis of resources available (which may be facilitated through personal social services, etc.). Second is an identification of the 'quantity' of goods within these categories required to permit or sustain inclusion within the society. Third, a specification of the rights which would be required to guarantee any individual access to these goods. Fourth is a positive commitment to distribute these rights equally; that is to say, the fact that they are distributed equally should be thought of as having independent moral value.

The reason for asserting that the equality of the distribution of rights has independent moral value may be illustrated by the following example. Suppose that we start with a society in which all are integrated on the basis of equally distributed social rights. A new wonder-drug is invented which enriches the quality of life for persons suffering from a range of painful and debilitating diseases. This drug means that those individuals who receive it can engage in the practices of life valued in this society, whereas previously they could not. Unfortunately, this drug is in scarce supply. It is not only expensive, but production of it is physically limited. Let us suppose that the society resolves the decision into two choices: either to maximize the production of the drug and to find a way of distributing it, or to produce none of it. This second is a conceivable view which might be adopted by someone operating within a citizenship framework on the grounds that at least this way equality is protected. What could be argued is that *equality* of status is what counts and to allow medication which necessarily introduces an inequality of status by implying that the lives of some members of the society are more worthwhile than others is an intolerable affront to those who need but cannot have the drug. Better then to forego the drug than permit inequality; a positive entitlement to equality dominates other considerations. It might well be felt that there is something unattractive and counterintuitive about this argument. Indeed, the temptation is to find a way of permitting production of the drug in a way which does not compromise the principle of respecting equality of status. The problem then is to find an acceptable method of distribution. An acceptable method would be one which reflected the belief that each person's membership of, and participation in, the society is just as valuable as any other's. It is perhaps easier to identify the sort of condition which would satisfy this principle by examining one which does not. Consider a case in which enough of the drug exists to cure three people and there are ten in need. All ten happen to be the same age – let us say, thirty – but three are outstanding members of society with great gifts, known and respected by millions, while the others are average unknown citizens. The utilitarian answer to this problem is obvious. Save those who will make the biggest contribution to the welfare of the society. This, however, is an evident violation of the equality-of-status principle, since some are judged more valuable than others and receive differential treatment on that basis. What needs to be found, therefore, is a method of distribution which does not incorporate inequality in this way. One possibility would be to rely on a lottery which gave each person an equal chance to receive the drug, thereby shifting from a principle that equal status as a member of society requires equal satisfaction of needs which by hypothesis cannot be satisfied here, to a principle of equalizing the risk that a need will not be satisfied.[32]

In cases of this kind independent moral value is attached to the idea of equality, via the principle of respecting equality of status. And on this, there is no division of principle within the citizenship school. If it is reasonable to attribute a view favouring positive entitlement to equality to one group, it is equally reasonable to attribute it to the other. In fact Marshall is quite explicit in committing himself to a principle of 'equality of status' and it is my view that understanding the role of equality in this way makes best sense of the Titmussian side of the school too.

In this chapter I have examined the role of a principle of equality in supporting the social policy objectives of citizenship writers. I have argued that an understanding of equality as equity, or attempts to defend equality on the grounds of a presumption, or of rationality, offer little support to these writers' conclusions. Equality, if it is defensible, must be defended by direct moral argument. Equality is an important value within citizenship theory and no principled division between 'egalitarian' and 'nonegalitarian' writers exists. There has, however, been a tendency to misconstrue the place of equality in the argument for an extensive welfare state. Equality is often only an instrumental value; the real objective is something else. It is the fact that the failure to achieve these other values is associated with the persistence of inequality that has led to the emphasis on equality. In the succeeding chapters I begin to deal with the defence of some of these other values more directly.

6

Market Exchanges and Welfare Rights

An important claim made by citizenship theorists is that there is a moral right to welfare. Welfare or social rights stand alongside civil and political rights. Taken jointly, the imperative to recognize and enforce this set of rights is the implication of the demands of justice. In the preferred version of citizenship theory, welfare institutions stand alongside the market place. Freedom, productivity and efficiency provide powerful reasons to rely on the price mechanism and free exchange, but without the corrective of a welfare state the benefits of the market cannot be justly distributed, and cannot therefore be accepted as legitimate.

The notion that there can be a moral right to welfare rooted in the requirements of social justice has been the target of the heavy artillery of the new right. In chapter 1 I rehearsed most of the principal arguments designed to explode that idea. In this chapter I consider whether market liberals have shown that social rights cannot exist or ought not to be recognized in a satisfactory moral theory. I deal first with the issue of exchange. Many market liberal arguments boil down to the claim that the outcome of a series of market exchanges ought not to be coercively interfered with. Coercive intervention is ruled out for a variety of reasons. Individuals may be taken to have freely entered the exchange and thereby consented to the outcome, or participation in the system of free exchange may be taken to be in the interests of individuals even where they incur heavy losses, or because, in some other way, fairness requires that the results of market transactions be respected. My conclusion is that none of these reasons is sufficient to eliminate the morality of recognizing a right to welfare. Secondly, I focus on the question of whether the very nature of property rights or traditional human rights exhausts the scope of rights-based considerations in social morality, thereby eliminating any possible 'space' for the existence of social rights. I argue strenuously that no obvious conceptual, linguistic or moral error vitiates the defence of social rights. Indeed, I conclude, there are excellent reasons to justify enforcing welfare rights. Having cleared the ground, the way is now prepared to articulate in the final two chapters the foundations of social rights.

The Problem of Risk in the Market

The first proposition to consider is the claim that if an individual freely enters an exchange relationship he consents to the outcome of the exchange and there is no reason therefore to interfere with the result. For the moment I put to one side the specification of the circumstances in which it may properly be said that a person has freely entered an exchange.

Richard Posner has stated this position most clearly:

> The notion of consent used here is what economists call *ex ante* compensation. I contend . . . that if you buy a lottery ticket and lose the lottery . . . you have consented to the loss. Many of the involuntary, uncompensated losses experienced in the market . . . are fully compensated *ex ante* and hence are consented to.[1]

There are several difficulties with an argument like this. First, even if it were true that to buy a lottery ticket is to consent to the loss, losses in the market are different. My market position is affected by many more unknowables than my position in the lottery. In a lottery I probably know that I am taking a risk and am probably aware that the chances and size of winning are affected simply by the number of other people playing the game. Quite likely I know or at least could find out what the statistical probability of winning is. In these circumstances it might seem plausible to say that I consent to the loss. In the market, on the other hand, the uncertainty is much greater. Much more knowledge is required to estimate and successfully reduce risks, and it is implausible to assume that market behaviour is evidence of preferences towards any particular outcome that might occur. Hence, if I lose my job because I worked for a company that hit bad times, it is wildly inaccurate to say that I consented to that on the basis that I freely chose to work in a risky industry. Quite likely I had no knowledge that the industry was a risky one, let alöne how risky it was. If I falsely believed employment within that industry and within my firm to be secure, it can hardly be said that I have consented to lose my job simply because I took it.

The point is a general one. Consent to the existence of a state of affairs requires a certain mental attitude.[2] Normally it is improper to infer the presence of a mental state simply from behaviour. This is especially so where behaviour is being used as a proxy for consent to outcomes which are often remote from the behaviour itself and where the outcomes are significantly affected by unpredictable factors beyond the control of the agent. The most that one can say, even in the case of a lottery, is that the risk of a loss has been consented to. But consenting to a risk is not the same thing as consenting to the loss. Moreover, whether one's behaviour correlates with actually consenting to a risk is something that can be settled only by empirical enquiry. There are no necessary truths here. If I am unaware of the existence of magnitude of a risk it is unlikely that I have consented to it. Even where I am aware of a risk and act freely in ways which happen to incur it, it does not follow that I have consented to it. I might cross the busy High Street every day on the way to work knowing fully that I run the risk of being struck by a passing car, but it does not necessarily follow that I consent to the risk of being injured. Indeed, I might well be a campaigner in my spare time for a traffic-free High Street precisely because of the danger to pedestrians. Knowingly incurring a risk is not necessarily equivalent to consenting to it.

The same difficulty underlies the claim that to accept compensation, whether beforehand or afterwards, is to consent to the treatment that has been received. Hence if a dangerous job is highly paid it may be true that I am compensated for running the risks of the trade, but it does not follow just from this that I have consented to the welfare loss I suffer if the risk materializes.

My concusion, therefore, is that it cannot be said that uncoerced participation in market transactions amounts to consent to whatever outcomes the market generates. It is illegitimate to rule out interference with markets on the ground that to do so fails to respect results which have been consented to. As it stands, however, this is a limited conclusion for it is possible that other reasons render interference illegitimate. Notwithstanding that I did not consent to lose in the lottery, for example, it is fair that I bear the loss provided I was not tricked or coerced into buying the ticket.

The second line of argument is to suggest that market-generated losses should lie where they fall because they are the result of engaging in a practice which it is in the interests of actors to support. This argument takes two forms. One way of putting it is to say that the results of the market can be justified to representative individuals as being in their interests, notwithstanding the apparent damage to their interests done by bearing particularly heavy welfare losses. The other formulation is to cast the argument in the terms of consent. Hence, rational self-interested agents would choose the principles that govern a market order if they were to choose rules to order their community. Because these are the rules that would be chosen it is argued that it is proper to infer that consent to them can be implied. From the point of view of consent, implied is as good as real; either one is sufficient to bind actors to the results.

Most of the difficulties with this second argument are well known. Even supposing that rational agents would indeed have consented to these rules in carefully specified circumstances, it does not follow that their hypothetical consent can bind them in different or even the same circumstances. As Dworkin has noted, the fact that you would have consented to sell me a painting yesterday for £10 had I asked to buy it is no reason why you should sell it to me today when I do ask. The point is not just that the circumstances are different – today is not yesterday, now you know the artist is Turner and then you did not – but that, more radically, hypothetical consent simply is not consent; only actual consent binds.[3]

If this is true then the issue narrows. It becomes critical to ask whether the rules of the market order are capable of being justified to participants as being in their interest and whether generalized self-interest is a sufficient foundation for a theory of fairness. Here the argument has two branches. The first is the utilitarianism of neoclassical welfare economics; the second is more of a rights-based libertarianism. I will suggest that of the two the second has morally more satisfactory foundations.

As we saw in chapter 1, one defence of a society which relies on free markets and restricts intervention to the development of common law rules which mimic the market by distributing the entitlements to property to those who may be taken to value them most is rooted in the concepts of efficiency and pareto optimality. It is clear that this approach to defining the rights that people have is at least radically incomplete, if not fatally flawed. Standing alone, the approach cannot define a set of social arrangements that it is in the interests of representative individuals to live under. Put another way, efficiency is not the goal that contractors would select in a hypothetical contract as the foundational principle to be used in determining the pattern of rights in society.

The problem is that pareto optimal or efficient outcomes are indeterminate until an initial assignment of rights has been made. It is not possible to specify what trades will occur until it is known what endowment of resources individuals bring with them to the market place. Individuals cannot know how to order their preferences across a range of goods until a set of relative prices is known. Nobody can know what they are willing to pay for something or what they require to be persuaded to part with something, until they know what their wealth is. What their wealth is is a function of their initial endowment and the way in which that endowment is affected by successive rounds of trading. A major factor in determining the size and nature of that endowment and the consequences of trading upon it is played by the structure of rights.[4] The appropriate structure of rights is not a function of the requirements of efficiency or wealth maximization; rather, the appropriate distribution of rights has to be independently justified.

What this means is that the first priority of a representative individual is going to be with both the specification of the initial distribution of rights and with the rights which bear upon his market position as trading continues. This point expresses the frequently noted observation that efficiency is an aggregative notion which is indifferent to distributional concerns. It is important to note that both of these elements are essential.

As a representative individual, I might be persuaded that it is in my interests to support some kind of market economy rooted in individuated property rights, if I can be convinced that such a system is more productive than alternative economic systems. But my interest is in how the system is likely to affect me. Probably I will seek to maximize the size of my initial endowment. Ultimately I might be persuaded that an equal distribution of wealth is the fair starting-point since this is the only initial position that everybody can agree on. I might accept this because it is fair or because I recognize that it is in my interest to get the game started and the only footing to start on is equality, because then each individual has given up the minimum it is necessary to concede while retaining the maximum it is possible to retain, consistent with actually commencing to trade. But this does not exhaust my interest because I know that my wealth is going to fluctuate as a result of market trading. Pretty soon the wealth I have is going to be determined more by my fortune in the market than by the starting point. Moreover, the wealth of subsequent generations will be only tenuously connected to the initial fair position. Even if the initial position is fair for the original participants in the market, it is not necessarily fair to later entrants. As a representative first trader I will be concerned with whether I am protected from the vagaries of market exchange. It cannot be presumed that I will be indifferent to this. It cannot be assumed that I will not be risk-averse and identify an interest in entrenching into the basic structure of society rights to protect me against heavy welfare losses, even if I know that the overall productivity of the system may be lowered or if I know that probably I would be able to insure myself against those risks in the market itself. As a first trader and probable parent there is nothing to prevent me having an interest in a structure of rights which protects my children from entering the market at a disadvantage because of my own market failure, even if, as before, productivity is reduced. As a later entrant there is nothing illegitimate about my having an interest in requiring that each generation enter the market with a fair initial endowment rather than one determined randomly by a multitude of previous rounds of trading. Moreover, as a market participant there is nothing irrational about noticing that my interest lies not just in being free to engage in trades or behaviour that are worthwhile for me viewed in isolation, but that it is necessary to observe how the activities of others similarly engaged affects me. This last point simply expresses the liberal fallacy. Hence, for example, it does not follow that because it is in my interest to drive to work when no one else drives, that it is in my interest to drive if every one else drives. In that case it is necessary to consider whether the market is in fact the most efficient device for satisfying my preferences. It could well be that reliance on markets alone subjects us to the tyranny of small choices under which the effective capacity to choose between different end states is denied.

These examples show that it is not irrational to have an interest in the structure of rights that goes beyond the initial distribution of assets necessary to set market mechanisms in motion. Moreover, to accept revealed preferences within the market as sufficient to identify the interests which are relevant to assessing the fairness or efficiency of the market is question-begging. Viewed from the point of view of self-interest or fairness it is just wrong to treat the consequences of trading after the initial fair starting point as unproblematic. It is simply not correct to suggest that by definition a trade from a fair starting point preserves that fairness for subsequent rounds of trading. It has become commonplace to observe that Nozick, for example, seems to believe either that the outcome of a series of mutually satisfactory individual transactions will necessarily be a social condition that the participants in the series would desire to see, or that if undesirable outcomes do occur they are not important enough to interfere with. Neither of these assumptions is obviously correct.

If we look at the matter simply from the point of view of self-interest, it is difficult to accept that an unregulated market can be justified to representative individuals as being in their interests. Certainly observed behaviour suggests that many if not most persons do believe that they are better off with intervention than without it. Of course this can be decried as an example of the irrationality of individuals who are unable to see the opportunity cost of such intervention. Intervention for them may mean a big gain, but intervention on behalf of other groups produces thousands of tiny losses which outweigh the one big benefit. The point might be that interfering with the market is something that it is rational to do as a way of minimizing your losses if everybody else is seeking advantages, though it would be in everybody's interests not to interfere. If this is so, the problem for the market liberal is a game-theoretic one, rather than one involving lack of rationality, and so the issue is to find ways of providing conditions in which long-term self-interest can flourish. But even this is not very persuasive. Enough is known about the operation of markets to suggest that welfare losses are frequently heavily concentrated on particular sections of the community and welfare gains are similarly concentrated. Thus gains accrue, on average, to those with talent and skill. The biggest gainers from markets are those who can offer abilities which are scarce. Such persons can accumulate resources and improve their bargaining position, and thereby engineer themselves into a position where they have a major impact on the purposes that markets serve. Through the accumulation of capital they can determine what others do; they make it profitable for others to devote themselves to fulfilling the purposes of the rich. This may all be fair, but the issue is whether self-interest alone is sufficient to persuade the untalented that it is in their interest to support this system. It is by no means obvious that it is. The issue reduces to a question of what the bench-mark is against which to judge self-interest. Market liberals tend to assume that the bench-mark is provided by a state of nature; that is, a world in which there are no property rights. Such a world is unproductive. Introducing property rights leads to growth. Providing that your property rights have not been interfered with, it is in your interest (or fair) to put up with any welfare losses provided they don't leave you worse off than you would have been in a state of nature. It is difficult to see what would damage you that badly; so, as if by magic, the market is justified.

It is, however, not at all clear why this should be the starting point. What needs to be compared is a series of possible worlds, each of which sets the base level of losses at different levels. I have already suggested that citizenship theory offers a defence of one such level. The acid test is which of these possible worlds individuals would choose as being in their interest to live in. Presumably some constraints would have to be placed on what it is proper for individuals to know. But any theory which limited knowledge to such an extent that only one society could be chosen would obviously be unsatisfactory. My belief is that even where individuals were possessed only of knowledge it is proper for them to have (if it is possible to determine that), there would be a range of societies open for choice each with different structures of property rights, and that it would be in the interests of some members of society to choose one society and others to choose another. Alternatives will range from structures of property rights which offer high rewards to the skilful by permitting individuals full control over the use and disposition of the fruits of their labour. Others will offer more security against the risks of market changes and relatively higher rewards to the relatively unskilled or risk-averse, coupled with periodic redistributions to even up the starting points of new entrants.

One last issue is to define who the representative person is. It begs the question to treat him as the average person in society, if only because there is so much variation around the average that not everyone is going to be prepared to pin their hopes on being average. Historically, market theorists like Adam Smith (and this is seen in Hayek too) have argued that the worst-off day labourer is better off in the market than in any other system. But it is illegitimate to treat the comparison as being between an African kingdom and a developed economy; the proper comparison is between varieties of modern economic systems.

Only if it could be shown that despite appearances all individuals would be better off under the first regime can it be said that such a society is in the interests of all. It is to show this that some market liberals go to such lengths to deny that mixed economies can be stable in the long run and to explain away the economic success of societies that do not rely on full property rights. These arguments are unconvincing. It does seem that there is a variety of possible worlds from which to choose which are stable in the longer run. Given this, it is implausible to take the state of nature as the appropriate bench mark for judging self-interest. There is no such uniquely privileged starting point determined by reference to self-interest. If the state of nature is the relevant starting point, it must be shown that it is because morality requires it to be.

What all this tends to show is that self-interest is not enough to justify a system of full property rights. I do not believe that market liberals can succeed on these grounds alone. What they require is a convincing demonstration that their morality is correct. This can be provided by using notices of fairness, rights and so forth. It is to this that I now turn.

Property Rights and Taxation

A series of different arguments can be offered for a regime of full property rights. It is important to note that such rights have to be argued for. As Miller, Scanlon and others have rightly pointed out, a major weakness of Nozick's *Anarchy, State and Utopia* is the absence of a defence of the rights he puts forward.[5]

We saw in chapter 1 an equivocation between those in the new right who believe that it is necessary to give the distribution of market outcomes a moral defence and those who do not. An aspect of this problem is the need for social stability, that is to say, the problem of securing allegiance to the principles of a market order by the participants within it. But this issue has an affinity with another, namely the kind of defence that can be given for full property rights. Miller has correctly noted that more recently market liberals have argued as if the notion of justice is to be understood as explained by reference to property rights.[6] On this view, property is treated as the fundamental concept and justice is explained by reference to it, rather than the concept of justice being fundamental and the institution of property being defended on the footing that it is required by justice. Miller argues correctly, I think, that Nozick relies upon an undefended notion of full ownership and that this is unacceptable since that understanding of the nature of property is not an essential element of morality *per se*, and it is possible to imagine alternative systems of property rights for which moral support can be provided. To suggest as Plant, for example, has done, that a defence of full liberal ownership is given in terms of the Kantian requirement not to treat individuals as means but as ends, seems to be incorrect since, at least in Nozick's theory, what it is to treat as a means is defined by reference to the violation of rights.[7] Treating someone as a means is improperly to cross their boundaries; the location of that boundary is determined by the specification of the rights, not by the Kantian principle by itself.

The problem with giving a defence of property rights stems from the fact that property and ownership are not fundamental moral notions but derivative ones. In other words, if property is justified as an institution, it is because it is required by other principles, such as freedom or utility maximization. Thus it is necessary to spell out the relationship between more fundamental moral categories and property. It is possible in principle that the connection between the basic principles and property is so close that full property rights can be thought of as entailed by these principles. If this were the case there would be little point in debating whether property rights are natural rights, because to deny that full rights are required would be just to have made some kind of mistake. However, it is clear that the issue cannot be resolved so quickly. As I have already noted, moral arguments can and indeed have been made for a variety of different types of property system without there being any very obvious logial mistake.

The task, then, is to see why we should believe that full property rights are required and why these property rights exclude the recognition of rights to welfare. The first thing to note is that moral advantages do accrue from having some institution of property. Such rules define protected spheres and create stability. Individuals can have some confidence that their relationship to the world is predictable and within these protected spheres they are free to go about and fulfil their ends. Equally, however, these protected domains have the effect of limiting freedom. The space that has been protected for A is a space B is not free to enter.[8] Hence any system of property rights sets up a system of freedom and unfreedom, and what needs to be assessed is the justice of the distribution so established. Secondly, just to say that freedom requires some stable set of rules if it is to be exercised in worthwhile ways, is not in itself an argument for any particular set of rules. Probably it is not unreasonable to expect that the relevant rules will have something to say about the relationship between the individual and the external world, for the ability to control and plan, to make use of bits of the external world is necessary if individuals are to be able to act in the world with confidence. This, however, does not entail that full liberal ownership is necessary on these grounds alone. Probably not much more is necessary than a right of use. Other more utilitarian arguments about incentives and so forth may be relevant here, but they can be put to one side just now. Noting that the relationship between freedom and property is important draws attention to another crucial point, namely that the working of the practice on the distribution of freedom needs to be critically appraised.

One popular suggestion used to justify full liberal rights is the idea that one is entitled to the fruits of one's labour and that that entitlement carries with it the right to be sovereign in deciding how to use what has been earned. Historically, the most famous defence of this argument was given by Locke. In his version a property right in the fruits of one's labour is derived from a prior property right in one's person and is transmitted to the fruits of one's labour by the process of mixing labour. As has frequently been noted, it is not clear why mixing labour is not just a way of losing your labour rather than acquiring property. Becker, for example, concludes his discussion of the labour theory of acquisition by suggesting that in its most plausible form the theory trades on the idea that it would be unjust to deprive someone of the expected benefits of their labour where they have taken pains to work beyond what they are morally required to do for others, and by so doing have produced goods which would not have existed but for their labour.[9] This principle is subject to the provision that no-one is harmed in the process, as for example they would be if they were put at a competitive disadvantage or in other ways found their opportunities restricted. In this form the principle suggests nothing stronger than that you are entitled to a property right in what you produce simply because no-one else has a stronger claim. Becker goes on to suggest that the principle can be understood as a desert principle where what is produced is of social value and where recognizing a property right, rather than praising or expressing gratitude, is a fitting reward for the services produced. But note how weak the principle is. It operates subject to what morality requires us to do for others and subject to the constraint that others are not harmed. If this is a plausible account of the way desert and entitlement to the fruits of one's labour operates, then it is perfectly compatible with the recognition of welfare rights. Secondly, even though it suggests that desert may have a role to play in justifying rewards, desert, as understood by Becker, is a limited notion. Whatever else is true, it is clear that the distribution in the market does not correlate with desert at all well. Due to the role of luck in the market, many market rewards are not deserved on any plausible account of desert rooted in effort or skill or diligence, and equally, many deserts are not rewarded. Modern liberals are correct to notice that full property rights cannot be justified on the grounds that market returns reflect moral virtue, even if moral virtue were sufficient to justify full property rights. Something else has to be put in its place.

What can work here? Hayek has suggested that we should accept rewards according to market valuation, but it is difficult to see that this amounts to anything more than a type of entitlement theory unless it is rooted in utilitarianism of some form. If the pattern of returns is to be treated as just, there must be some kind of correlation with some characteristic of the agent. Desert is an obvious candidate; perhaps the value of contribution is another. But this raises the thorny question of whether the value of contributions can be individuated in the appropriate ways. In a complex and independent economy it is by no means obvious that they can. Moreover, it is impossible to evade the question of the value of the contribution to individual rewards made by the provision of the structure of property rights and the pattern of profitable opportunities that that makes available. As Kearl has shown, taxation is not necessarily a form of theft.[10] It may be nothing more than a claiming back by the state of that portion of wealth which state institutions have created. On this view taxation is little more than a means of recovering a contribution made. Now, this is no knock-down criticism of Nozick since he does not rest entitlement on contribution, and he could thus allege that Kearl's criticism is beside the point. If he takes this view, however, the problem seems to be that he is simply assuming the truth of what he needs to prove.

These remarks suggest the following. First, freedom may require some kind of property system, but this does not show that either full property rights are required or that they are required in capital. Secondly, if freedom does underlie property it must be recognized that the system creates a structure of freedom and unfreedom and that it is necessary to assess the working of the system from the point of view of justice. In other words, we must examine not just the formal structure of rights which *qua* rights may indeed be equally distributed, but also the operation of the system in practice. Thus, freedom may require interference with property to protect the very values that property was set up to secure. Thirdly, if justice enters into the account of property it does so as a more fundamental notion than property itself. Neither desert nor contribution justify untrammelled property rights. They may rather require interferences. Fourthly, a requirement of stability and a desire not to frustrate expectations lends support to reliance on property rights, but it is not clear that they justify any particular structure of property rights rather than a stable one in which changes are not made too quickly. The point is that it is the stability of expectations that count; there is no right that particular expectations be recognized as binding.

In the end, probably the best way to treat property rights is within a broadly utilitarian framework. As Ryan has suggested, it is incorrect to think of an injustice being done to individuals if a particular set of property rights is not recognized, even though not to set up a system of property rights may be to forgo any number of advantages in terms of wealth and freedom.[11] If this is correct then the moral constraint upon redistribution in the name of social rights will not be provided by the existence of prior rights of ownership but by its effect on the incentive structure, and this of course is in part going to be a function of the beliefs which individuals have about what are the proper claims a society may make upon them.

It is useful to notice that this suggests the significance of a scheme of fair taxation. My suggestion is that we do not have an entitlement to keep full control over what we earn. What we may keep is in part determined by our obligations to others. Where this is so, it is plainly wrong to regard a scheme of taxation as the moral equivalent of forced labour or as violating the distinctness and separateness of persons. All that is being done is the enforcement of duties, not the violation of rights. In principle, the requirement to pay taxes which reflects, for example, a duty to compensate others for bearing the burdens of insecurity in the market is not much different from a duty to work to repay contractual debts. To claim that to be required to pay compulsory taxes fails to recognize the moral separateness of persons and so forth, is to presuppose the truth of what has to be shown, namely that the rights which individuals have are full property rights and that apart from the general duty not to interfere with the rights of others the only enforceable obligations are ones which have voluntarily been incurred. Once this assumption is challenged, the claims concerning the moral evils of taxation are revealed to be hyperbole. But, having said this, there may well be constraints on the way in which it is proper to raise the funds to discharge those obligations, and often no doubt it will be very difficult to weigh and balance competing considerations. There is no lexical ordering under which resources needed for redistribution have a first claim and then and only then resources are available for private use. Sometimes, when the factors justifying redistribution are especially urgent, it is right to treat this demand as a prior one, but this will not always be so. Occasionally, there may be a fine balance between the reasons favouring redistribution, and those suggesting that the demands being placed on the pockets and loyalties of those whom the market has provided with means have become too onerous.

I do not have a theory of fair taxation to offer except to note that the tax system will have to meet some moral criteria. It is doubtful whether any system will be fair in the sense of completely non-discriminatory between individuals and different plans of life or preference schedules. Any system of taxation is going to change the relative costs of engaging in different pursuits, if only because it is difficult to see how everything that is a source of pleasure can be taxed; as a result whatever is left untaxed will therefore be cheaper to engage in and take pleasure from. Nevertheless fairness does impose some kind of constraint on the way resources can be extracted. Taxes are fairer than compulsory labour because they minimize the extent of coercion required to get the job done by leaving maximum freedom to individuals to choose how and at what to work. They also leave open a greater possibility to decide how much contribution to make in the sense that it is possible to avoid taxes by not earning very much. Furthermore, different systems of taxes affect choices in different ways and this should be taken into account. So in sum, provided the reasons justifying an enforceable obligation to facilitate redistribution are good ones, taxation is the most acceptable means available to carry out our mutual duties. Taxation is not an immoral means independently of the ends it serves and, provided efforts are made to make the scheme as fair as possible, its use is inevitable and morally acceptable in a just society.

Before leaving my discussion of the operation of the market system, it is worthwhile drawing attention to the problem of exploitation. As markets operate inequalities emerge and tend to become cumulative. Individuals of widely disparate economic power contract with each other. At some point differences in economic endowments cease to be merely the basis for mutually advantageous trades and begin to affect the fairness of the bargains reached. In these circumstances one party is able to take advantage of the other. Enough has been said in this chapter to support the claim that markets are not simply neutral devices operating equally in the interests of all rational individuals. Markets do not serve all purposes or all individuals indifferently. Because of the insecurities and inequalities of the market it is necessary to examine bargains from the point of view of fairness.

The theory of fairness relied on by citizenship theory may be simply stated. Bargains will be unfair or exploitative to the extent that individuals are effectively unable to resist entering exchanges which compromise their status as full members of the community. A central purpose of social policy, therefore, is to redistribute resources so that citizens are able to resist being forced into exploitative exchanges. Once that is done, it is possible to be more sanguine about the bargains that people strike.

So far in this chpater I have considered various arguments based on consent, fairness, self-interest and the morality of property rights which might be thought to exclude the possibility of recognizing welfare rights. My conclusion is that none of them can support that result. An important point emerges from my discussion. Much of the argument of the new right presupposes that it is possible to define a set of procedural rules which all persons would or should accept as legitimate. Provided that transactions do not breach these rules, the outcomes of the process are acceptable in the sense that they are at least not unfair. It is also assumed that it is easier to gain support for the rules that define the game than for the outcomes of the game itself. In this way reliance on the market avoids the need to attempt the impossible task of generating consensus on the moral criteria to apply to market outcomes. Political conflict is thereby reduced and stability fostered.

If I am right, this new right theory is exposed as a sham. The assessment of the rules cannot avoid taking account of the results they facilitate. Outcomes and process cannot be so neatly divorced, especially since the outcomes feed back on the real, if not formal, character of the process. The need to generate some kind of consensus on the morality of market outcomes is inescapable if society is to be based on something more than brute power. The 'depoliticization' of distributional issues is itself as difficult to achieve as the creation of a social democratic consensus on social justice. And, if it is achieved, it would be the moral equivalent of sweeping dirt under a carpet.

Do We Have a 'Right' to Welfare?

I turn now to the final set of arguments designed to show the impossibility of claiming a moral right to welfare. The first claim is that to assert a right to welfare is to make a conceptual mistake. Logically, the ascription of rights belongs to one moral domain; a concern with welfare to another. To claim a right to welfare is to conflate two logically distinct domains of moral discourse. Rights, it is asserted, are conceptually connected to the idea of freedom and impose obligations on others not to interfere with the actions of the holder of the rights. As Hart writes:

> the concept of a right belongs to that branch of morality which is specifically concerned to determine when one peson's freedom may be limited by another's and so determine what action may appropriately be made the subject of coercive legal rules.[12]

Obviously if this approach is correct there is no possibility of claiming welfare rights because the only obligations rights create are duties of non-interference rather than duties to assist. Any positive duties must, as a matter of logic, be created through the exercise of freedom. Duties to aid and rights to be assisted can exist only if they have been voluntarily assumed, for example, through a contract. There can be no general rights to be aided which exists independently of consent.

In my view, linking the idea of a right exclusively to the protection of the opportunity to act freely is unnecessarily restrictive. Extending the concept of rights to rights of recipience breaches no obvious conceptual truth about morality, nor does it violate ordinary usage or any privileged historical paradigm. What is conceptually wrong, for example, with the notion that an elderly person has a right to be treated with respect? True, a breach of this right does not ground a cause of action but there is no conceptual mistake in saying that someone has a moral right to receive respect. There are many examples where it is surely wrong to say that talk of rights is simply out of place. Parents often have a moral right to be assisted by their children. The right to a fair trial involves a right to receive. And if other non-interference rights are to be enforced or protected the state has a duty to provide resources in the form of a police force to do so.[13]

A second line of argument is to say that rights to welfare are ruled out because they breach the requirement that rights and duties are correlative. Here the notion is that for every alleged right there must be a corresponding duty. To say that X has a right is at the same time to imply that there is a Y who has the duty to satisfy it. My right to life entails that you have a duty not to kill me. The agents who bear the duty are readily identified (in this case everyone), and so is what they must do to fulfil their duty (in this case literally nothing). But if I have a right to welfare, who is obliged to respect it and what must they do to do so? If the bearers and nature of the obligation cannot be identified, the correlativity requirement is breached and the attempt to establish the claim to welfare as a right fails.

Whether the correlativity thesis is correct is a matter of some doubt, but it is more useful to show that rights to welfare satisfy it. If they do, a more rigorous foundation for state welfare can be provided. Raymond Plant has persuasively shown that claiming there are rights to welfare is consistent with the correlativity principle.[14] His suggestion is that the right is held against society in general rather than against specific individuals and that, more particularly, it is held against the government. It is the government that bears the strict obligation to satisfy welfare rights. The strict duty of individuals, therefore, is not personally to provide resources to specific needy people, but to support the institutions that do so. The strict duty is primarily to pay the taxes required by government.

It is doubtful, as a general proposition, whether substantive moral arguments can be resolved by resort to conceptual or logical truths about morality. Substantive moral issues can be resolved only by recourse to substantive argument. The possibility of rights to welfare cannot be eliminated on conceptual grounds alone. This point is reinforced when we consider the function of rights in moral theory.

Rights are a particular type of claim; they define an entitlement to be accorded a certain type of treatment. Rights are a moral protective device. They serve to protect a substantial moral interest of the bearer of the rights against the claims of other persons, the collectivity and the general welfare. Rights are typically ascribed to individuals and serve to guarantee to them specified goods in the form of resources and opportunities for action. They can be used by individuals as devices to deploy in the control of the external world. Rights are very useful in subjecting the world to human purposes in a predictable and secure fashion. Without the ascription of rights the conditions of individual flourishing would be eliminated.

It this view of rights is accepted, the question of what rights there are is to be considered in relation to a view of the basic moral interests of persons. Put in this way the claim to recognize the possibility of welfare rights is compelling. The moral relevance of much need speaks for itself. Welfare rights can provide the framework for the elimination of individual suffering. They can also make available to individuals the resource base to permit the effective use of other civil and political rights. Welfare rights support liberty. Indeed, at bottom, their justification draws upon precisely the same conception of individuals as potentially autonomous agents as does the justification of property rights. Without welfare rights, the value to a significant group of persons of their liberal opportunity rights would tend to be greatly reduced. Welfare rights make the opportunities to act freely worth possessing and help sustain self-respect. There can be little doubt of their value.

But this, it may be suggested, is insufficient to show the existence of welfare rights because they, unlike traditional human rights, require that governments command and deploy substantial quantities of resources. The sheer impracticability of expecting that most governments in the world could command the necessary resources to provide their population with a decent standard of living shows that welfare 'rights' do belong in a different moral domain to traditional human rights.[15] The difficulty with this argument, of course, is that a posits a sharper distinction between the practicability of satisfying traditional human rights and welfare rights than actually exists. Both sets of rights require the positive outlay of resources. In many societies what is needed to defend the core human right, the right to life, stretches the resources of the community to the limit, though that does not make the right to life any less a right. Practicability is a matter of degree and, as Plant has suggested, it is more appropriate to 'say that governments ought to respect all these rights so far as they are able "in accordance with the organization and resources of each state" '[16], than artificially to identify categories of practicability and deny the status of rights to claims falling within certain categories.

For all of these reasons there seems nothing particularly muddled about claiming rights to welfare. Not only can they exist, but there are powerful reasons to suggest that any satisfactory moral theory ought to recognize them. As I have sought to show in this chapter, the characteristic arguments of the new right do not succeed in eliminating welfare rights. The question, 'what are rights to welfare rights to?', remains open. In the final two chapters I say more about this issue. Chapter 7 considers and rejects the theory that need standing alone defines the content of welfare rights. In the final chapter I defend the principle that welfare rights are to be understood by reference to what is required to guarantee the status of individuals as full members of the community.

7

Need

The search for a moral foundation for the welfare state often begins and ends with the notion of need. The moral imperative to satisfy needs presses urgently; failing to respond to unmet need leaves individuals extremely deprived. Unmet needs, therefore, ground the first claim on available resources. The nature of needs allows them to be distinguished from mere preferences. Needs are basic and fundamental to any human functioning. They are immutable. An individual does not choose his needs nor can he change them as he might a suit of clothes. For this reason needs are not simply important preferences, but something quite different and morally more fundamental. They cannot be chosen or developed; more crucially, they cannot be escaped.

If this account works it has several important implications. First, the priority of need-based claims against those of wants, desires or preferences is defended. Whether the moral imperative to satisfy needs is viewed as a feature of benevolence or justice the upshot is the same. A morally acceptable society is one which guarantees the satisfaction of the needs of its members as its most basic obligation. Once this obligation has been fulfilled society is free to facilitate the fostering and satisfaction of preferences. In this way need operates as a principle of distribution.

The distinction between needs and preference is therefore crucial.[1] A person in need has an enforceable claim on the resources of others, whereas when it comes to the satisfaction of preferences, that person must fend for himself in the marketplace, fulfilling his desires if he can through the arrangements he can create with others. In this way, the notion of need serves to mark off the domain where markets must be regulated or replaced from that where they may be allowed free play. 'Need' provides one element in a principled foundation for a mixed economy.

Secondly, need grounds only a limited claim on an affluent society's resources. An individual's need for clothing, or food, or shelter can be readily satisfied at limited expense. Organizing society to guarantee that needs are met is not like organizing for total war in which every fibre of every muscle strains to achieve victory. Rather, all that is necessary is limited effort to devote a relatively small portion of total resources to forestall the development of needs or to pick up cases that become urgent. One reason to stress the contrast between need and preference is precisely to head off the risk that individuals could develop a taste for expensive ways of life and claim that they 'need' the resources necessary to participate in them. No matter how important a preference is to an individual, no matter how sincere his taste, his claim on society to provide him with the resources to satisfy that preference is not a claim to meet a need. Needs are objective facts; they are not constituted by subjective preferences. For this reason society's resources cannot be 'hi-jacked' by those with expensive tastes. There is no obligation on society to distribute resources to satisfy expensive preferences. It is up to each individual to fend for himself in that regard.

Thirdly, because 'needs' can be identified objectively, a clear and unambiguous foundation can be laid for welfare institutions. Once we acknowledge that needs should be met – surely a difficult claim to resist – moral controversy is replaced by social science. As Plant and Lesser have suggested, 'the argument ought to be a factual and empirical one, concerning the most efficient way of meeting these needs'.[2] If this view is correct, it is very attractive. It suggests that by focusing on 'need', moral disputes can be dissolved. 'This means that a very important part of social policy . . . could be decided without reference to overall views of what society should be like.'[3] Individuals with widely divergent moral views who disagree about much else ought to be able to agree about the existence and priority of need-related claims.

But how plausible is this view of need? There are some good reasons to suppose that the concept of need cannot function within a political theory in the way this account assumes. In this chapter I question whether need can function as the basis of an independent principle of justice. In my view it is not possible to identify a limited and objective set of needs that can act as a uncontroversial foundation for a welfare state. A consensus, rooted in the demands of logic or philosophical analysis, on the categories of need that society ought to protect through a structure of rights, is probably not available at all, or if it is only at such a high level of abstraction that few policy implications flow from it. Any consensus that could be achieved would flow as a practical matter from a vision of the nature of the political community and the community way of life, shared by it members, and forged by them.

A first difficulty with the account I have outlined above is whether it is reasonable to treat need standing alone as a principle of distribution. Clearly a principle of distribution according to need is plausible only if an account of 'need' can be given so that there are sufficient resources available to meet needs so defined. It is evident that if the claims of those 'in need' exceeds available resources, then those resources will have to be distributed according to some supplementary principle of distribution. Under conditions of scarcity, as Weale has persuasively argued, 'the satisfaction of need is itself a benefit to be distributed in accordance with some principle'.[4]

If we wish to hold on to the notion that it is important to satisfy needs, but recognize the implications of resource scarcity, it is possible to conceive of several candidates as a supplementary principle of distribution. Probably least attractive would be to distribute an equal quantity of resources to anyone in need. The obvious weakness with this is that individual variations in neediness are ignored. Alternatively, urgency of need suggests the plausibility of a principle requiring satisfaction of the most pressing needs first. Thus, if Joan is three times as needy as Jill, the obvious thing to do is to concentrate our efforts on Joan until such time as she becomes only as needy as Jill. Thereafter, resources might be distributed to them equally.

Attractive though this solution seems, there are several difficulties with it which tell against its acceptability as a distributive principle. First, it assumes what is by no means obvious, namely, that it is possible to rank degrees of neediness on some common or single scale. Only if need can be ranked in this way, for example, as if on a scale from -100 (utter deprivation) to 0 (all needs satisfied), can unambiguous imperatives be produced.[5] Often, however, I suspect it will be impossible to rank different persons according to a scale of neediness where these needs are of significantly different kinds, or where, even though placed in similar circumstances, the respective individuals perceive their situations quite differently. Secondly, the principle of urgency seems to assume that individuals are equally effective at converting resources into need-reduction. It is surely likely that many of the most needy members of our society are either inefficient at meeting their needs, or have needs that require massive outlays to produce quite minor reductions in need. Certain medical conditions, for example, are so crippling and intractable that huge quantities of resources do little to improve well-being. In these circumstances it is necessary at least to consider whether the best use of resources requires distribution in accordance with urgency of need alone, or whether it is necessary to consider also the efficiency with which those resources actually satisfy needs. Sometimes it would be preferable to cast the principle in terms of minimizing the amount of need left after resources have been distributed, even though that might mean that some extremely urgent needs are left alone. Thirdly, this approach does not touch on the problem of resource scarcity. If resources are scarce relative to need, either because the resource required to satisfy needs eat up more than the total pie, or because it seems morally incorrect to deny that at some point the claim of needs to first call on resources must give way to the use of resources for other purposes, then it follows that some further principle of distribution is required. Urgency, perhaps qualified by an efficiency of need-reduction criterion, could act as a sufficient principle of distribution only where the quantity of resources available for need satisfaction had been determined in some way. And the determination of that very question requires, of course, the specification of some distributive principle or some set of principles with distributive implications.

Is 'Basic Need' a Distributional Principle?

The problem of the scarcity of resources for need satisfaction is not a false one, and bedevils another initially plausible way of thinking about distributing according to need. According to this perspective, the problem of scarcity can be overcome by distributing only to *basic* needs, at least in the first instance. The trick is to classify certain needs as basic and others as not basic. Effort is then to be concentrated on satisfying basic needs. The intuitive attraction of this approach is that it would seem to require far fewer resources to satisfy basic than all needs.

There are, however, difficulties with this approach too. Insofar as urgency is used as a criterion to classify a need as basic, some of the problems have already been outlined above. Beyond this, however, even if we assume a consensus on the categories of basic need, not all basic needs are necessarily satiable. Medical needs, for example, are not satiable in the required sense. The history of medicine is a story of developments leading to the control, cure or eradication of certain types of diseases, only to find new ailments becoming major and increasingly expensive problems. Thus heart disease and cancer have replaced typhoid or tuberculosis as major killers. It is, therefore, unclear what determinate meaning can be given to the notion of satisfying a basic need for medicine. How many kidney machines or heart transplants would this require? In the twentieth century we have become increasingly aware of the extraordinarily high costs of modern medicine. The crisis of medical funding which has occurrred in many Western countries reveals the naivety of treating medical need as a sufficient criterion for distribution. For this reason Weales's suggestion that resources be distributed so that there is 'an equally distributed risk of unsatisfied need, where the appropriate degree of risk is socially determined and agreed' seems seems attractive.[6]

The insatiability of certain basic needs does not exhaust the problem of using basic need as a distributional principle. A second difficulty is that even identifying a certain *category* of need as basic and insatiable is not sufficient to determine what would count as satisfying it. It is one thing to identify a certain category of need as basic, but it is another to specify what is required to satisfy it. The problem is that any attempt to satisfy a basic need will involve the use of standards of evaluation which themselves are not basic. The category of a basic need is formal and abstract whereas a decision about when that need has been satisfied invokes specific, concrete interpretations of appropriate standards.

An example will make this point clearer. Consider the basic need of shelter. If we all accept a principle that we should distribute resources to satisfy basic needs, we would agree that our society has a responsibility to do something about those people without shelter. We know, of course, that if we are to do something this will involve diverting resources towards that end. But do we know any more? It is difficult to see that we do. We know we have to provide shelter; but how much? How many cubic metres of space per person is necessary? Do we have to use materials of a certain quality? And so forth. A principle which specifies distribution in accordance with basic needs seems to say no more than that there are distributional implications of making responses to certain categories towards which we ought to respond.

This argument has two implications for the idea that basic needs can define a principle of distribution. First, the notion of basic need is not doing all the work in accounting for the distributional implications of the principle – non-basic standards play an irreducible role. Second, as a result, the distributional implications may be more far-reaching than at first appeared likely in adopting a basic need criterion. Consequently the probability of running back into the scarcity problem re-emerges, and with it the risk that the need principle may conflict with, and have to be traded off against, other competitive moral principles.

Finally, one further problem with the idea that basic need *simpliciter* can act as a principle of distribution should be noted. This is that commonplace intuitions do not support the view that all basic needs ground claims to be met. Consider, for example, the case of a spurned lover. Nothing one could say would shake him out of his belief that the most overriding need in his life, the only thing capable of making life worth living, is to regain the affections of his erstwhile mate. But it would be surprising, to say the least, if anyone would go so far as to argue that the love of Martha (or whoever) *ought* to be distributed towards him.

This point can be generalized. The need for affection and for friendship appears to be as good a candidate as any for being ascribed a status as a basic need. But whereas in the case of material deprivation many would accept that that deprivation ought to be eliminated, few would accept the same in the case of personal affection. The reason is, of course, that to do so would impose an intolerable moral burden on the suppliers of affection in a way that is not implied in the case of material resources. At most, compassionate societies seem to be prepared only to go so far as coping with some of the worst fallout of 'affection-deprivation' by providing social workers who might inculcate or encourage the development within such unfortunate people of the personal attributes which might tend to lead others voluntarily to display affection and friendship to them.

It is clear then that need, standing alone, does not constitute a satisfactory principle of distribution. Moreover, as the example of deprivation of affection shows, not all (basic) needs automatically ground a moral claim to be met. At best a principle of distribution according to need is incomplete. And this much is true even if the identification of the existence of need is inherently uncontroversial and if it is acceptable to treat need as grounding an independent principle of justification.

This latter assumption has been challenged by Brian Barry in *Political Argument*.[7] His claim is that need statements are essentially triadic, taking the form, 'X needs A in order to do Y'. Needs, on this view, are instrumental to the achievement of particular ends or purposes and 'only when the ends or purposes for which things are needed are both articulated and found to be justified does the appeal to need have any moral force'.[8] If this is correct, it seems to follow that need claims have no independent justificatory force. Our sense that X ought to receive A just because he needs it trades on an unarticulated and implicit knowledge and acceptance of whatever it is that A is needed for. Thus it appears redundant to ask why a starving man needs food, for the answer that he needs it to stay alive seems so obvious as not to require stating, just as the implications of recognizing the need seem, at least to most people, clear-cut.

The question this raises is whether the view that need claims are instrumental (even where it is not necessary to specify what something is needed for) and the claim that the justification for acting in a certain way depends on the ends or purposes in question, have damaging consequences for a view which seemed to want to make the existence of unmet need sufficient moral reason for action? Raymond Plant and Harry Lesser discuss one damaging possibility. In *Political Philosophy and Social Welfare*, they argue that an instrumental account of needs, by identifying a requirement to justify ends and purposes, introduces into the notion of needs the full range of moral controversy. On apparent advantage of needs-talk in social administration is revealed to by a myth, namely, the implicit assumption that needs could be identified in a neutral fashion through the practice of social science. By rendering the satisfaction of a need contingent upon the purpose which it serves, the moral significance of needs is thereby made relative to the values that the needs serve and the apparently solid objective basis for identifying the sphere of the welfare sector is lost.

The spectre raised by the instrumentality of needs is that the problem of justifying policies designed to satisfy needs is going to be doubly difficult, for not only does a principle of need satisfaction have to be defended against the claims of other moral principles, but the identification of need itself is subject to controversy. Indeed rival accounts of need very likely would be penetrated by those other values, such as freedom, which, on a simpler view, would be in conflict or competition with need. The problem then is that argumentation becomes complicated and that a needs principle has to be interpreted in the light of a spectrum of ends to which those needs contribute.

Two significant responses have been suggested to deal with this difficulty. In the end neither succeeds. David Miller has sought to deny the instrumentality of needs, in order to claim that a needs principle can operate as an independent principle of justification.[9] A different line of attack has been put forward by Raymond Plant and Harry Lesser, whose suggestion is to accept the view that need claims are instrumental, but to deny the stronger claim that the essentially contestable character of morality rules out the possibility of providing an account of basic needs which not only is objective, but also provides a sufficiently firm substantive basis for grounding the basic apparatus of a welfare state.[10] They do this by arguing for the existence of a range of basic needs which are instrumental to any moral purpose or end, According to Plant and Lesser, needs identify conditions which are instrumental to any kind of moral action, in the sense that their satisfaction is required if any kind of moral action is to occur. They neatly summarize their argument as follows:

> If there are necessary conditions of moral action, irrespective of particular moral codes, there will be some things that must be classed as needs whatever one's moral position. These conditions include physical survival and autonomy, i.e. freedom from arbitrary interference, ill-health and ignorance; and members of any society have a duty to create a social system that will satisfy these needs as well as possible.[11]

An important variant of this type of argument has been made famous by John Rawls[12] and extended by Albert Weale.[13] The basic idea is the same, and involves identifying as needs a class of means which are instrumental to any end or purpose. It is these means which Rawls calls primary goods and which stand as a proxy for basic needs. The upshot of the argument is similar to that of Plant and Lesser, although the strategy of argument differs in each case.

Miller's Defence of the Non-instrumentality of Needs

In *Social Justice*, Miller draws a distinction between three different types of need statements:

1 'instrumental' needs (e.g. 'he needs a key', 'she needs a driving licence');
2 'functional' needs (e.g. 'surgeons need manual dexterity', 'university lecturers need books');
3 'intrinsic' needs (e.g. 'men need food', 'he needs someone to understand him').[14]

Miller accepts that claims of the first kind require an independent statement of the end for which something is needed. Thus, for example, someone 'needs a key in order to enter his house'. But this, he argues, is not true of statements of 'functional' or 'intrinsic' needs. The statement that 'surgeons need manual dexterity' is complete as it stands.

In an attempted expansion:

> One might try 'surgeons need manual dexterity in order to be surgeons' or 'surgeons need manual dexterity in order to do their job', but one has hardly added any new information in either case. Of course it is possible for someone to ask 'Why do surgeons need manual dexterity?', but in giving an answer one would be involved in explaining what it was to be a surgeon to someone who knew little about the role, not in supplying distinct ends *for* which the surgeon's dexterity was needed.[15]

Miller suggests that the same holds for the third category, and argues that the 'means-end form distorts the sense of the original claim' for 'if one undertakes to supply an end here, one is simply filling out a whole of which the thing needed is one part'.[16]

Does Miller's account resolve the principal difficulty which an instrumental account of needs created, namely, that understanding the notion of needs instrumentally rendered any justification grounded on needs dependent on those ends for which the needs in question were means? Does Miller's non-instrumental account avoid opening up the defence of need-claims to the full range of moral controversy? Or has he successfully insulated them?

The answer to these questions turns on the account Miller gives of 'harm', for to claim that someone is in need is to make a claim about the consequences of depriving him of certain resources. Miller suggests the following as a definition of need: 'A needs X' = 'A will suffer harm if he lacks X'. This view is elaborated by relating the notion of harm to that of a plan of life. Miller's final position is worth quoting in full:

> Harm, for any given individual, is whatever interferes directly or indirectly with the activities essential to his plan of life; and correspondingly, his needs must be understood to compromise whatever is necessary to allow these activities to be carried out. In order, then, to decide what a person's needs are, we must first identify his plan of life, then establish what activities are essential to that plan, and finally investigate the conditions which enable those activities to be carried out.[17]

Does this provide the foundation for identifying basic needs in a neutral (perhaps non-normative or empirical) manner? If it did, we would have a uncontestable account of human needs which could fulfill an important role in building a defence of citizenship theory.

Plant and Lesser address this issue specifically in *Political Philosophy and Social Welfare*. Their object is to criticize the view that a neutral account of harm (or ailing, etc.) is available. In summary, they show that such an account is itself dependent on a specification of further ends:

> The concept of need is essentially contestable just because the ascription of need is related to a norm of harm that is essentially normative and is going to vary from morality to morality and from culture to culture.[18]

This conclusion is supported by quoting two examples developed by Mounce and Phillips in 'On morality's having a point', which shows that even the notion of physical harm is contestable.[19] In both of these examples a basic intuition that an individual has been harmed is overturned by a recognition of the implications of the injuries as interpreted within an individual's *Weltanschauung*. The first case concerned the philosopher Brentano, who went blind at the end of his life. Brentano dismissed his friends' commiserations, claiming that his blindness was beneficial to him because it allowed him to concentrate on philosophy, whereas previously he had allowed himself to cultivate too many diverse and distracting interests. The second case is that of a Catholic woman, unable to comprehend that the consequences of the birth of additional children could be described as harmful, because bearing children is a gift of God and cannot therefore be damaging.

It seems to me that these cases are sufficient to defeat any view which rests on the claim that an entirely universal and neutral account of harm can be offered, so as to ground a non-normative account of basic needs. But is Plant and Lesser's criticism of Miller to the point? Miller's claim is surely not that need is neutral in this view. Plant and Lesser's argument tells against any view which claims that for any A, if X is absent, then A has been harmed. For Miller, there is no description of X which is universal and neutral, so that when X is absent for any A, A has been harmed. The reason for this is that the specific description of X is dependent upon the ideals and standards adopted by A. Miller, therefore, does not *assume* that there is any strict analogue of a set of primary goods which would be identified by X, just because what X is, for any A, will vary with differences between the plans of life of individuals in a society. Plant and Lesser are correct to argue that Miller's account of harm and needs is not a suitable basis for establishing a *neutral* foundation for a welfare state, but this is not a startling conclusion because it is no part of Miller's thesis that it is.

Miller's argument is a more subtle one than that portrayed by Plant and Lesser. Miller wants to argue that the establishment of a welfare state grounded on the satisfaction of need, can itself be represented as a demand of justice and that need can operate as an independent principle of justification. Furthermore, the claim is made that the identification of need is only 'weakly evaluative'. In other words, the question, 'What basic needs are there?', can be answered, even though the existence of these needs depends on the specific ideals of individuals within society. What is required to give an account of needs is the ability to identify and describe the individual's plans of life. The account becomes weakly evaluative because Miller imposes the constraint that for something to count as a need, the plan of life of which it is part must be intelligible to us.

This exposes one way in which the claim that the non-neutrality of needs destroys the basis for justifying a welfare state has moved rather too quickly. Plant and Lesser assume that, if it is to be possible to justify social policies based on need, then it must be possible to identify needs in a way which makes no reference to normative criteria. It is assumed that, if normative criteria enter into an identification of the existence of a need, then any justification of a policy designed to satisfy needs must depend on those normative criteria. Moreover, it is assumed that for need to operate as the foundation of social policy, a standardized account of need must be offered. In other words, needs must be common. If X is Tom's need, it is also a need for Dick and Harry. Finally, Plant and Lesser trade on an unargued premise that, if the identification of need involves normative elements, then an account of what needs there are becomes controversial. This assumes that the very identification of the existence of needs involves *adopting* the normative perspective associated with those elements.

None of these assumptions is obviously true and Miller's account avoids these potential problems. Miller recognizes that a description of what needs there are will depend on a knowledge of what plans of life there are. The needs of different individuals will vary according to their plan of life. Nevertheless, it would still be possible to operate a welfare state based on need satisfaction, provided that the type and range of need was known. The fact that needs may be in part normatively constituted does not by itself imply that a neutral description of the existence of needs could not be offered. A welfare framework could be established that allowed individuals a wide degree of choice in policies that satisfied different types of needs. In other words, the possibility is open that a framework which neutrally satisfies needs can exist, but which does not assume that all individuals have the same needs. It has not been closed by noting that needs are in part normatively constituted.

Furthermore, the justification of satisfying needs is not directly dependent on those normative elements which enter into the identification of a need. If we adopt Miller's terminology of plans of life, we could say that the reason for satisfying needs is derived from a principle of respecting and/or facilitating individuals in their plan of life. The defence of this principle presumably makes use of arguments for the value of self-determination, and so forth. It would not necessarily draw upon the reasons why an individual's plan of life was specifically of value to him. Thus, for example, the reason for providing Ludwig with a hearing-aid and a piano would be that Ludwig needed them in order to carry out his plan of life. The reason would not be that playing the piano was a good thing, even though that may be the reason why Ludwig needs it. In other words the *reason* why X is of value to A, as essential to A's plan of life, and hence the reason why it is a need for A, is not the direct reason why X is given to him. This latter reason may just be that X is of value to A, without asking *why* it is.

It should be noted, however, that there is no strong sense in which need provides an independent principle of justification here. What seems to count is: (1) the character of the plans of life, coupled with; (2) a principle that plans of life should be respected or facilitated. This principle must itself be justified by reference to a concern with self-determination, autonomy, freedom or respect for persons. The structure of the normative argument remains triadic in the sense that the value of the need is determined by (1) and (2). This instrumental character of need statements is, in fact, quite clearly given away in the passage from *Social Justice* which I have quoted above.[20]

The point brought out by the Ludwig example is that even where needs vary, and vary in accordance with differing moral outlooks, it does not follow that building a defence of a welfare state directly related to need necessarily involves being morally partisan and adopting one, rather than another, moral system. In order to show that holding a view which begins from the premise that need could, in principle, be incorporated within a defence of the welfare state is necessarily partisan, involves substantiating further claims. In particular, it involves grounding the claim that no *framework* of need satisfying policies can exist which is neutral with respect to the needs satisfied. Here it is not enough to show that any *particular* policy would satisfy some needs but not others, for the whole point of this framework is that it allows selection *within* it. What has to be shown is that the satisfaction of some needs necessarily precludes the satisfaction of others.

So far, then, Plant and Lesser have given us little reason to believe that it is not possible to incorporate into a defence of the welfare system an account of need which avoids the moral complications they suggest follow from the normative constitution of the concept. My elaboration and extension of David Miller's approach has led to the suggestion that if a principle of respecting and/or facilitating an individual's plans of life is accepted, it might be possible to imagine a framework of need-satisfying policies which would be neutral with respect to (that is, would not discriminate between) the plans of life of individuals. Here the idea is that each individual – in a state of nature, perhaps – could be offered a guarantee that a framework of policies would exist, so that whatever his plan of life happened to be, policies would exist which would, if they are needed, make the appropriate resources available to him. Each individual would be able to select a policy within the framework which would be appropriate to his needs, as constituted by his plan of life. In this way the presence of moral diversity would not rule-out, *tout court*, the possibility of achieving a consensus on the need for, and characteristics of, a morally adequate welfare system.

A further point should be noted. My interpretation of Miller indicates a similarity with a Rawlsian primary goods approach, in that both are related to the provision of means to the individual's ends as defined by plans of life. One important distinction remains, however, and that is that, unlike Rawls's, Miller's approach does not assume that a definition of primary goods as generalized means can be offered. In Rawls's account a primary good is something that is wanted whatever else is wanted. A primary good is a means to an end; even though A and B have different plans of life, a set of goods exists which is equally instrumental to their respective plans. Miller's position does not presuppose this. Those things which are needed by A, as defined by his plan of life, may, and probably will, differ from those things needed by B. On this view there is no single set of primary goods; rather, at most there would be sets of primary goods.

Before examining this view more closely I want to consider the argument of Raymond Plant and Harry Lesser to see whether it provides a more direct and attractive foundation for the moral claims of a citizenship approach.

The Plant/Lesser Solution

As we have seen, Plant and Lesser believe that, if the existence of a need is in part dependent on the ideals or values of individuals (which it is), then no neutral account of needs can be offered which is capable of providing an uncontroversial basis for a welfare state. On the other hand, they believe that such an account is not only viable but necessary to a defence of publicly organized social policies. The circle is squared by arguing that certain types of need exist and can be recognized without invoking any specific normative framework. In other words, an account of needs can be offered which is neutral with respect to differing ideological perspectives. The key argument was outlined earlier. Its central proposition is that 'if there are necessary conditions of moral action, irrespective of particular moral codes, there will be some things that must be classed as needs whatever one's moral position'.[21] Plant and Lesser base their argument on the assertion that any logically self-consistent morality must recognize certain things to be human needs. They want to go further than just this, however, for they want also to claim that the same argument entails that 'the duty of members of a society appears to be to set up a system that will make the satisfaction of needs possible'.[22]

The argument is as follows:

1 'the existence of moral agents is a necessary precondition of moral activity'.

If

2 'human beings have moral duties',

then

3 'they have a need to survive'.

and then

4 agents have a 'duty to help each other to survive and preserve life'.[23]

The suggestion is that this chain of reasoning could be denied only if we assume that there are no moral obligations at all. And it is averred that the argument rests on just 'two purely logical principles of ethics'.[24] These are, firstly, that a moral code must be consistent, and secondly that, if A ought to do X, then he has a right to do X.

These arguments do not seem particularly convincing. Consider the move from the first point to the second. Why does it *logically* follow that, if A has any moral duty, then he has a need to survive? This may often be the case, just as a matter of fact, but under certain circumstances it may not be. Take for example the case of a hunger striker. It is not unimaginable that someone might regard starving himself to death as a moral duty, for example, as part of a strategy to attract public attention to an outrageous government policy. Survival is a need for this individual in only a very odd sense. The same might be said of any deeply religious person who regarded earthly life simply as a preparation for the life to come. If his view included the belief that blood transfusions were morally repugnant and sinful it would be difficult to persuade him that he needed blood. How persuasive would it be to argue with a Jehovah's Witness, for example, that blood was needed as a precondition of moral activity and that recognition of this need was required to make his moral code logically self-consistent?

It is not obvious, therefore, that every moral code must recognize survival as a basic need, if only because a moral code may require the extinguishing of life as a moral act. A moral code may fail to recognize survival as a basic need in other ways too. The Plant/Lesser thesis depends crucially on the assumption that, if A ought to have X (presumably all things considered), he has a right to X. But the problem is that, from the fact that A has a right to perform his duties, it does not follow that A has a right to be helped to perform his duties. Now this is crucial to the argument of *Political Philosophy and Social Welfare*, because Plant and Lesser want to use the argument of logical consistency to account for an obligation to provide certain welfare rights, which must be recognized by any moral code if it is to be self-consistent. But it is just not true that a welfare right can be grounded in this way. I have already given some examples of cases where, at least under certain circumstances, survival would not *necessarily* be recognized by particular moral codes. It is no more obvious that consistency requires the recognition of a right to be aided in the fulfillment of one's moral duties.

Plant and Lesser need to show that a moral code which does not include a duty to aid individuals in the fulfillment of their duties is logically inconsistent. If this could be demonstrated it would follow that any moral code which restricted duties to negative duties of forebearance was inconsistent. But this is clearly not the case simply as a matter of logic, because individuals do not always have a right to be aided in fulfilling a duty. Consider, for example, the case of Tom who has borrowed £10 from Dick, having promised to repay it on 1 July. In June, Tom suffers a misfortune and is left impecunious. On 1 July, Dick requests the £10 from Tom, who declares himself unable to pay. It is clear that Tom does have a duty to repay Dick, but also that, through no fault of his own , he is in no position to fulfil it. Dick meanwhile has also suffered a misfortune and is in no position to waive the repayment. Tom appeals to Harry with the argument that, as he, Tom has a moral duty to repay £10 but cannot fulfill his duty, Harry should give him £10 to pay Dick, just because, if you have a duty, you have a right to be aided in fulfilling it. Not surprisingly Harry claims that aiding the fulfilment of Tom's duties is not a morally obligatory reason for him to hand over £10, though of course he would be under an obligation not to interfere with Tom's repayment, if Tom could afford it.

Given this, it is not logically inconsistent for a moral code to deny that an individual has a right to be aided in the fulfilment of a duty. The implication is that a putative right to welfare, in response to a need for survival, cannot be established, solely as a requirement of reason in this way. Rather, argument for such a right must use normative or substantive moral reasons in a more immediate and direct way.

Implicitly this is recognized in the Plant/Lesser thesis, for an argument is offered to show that positive duties, rather than purely negative ones, are required. The argument, however, does not take place on the appropriate ground. What needs to be shown is that premise 4 above, (that is, that agents have a duty to help each other and preserve life), is justified as a condition of an agent fulfilling his moral duties. Instead, what is offered is direct substantive argument to show that the case for restricting duties to negative ones only cannot be justified on the ground that first, negative duties involve no sacrifices in their fulfilment, whereas positive duties do, or that, secondly, negative duties are always more important than positive duties. Their argument is compromised yet further when it is conceded that there is no unequivocal obligation to prolong life, if lives so prolonged are not judged worthwhile:

> it seems clear that there is no obligation to provide costly medical treatment whose success is uncertain or which can prolong life but not under conditions that make it worthwhile.[25]

This argument is, however, precisely the kind that Plant and Lesser should not use, because it draws attention to irreducibly normative and contestable elements within the obligation to aid survival. If there is a moral obligation to aid survival, for the reasons identified by Plant and Lesser in their formal thesis, then it must be derived from the requirement to aid someone in the fulfilment of their moral duties. The arguments based on the value of life and on aiding someone in the fulfilment of their duties are not even extensionally equivalent, for it is not obvious that fulfilling moral duties is what gives value to an individual's life.

The second part of the Plant/Lesser thesis concerns autonomy as a basic need. This argument is derived from the observation that freedom from certain hindrances, namely arbitrary power, ill health and ignorance, is required, if any moral action at all is to be possible. This argument fares no better than the previous one. Indeed Plant and Lesser themselves suggest that the agreement on the need for freedom in order to act morally is largely verbal, but, contrary to the requirements of their own approach, they do little to dispel the intuition that this observation is in fact correct.

It is not necessary to spend much time on this argument. It is enough for my present purpose to point out that the definitions of *arbitrary* power and ill health are not obviously non-normative, nor is protection against them a necessary condition for moral action of any kind. What, after all, is to stop an ill person acting morally? Under certain conditions moral action may be more difficult or painful or sometimes impossible, but this does not establish that health is a necessary condition for any moral action. Equally, the presence of arbitrary interferences does not make moral action of every sort impossible. The possibility of moral action is destroyed only if every action is determined by some arbitrary interference. The fact that there may be some arbitrary interferences in a society still leaves open the possibility of moral action where such interference does not eliminate all choice. Indeed, it remains possible that some moral action can take place even where arbitrary interferences have occurred. For example, were there no examples of moral action amongst the inmates of Nazi extermination camps?

My conclusion is, then, first that Plant and Lesser fail to provide any significant reasons for believing that a specification of the requirements of a logically consistent moral code can be used to support the claim that a set of basic needs can be identified and that this can constitute part of the foundation of a right to welfare. My suggestion is that any argument that X is a need will inevitably be partly constituted by reference to normative criteria, as was shown by the Brentano example. This *alone*, however, is not sufficient to show that a defence of need-based welfare services is necessarily morally partisan, because one could adopt a principle of satisfying needs without adopting an attitude towards the normative elements which partly constitute the existence of certain needs.

Does 'Need' Justify Welfare?

The discussion in this chapter so far has cast doubt on the possibility of providing a non-instrumental account of needs capable of acting as an independent principle to justify a welfare state. It has also questioned the possibility of developing an objective, non-evaluative account of need on the lines suggested by Plant and Lesser. The issue now is whether, as emerged from my discussion of Miller, it is nevertheless possible to envisage a morally neutral framework of need-satisfying policies and whether this could act as the foundation of a citizenship approach.

For there to be a morally neutral account of needs one or other of the following must be valid:

1 all needs are, as a matter of fact, common to all human beings;
2 some needs are, as a matter of fact, common to all human beings;
3 despite the fact that needs differ from person to person, it is possible that all of the differing needs can be satisfied simultaneously;
4 despite the fact that needs differ from person to person, it is possible that some categories of need (for example, plan of life needs) can be satisfied simultaneously.

It is not necessary to spend much time on 1 and 3. These claims are just obviously wrong. Hence, 1 does not allow us to say that the needs of Beethoven for the means to pursue his composing are different from the needs of Gareth Edwards to play rugby. Equally unpalatable is 3 because it implies that conflicts between needs can always be resolved. What if Mary's need for John's company can be satisfied only at the expense of John's need to be a hermit?

Claims 2 and 4 are, therefore, more plausible candidates. Proposition 2 looks rather similar to Rawls's notion of primary goods, or could be argued for by someone who believed that it is possible to give an unambiguous and universal account of a human nature possessed by all individuals of the species. Claim 4 is the kind of claim presupposed by Miller's analysis.

Rawls's notion of primary goods is well known and has been extensively discussed. All that is important to note here is that Rawls tries to abstract from acknowledged differences in the things men value in an effort to define a set of means that it would be rational for everyone to want irrespective of whatever else they wanted. For Rawls, primary goods include wealth, income, liberties (civil and political) and the bases of self-respect. Either Rawls is proposing an empirical generalization (primary goods are, as a matter of fact, universal means; for example, everyone values wealth), or else conceptions of the good life which do not presuppose that Rawlsian primary goods are a means to their realization are not rational. If we are offered an empirical generalization we are offered a false one. Not *all* conceptions of the good presuppose that primary goods are a means to their fulfilment; not *all* conceptions of the good which do accord primary goods an instrumental role would necessarily be ones in which the possession of more primary goods would constitute an improvement of position. If, on the other hand, we are not offered an empirical generalization, then, so the argument goes, the Rawlsian argument must be presupposing a view of what can count as a *rational* plan of life, and Rawls must be guilty of defining as *irrational* conceptions of the good which do not fit the model.

Rawls has, of course, several responses to the first criticism. At least so far as income and wealth, and hence the availability of shelter and food, are concerned, he can argue plausibly that primary goods are universal in the appropriate sense. First, it *is* difficult to imagine conceptions of the good to which the possession of *some* of these primary good would not be instrumental. The standard counter examples involve groups such as genuinely voluntary tramps and aesthetes – but even these do have certain minimal needs. More to the point, the availability of primary goods does not harm their interests even if they do not avail themselves of them.

But this reply has only limited force. It remains the case that primary goods are not equally instrumental to any conception of the good life, nor is it always rational for someone to prefer more of them to less. The analysis gains in force, however, if its application is restricted to advanced industrial societies which may well be characterized by a sufficiently widespread consensus to permit a range of primary goods to be identified.

My main interest in the theory of primary goods, however, is to ask whether primary goods can act as a foundation for the citizenship theory outlined earlier in the book. My conclusion is that they cannot. Rawls's analysis has at first sight implications only for the distribution of income between social classes. Minimally what would be required if primary goods were to act as the basis of a citizenship theory is either that the primary good, the bases of self-respect, turned out to require the citizenship type of welfare system, or that the idea of primary goods could be extended to include the requisite range of social policies. Some efforts in this direction have been made. Michelman, for example, has suggested that a range of specific welfare rights can be justified within a Rawlsian framework if it can be shown that they are essential to self-respect.[26] Weale has argued the case for treating social services, including 'social security payments, education, health and personal social services, and some special provision for housing',[27] as primary goods.

My difficulty with these arguments is that it is not clear that they retain an appropriate level of neutrality. In other words, they fail because they end up inevitably discriminating between alternative conceptions of the good. Miller's version, also, runs into the same problem. The reasons for this have been widely rehearsed. At best Rawls's version is neutral between *individualistic* conceptions of the good – that is, those it is possible to articulate in abstraction from, or independently of, the conceptions of the good of others. However, to quote Thomas Nagel:

> The primary goods are not equally valuable in pursuit of all conceptions of the good. They will serve to advance many different individual life plans (some more efficiently than others), but they are less useful in implementing views that hold a good life to be readily achievable only in certain well defined types of social structure, or only in a society that works concertedly for the realization of certain higher human capacities and the suppression of baser ones, or only given certain types of economic relations among men. The model contains a strong individualistic bias, which is further strengthened by the motivational assumptions of mutual disinterest and absence of envy. These assumptions have the effect of discounting the claims of conceptions of the good that depend heavily on the relation between one's own position and that of others . . .[28]

This argument is fatal to the nondiscrimination claim in all the versions I have mentioned. Even the Miller position, as I have glossed it, cannot provide a neutral framework of need-satisfying policies if different individuals have mutually exclusive life plans. Where this kind of case occurs it is impossible to avoid making a choice between different life plans which is morally partisan and requires a direct normative defence.

Consider, for example, a society which includes several Robert Nozicks and several Richard Titmusses. The Titmuss group would put forward arguments for the ordering of society which would necessarily violate the principle of mutual disinterest. Its members would argue that the kinds of plans of life which they valued depended for their realization on society undertaking to preserve certain patterned relationships between people, or on individuals regarding their society and their fellows in a certain way. The values of equality and fraternity would figure prominently in their account. Furthermore, they would contend that certain types of inequality undermined the self-respect of the worst-off and prevented them from developing plans of life or conceptions of the good which were of value to them. Hence the need for the full range of social policies. Nozick and clones would regard the matter differently. They would argue, against the 'Titmice', that such a society treated them unfairly, violated their distinctness and separateness of persons, gave society property rights in their bodies, and so forth. The only society in which they could form and act on plans of life of value to them would require a minimal state. A developed welfare state would be as damaging to them as its absence would damage their opponents. Only if they knew that were solely responsible for themselves and would not be treated as means to the ends of others could they lead self-respecting lives.

How can these views be neutrally reconciled? The answer is that they cannot. Depriving individuals of the knowledge of their social position in society would not helped, nor would juggling with their social positions. A Titmuss could still reasonably maintain his position, even if he knew that he would never be ill, unemployed or poor, and that his need for fraternity would be met by his siblings in a large family. A Nozick could still argue in favour of the minimal state even if he knew that bad luck would bankrupt him. Holding Nozickian or Titmussian views is not necessarily a form of special pleading which can be overcome by denying individuals morally arbitrary information.

It seems to me clear that, no matter how long the argument proceeded, no reconciliation could be found which would be equally fair to both sides. In this kind of case it is not even possible to bargain towards an acceptable compromise. The points of view are mutually exclusive. Appealing to Rawlsian devices must fail since both sides would not accept the same definition of morally relevant knowledge, nor the principles of rationality. Although both would accept the importance of self-respect they would not agree on which pattern of institutions best safeguarded it. Albert Weale's suggestion, that in the original position a principle of equalizing unmet needs would have direct ethical appeal to all, would not meet with the approval of the Nozicks. And the idea of a neutral framework of need-satisfying policies would be unworkable.

The problem is raised in other ways too. If need-satisfying resources are in relatively short supply, decisions have to be made about principles of distribution. Intuitively, these principles are, it seems, likely to be discriminatory, that is, they are likely to favour some types of life over others. They might, for example, discriminate against 'expensive' conceptions of the good and in favour of 'cheap' ones. The needs of chess players may be more readily catered for than the needs of athletes, for instance. At a more substantial level, decisions on how to distribute funds within a medical service, between research and care, between preventive and curative medicine, and so forth are certain to affect individuals differently.

It seems that the only possible but ultimately unsuccessful way to retain the notion of non-discrimination is to argue that the fact that, in practice, some are more favoured than others disguises the fact that at a higher or more abstract level the principle of distribution turns out to be non-discriminatory. One example could be the utilitarian principle, 'everyone is to count for one and nobody for more than one'. On this principle it would be possible for some individuals to come off very badly even though the principle had been fairly applied. But the difficulty with this suggestion is that it is hard to see how parties would ever agree on a particular abstract principle as being the right one to apply in a social order. In other words, this suggestion falls foul of the analysis considered above.

Finally, non-partisanship would be preserved only if the *mode* of satisfying needs did not discriminate between plans of life. But it is difficult to see how the method of satisfying needs can avoid invoking specific normative principles. This problem has already been discussed above in connection with basic needs. Moreover, it is questionable whether the policies used to make need-satisfying resources available (for example through taxation) can avoid prejudicing plans of life amongst the contributors. Not every activity which individuals enjoy participating in can be taxed. Some untaxable activities may well be central to an individual's plan of life. It seems inevitable that taxation will change the relative costs of choosing a plan of life. If this is so, then it is difficult to see how any framework for satisfying needs could avoid being discriminatory.

The purpose of this chapter has been to examine whether 'need' can provide the foundation for a defence of the welfare state which both defines its role and dispels the apparently intractable controversy which accompanies discussion of moral principles. It is clear, I think, that 'need' is not a hard-edged concept that can be objectively identified and clearly distinguished from 'preference'. Once we recognize the instrumentality of need-statements and the relation that need has to notions of harm and plans of life, it becomes implausible to think of a need as something that is necessarily either inescapable or categorically different from an important preference. What good reason is there for saying that the prerequisites of artistic endeavour are not 'needs' (for public policy purposes) of an artist because they reflect a reversible decision to be an artist? Surely it is more satisfying to treat them as needs when they are so closely bound up with, and essential to, a person's plan of life; when they are inextricably bound up with a person's conception of his identity and his fundamental purposes.

The upshot of all this is that 'need' standing alone does not offer the fabric for a morally secure grounding of the welfare state. It does not supply a distributive principle against which the social justice of a society can be assessed nor does it supply an objectively valid bedrock upon which a defence of social rights could be constructed. Need is important, indeed vital, in the argument for a welfare state, but what has to be called upon is a morally partisan notion of need which takes its bearing from a larger moral theory. It is to that larger theory that I turn in the next and final chapter.

8

Reconstructing Citizenship Theory

The core of the citizenship theory of the welfare state is community membership. Community membership is the good to be promoted by welfare institutions in a market economy. It is also the source of the claims we have against each other. From our membership in our community flow the welfare rights we can assert and the duties we owe to contribute to the support of our fellows. The role of community and community membership in all this is irreducible. The theory of the welfare state I defend in this book is therefore intrinsically communitarian. Whatever moral appeal this theory has derives ultimately from the moral significance of consciously making over our social institutions so as to preserve and enrich the reality of belonging to a community committed to integrating all of its members into its way of life. In the first instance, of course, this requires restoring the effective membership of those who are systematically excluded from access to the common patrimony. Obviously it also involves the use of preventive measures to forestall the operation of those forces which lead to exclusion. Perhaps less obviously, but no less importantly, it entails the development of policies and the provision of services which inculcate and draw on the potential communitarian sentiments of all citizens, not just those who might conventionally be regarded as 'poor' or in 'need'. The welfare state is, therefore, ideally an institutional recognition of social solidarity. No matter that the welfare state may have degenerated into parsimonious austerity and heavy-handed bureaucracy, and that moral vision has been blurred within the maze of conflicting policies. Like it or not, some kind of welfare state is an essential element in a market society. Hence, the political challenge is to regenerate the communitarian vision of welfare so that the welfare state can be an instrument through which a society can define itself and nurture its members. The alternative is to be reconciled to a permanent minority of our fellows forced to live outside the city gates without hope of reaching the warmth and safety within.

In the end, of course, the practical viability of citizenship theory does not turn on its philosophical but its political credentials. A sense of community membership and a perception of the other members of society as fellow citizens is a social psychological foundation for a consensual recognition of the moral importance of each person's entitlement to be treated as a full member of the community. This sense of community membership is something which needs to be fostered and nurtured. It needs to become part of the fabric of the society; an aspect of the constitution of everyday life. And the sentiment of community needs to be enlisted and regenerated not simply through passive support for the tax measures required to fund centralized bureaucracies, though this will inevitably always be a large part of the welfare state's activities, but also through active involvement in smaller scale self and mutual help projects. The future of the welfare state organized according to citizenship principles lies in my view in something more than a straightforward reaffirmation of traditional bureaucratic Fabianism. It requires a genuine commitment to infusing welfare services with opportunities for participation in flexible and decentralized structures rooted in local communities. There is more to satisfying needs than administering to them.

In this chapter I block in more fully the foundations of this approach. My intention is to describe and defend the key elements of the moral foundations of citizenship theory. As might be expected, the emphasis is on the notions of membership and community and the implications that follow from them. It will become apparent that my approach to justifying the welfare state differs from some other common strategies. I do not make recourse to the social contract or human rights. In my view neither of those approaches provides a satisfactory foundation for the welfare state. Equally, I do not claim that the welfare state can be defended by pretending that its institutions are institutions which it is in the self-interest of members of the society severally to support. The fact is that for many of the 'better off' a properly constituted welfare state is something that they would be better off without. The wealthy either have to be coerced into contributing or do so because they recognize it as their duty. Finally, I do not claim that a defence of welfare institutions can be grounded directly on 'need' standing alone. As we have seen, 'need' does not provide an independent principle of justification. Rather, reference must be made to the value of the ends to which needs contribute. It is my contention that these values revolve most convincingly around the idea of full membership in that community.

The Question of Full Citizenship

Social justice requires the recognition and protection of a range of citizenship rights possessed equally by all members of society. These rights include, alongside more traditional civil and political rights, a number of welfare or economic and social rights. Citizenship rights, as their name suggests, are held by individuals in virtue of their membership of the society in question. They are ascribed to persons *qua* citizens rather than directly or exclusively *qua* human beings. From this point of view a central question is: what set of rights (in this case welfare rights) is required to confer, protect and guarantee the status of persons as full members of society? When fully spelt out, this list of rights, within the context of a capitalist society, provides the moral foundation for an extensive welfare system providing universal services outside the market.

To defend this view it is necessary to show not just that it would be a good thing to recognize certain claims as rights, but also that it is morally permissible to impose the duties entailed by these rights on others. In my view the acceptability of imposing correlative duties on both welfare providers and recipients results from moral facts pertaining to community membership. Much of the argument designed to dislodge the claim that an individual has a right to full control over the use and disposition of resources legitimately acquired through consensual transactions has already been made out, and the duties of welfare recipients will be outlined later in this chapter.

The right to be aided is founded on one's membership in society. The purpose of a right to welfare is to guarantee that needs are met. The needs in question here are to be elucidated by reference to the notion of what is necessary to protect and preserve someone's status as a full member of his community. If these needs are not satisfied then the individual's effective membership of the community is threatened. To need something is to be harmed in its absence. Here the harm derives from the exclusion from the ability and opportunity to participate in a society's way of life.

Of course, this is not to say that the notion of being a full member of society is always an easy one to describe. Often it will be difficult to say whether a particular benefit is critical to one's membership, or whether it becomes critical only where one lacks both it and other benefits or whether it is really critical in any circumstances of relevance to public policy. I do not doubt for a moment that if there are any 'essentially contested concepts', the concept of being a full member of the community is one. But notwithstanding the uncertainties and the opportunities for philosophical dispute, I am confident that as an empirical proposition 'full membership of the community' is a notion which is widely understood and that there is, or there can be invoked, reasonably widespread agreement on the range of benefits and opportunities, denial of which will compromise it.[1]

Being a full member of society is tied to the effective ability of an individual to participate in a society's way of life. It is a function of two overlapping elements. First the practicability of an individual enjoying a certain style of life. Secondly, the life chances available to him in the society. If someone is deprived of certain critical life chances, or simply lacks the means to enjoy those social benefits and consumption opportunities which are generally available, then he is excluded from his society's way of life and has a *prima facie* claim on the resources required for him to secure readmittance.

This approach presupposes being able to identify a way of life which may properly be said to be that of the community or society. Naturally this involves a measure of abstraction from ways of life or styles of living which are specific to groups within the society. One requires a statement of general, society-wide standards or norms, such as that provided by Townsend in *Poverty in the United Kingdom*[2] and Mack and Lansley in *Poor Britain* which transcends the details of ways of life specific to particular communities whether they be rooted in class, religion, ethnicity or region. Talking of a society's way of life, therefore, suggests the existence of some kind of national culture which exists alongside or underlies cultural variation within the community.

All of this raises an immediate worry. On the face of it, abstracting from variation and difference in a richly pluralistic society identifies a common denominator; but it is a lowest common denominator. If public policy is oriented towards sameness, whether it reflects existing common standards or seeks to develop new uniform standards, the result is dull, plodding, mediocre homogeneity. Variety, spontaneity, innovation and fun are sacrificed whenever public policy is founded on commonness or seeks to foster uniformity.

The mistakes of the communitarian, it is alleged, are manifold. He seeks to develop something with little intrinsic worth at the cost of destroying or at least compromising something of real value. Cultural pluralism is valuable not only for its own sake but because it is the upshot of individuals acting on their preferences and seeking to enjoy styles of life which suit their purposes. Better a society in which the airwaves reverberate to the competing allure of Bach and the Rolling Stones than one confined to patriotic hymns. Moreover, it is doubtful whether a society has a way of life. The only ways of life there are are the ways of life of particular individuals and groups of individuals. Abstracting from these real ways of life does not identify a way of life actually enjoyed by any member of a society. It is nothing more than an empty abstraction with no real existence and no value.

At first sight citizenship theory does seem to be open to this line of criticism. The approach does involve abstracting from the range of different activities, patterns of consumption and types of relationships within the community. But it is not every common characteristic that is seized upon. Only relevant are those activities, relationships and consumption patterns which *are* highly valued and generally available within the community. What these are will of course vary from society to society, from period to period, and also with the level and character of the economic development of the society. The claim is, however, that notwithstanding variety and difference in a society, typically there are standards which are generally satisfied and which as a practical matter most people attach weight to. Again as a practical matter, an inability to live up to those standards or engage in certain patterns of consumption or types of relationship leads to a clearly recognizable and readily documentable exclusion and withdrawal from society. Where resources and life chances deviate too greatly from generally available resources and life chances, deprived families are relegated to the margins, cut off from the benefits enjoyed, and often take for granted, by the majority.[3]

So in the first place I believe it is to be a sociological truth of considerable moral relevance that there are common elements underlying cultural variation which can effectively define minimum standards below which individuals and families are cut off from the rest of society. Furthermore, there appears to be fairly substantial agreement ranging over all social classes about what those standards are. The basic elements of the society's way of life exist as concrete reality and not meaningless abstraction.

Secondly, claiming that a society has a way of life reflected in a national culture, that access to that way of life ought to be guaranteed and sustained for all persons, and that policies ought also to be aimed at reinforcing the general awareness of, and support for, that way of life, does not exclude or derogate from a recognition of the value of pluralism. The communitarianism I support here is perfectly compatible with variety and difference. Indeed, one of its goals is precisely to spread more widely the social foundations of individual flourishing. A recognition of the importance of diversity, a commitment to encouraging and facilitating the development of individual talents in a wide variety of ways can properly be part of a society's way of life, and that fact can readily be reflected in its social policies. For citizenship theory, the goal is not homogeneity; the enemy is not heterogeneity. The goal is to provide everyone with the wherewithal to enjoy and participate in the benefits of pluralism. The enemy is only those differences which are connected to the processes of exclusion and domination. So although part of the political project in a regenerated welfare state is to reinforce a national culture and support for it, it cannot fairly be said that this entails a commitment to grey uniformity. In fact, quite the contrary.

Being a full member of society involves more than possessing the same set of opportunity rights and rights to non-interference as everybody else. Of course, at the minimum, that much must be guaranteed. A society in which Catholics cannot hold public office, or in which certain professions or the right to vote are closed to particular races, does not treat all its members as full members of the community. But it is also necessary to be concerned about the value of opportunity rights to individuals. Many of those within the excluded class lack the resources necessary to make worthwhile use of the rights which all possess. Part of the function of welfare rights is to achieve some fairness in the distribution of the value to individuals of opportunity and non-interference rights. Empirical sociology by specifying the content of the society's way of life can give some idea of what types and quantities of resources are required to achieve this goal. Abstractly, one expects this account to refer to the guarantee of a minimum resource base to permit personal consumption at acceptable levels as well as a specification of a range of life chances which govern access to occupational, social and cultural benefits.

There is, moreover, reason to believe that this account would lend support to the tendency to rely upon universal services in kind. This is because the protection and preservation of a person's status as a full member of society is not simply a function of the quantity of fungible resources available to him. Rather, it turns more directly and immediately on the opportunity and ability to consume or gain access to particular quantities and qualities of specific resources such as medical care, education and housing. One reason for supplying services in kind is just that citizens have a right to that specific resource. The right extends that far and no further. Thus one may have a right to education, although not a right to income which may or may not be spent on education. One defence, therefore, of in kind services is that the rights a citizen has are derived from what is required to guarantee his status as a full member of society. If this involves an ability to command a certain package of resources, then the relevant rights are rights to those specific resources only. Thus a delivery system is required that ensures that what the individual gets is what he has a right to, for example, medical care.[4] Services in kind are one way of doing this. Furthermore, universal services in kind may help create some sense of community membership by encouraging common participation in their consumption and, to some degree, in their delivery. They may also serve to reflect a commitment to a principle of equal citizenship manifested by institutions designed to foster an egalitarian distribution of a specified set of basic goods. Finally, there is an argument for preferring services provided in kind to cash transfers if there is reason to believe that some persons may be imprudent or wasteful or be unable to make adequate use of cash. If the costs of this are sufficiently great, services provided in kind may avoid them. Services provided in kind may be defended on the grounds of justified paternalism.

There is, therefore, a natural inclination for someone committed to citizenship principles to look to universal in kind programmes as a way of achieving his purposes. But it would be a mistake, in my view, to see a commitment to universality and the provision of services in kind as a necessary consequence of adhering to citizenship theory. Whether a particular service ought to be provided either in kind or universally needs to be assessed in the light of all the relevant facts. On occasion it may make perfect sense, from a citizenship point of view, to rely heavily on cash transfers based on selectivist criteria.[5] Such transfers may often be the most effective way to integrate those who would otherwise be excluded. Indeed, there may often be powerful arguments for achieving redistribution in this way, especially where it can be shown that universality of provision is associated with, or part of, the replication of patterns of inequality which are unacceptable to a citizenship theorist. A flexible and pragmatic attitude towards cash versus in kind and selective versus universal services needs to be adopted. What distinguishes the citizenship approach to the welfare state from its rivals is the view taken of the origins of certain types of need and the values which it is argued society ought to publicly endorse and recognize through its institutional structures. The particular policy responses required to counteract the systemic forces generating exclusion and to manifest the commitment to guaranteeing each person's membership in the community must be empirically determined. In my view, the political and ideological identity of citizenship theory is not governed by any particular type of institutional response to need and the tendency to treat any concession in the direction of selectivity or the use of cash transfers, vouchers and user fees as heresy has done it harm.

The Familial Basis of Citizenship

In addressing the moral foundation of citizenship theory it is necessary to recognize that a number of different positions are wrapped up together. First, individuals can claim rights to welfare (the right to guaranteed participation in a society's way of life) because they are members of the society. Second, there is something especially important about being a full member of society. Third, given that a non-discriminatory framework of need-satisfying policies cannot be provided, a framework which guarantees full membership to those most likely to be excluded should be adopted.

The first position amounts to the view that one's right to be aided or to have certain life chances protected is derived from membership of the society per se and not from any prior hypothetical or actual agreements or contracts. On this view the rights and obligations which are involved are rooted in the moral significance of relationships between members of the same society, but these relationships are not thought of as voluntarily created, nor are the moral claims voluntarily incurred. On the contrary, the relationships and their moral implications are non-voluntary. Your claim is what it is just because you are a member of the society, even though you have not chosen to enter it nor have chosen to consent to its terms.

One way of approaching the foundation of this view is to note its similarity with the kind of moral claims most would agree exist within a family. Members of a family have claims on others and duties towards them. If a family member falls ill it is expected that his family will help. In fact, we commonly expect some members of a family to carry considerable burdens in caring for or aiding their relatives as, for example, when it is necessary to cope with elderly parents or handicapped siblings. The most that is usually offered to a family is assistance to ease the burden; rarely is the burden entirely removed from the shoulders of the family and this despite the fact that the member in need requires almost constant attention.

Wherein lie the claims of family members? It is clear that they cannot be reduced to consent or some form of contract, notwithstanding that marriage involves an exchange of vows and that generally one chooses to have children. The fact is that one can make claims against other family members and owe them obligations that cannot be traced back to agreement or behaviour tantamount to a voluntary assumption of responsibility. Rather, there are two major sources of familial claims. The first is that the family constitutes a scheme of mutual support. From it, as a child, one receives succour, language, education and the foundation of a sense of morals and worthwhile goals. For these benefits one owes a debt to those whose cooperation has facilitated their supply regardless of the fact that entering into this web of relationships has not been a voluntary choice. In part, then, one's obligations to other members of one's family are a reflection of what is their due as participants in this scheme. The suggestion is that obligations are rooted in reciprocity. The rights of my parents against me are accounted for by the services which they have supplied to me. But consider an implication of this. Debts, after all, can be repaid and once the debt has been repaid the obligation vanishes. Intuitively it seems likely that often children make more of a contribution to their parents than vice versa but yet we do not feel that they are therefore released from their obligations. A child's aiding a difficult, incontinent, senile and neglectful parent is not entirely supererogatory. His obligations extend beyond those implied by a contribution-based explanation.

Hence, in the second place, certain claims and obligations exist simply in virtue of membership and regardless of contribution. Nor is the explanation of this that, although contribution underlies the obligations, it is never possible to use contribution directly as a way of determining the specific content and extent of them, because individuated contributions cannot be identified. Rather, contribution plays no part in accounting for some of our obligations. Consider the case of obligations towards handicapped siblings. A common and strongly held intuition is that all family members, not just the parents, have special obligations to a handicapped child. The claims of the child are claims he has just because of his family membership. The obligations of others are not a recognition of something owed to him as a recognition of indebtedness nor as a form of compensation (as they might be if the parents were responsible not only for his birth but also his handicap – for example, as with foetal alcohol syndrome). Consider also the case of a parent who deserted his children before birth and who reappears in his dotage asking forgiveness and pleading for aid. Certainly his claim on his children is diminished by his action, but it is not extinguished. Moral implications still flow from their special relationship.

One way of supporting the moral claims of citizenship theory, therefore, is to invoke patterns of argument analogous to those used in the case of the family. Thus, just as with a family, one does receive a range of benefits from society and many are similar to those channelled through the family. Societies provide, amongst other things, language, the possibility of acquiring resources to meet needs or pursue other purposes, an 'infrastructure' that is a precondition of interaction, institutions through which individual projects can be carried on, and the matrix that makes the formulation of these projects conceivable and gives them content, and so forth. In these and other ways individuals are especially indebted to their society for the contributions it makes to them and therefore they are indebted to the other individuals in the society whose participation has made the production of these benefits possible. In part this indebtedness accounts for the obligations to aid other members of one's society, just because their participation in the society contributes to the existence of the society which has provided so many benefits. It is this general 'social' contribution which helps undermine the argument that one has an untrammelled right to use and dispose of as one sees fit whatever one has acquired through action within the terms specified by one's property rights. And it is the kind of principle outlined here that underlines the argument of Titmuss, discussed earlier, that many welfare rights merely institutionalize forms of compensation as a recognition of contributions made by some to the progress of others.

However, just as with the family, understanding that claims and obligations are a recognition of contributions or reciprocity captures only an aspect of the view. Certain claims and obligations within citizenship theory can be understood only if membership alone underlies them. In other words, there are cases which parallel that of the handicapped child or prodigal father. Not every occasion when welfare aid is needed is one in which it is plausible to regard the person in need as a bearer of costs created by the progress of others and therefore as someone not personally responsible for his condition. In these cases, citizenship theory is required to hold that their claim to be treated as a full member of society follows simply from the facts of their membership in the society.

Modelling the claims and obligations on the analogy of a family provides a different foundation for them than that implied by a contract approach. On the view suggested here, one's membership of a society is sufficient to ground a range of rights and obligations which are defined in relation to other members of the society and which one ought to recognize independently of one's having consented to accept them. The question then becomes: which rights and obligations and why? Just as with a family, the obligations which derive from membership are limited. Common intuitions clearly do not support the view that just anything can be claimed on the basis of common membership. Therefore, it is necessary to spell out the range of rights and obligations which can be so grounded.

The Language of Rights in Citizenship Theory

A plausible defence of citizenship theory involves claiming that an extensive range of social policies must be accepted as a consequence of seeking to respect the status of citizens as full members of the community. It is a short step from seeing certain basic rights and obligations as rooted in common membership to arguing that full membership is a good to be promoted. The idea of full membership connects with a notion of equality. Each member of the society is to be treated as equal in his right to enjoy and have access to those fruits of society which define full membership. Moral value is attached to the relation of equality as well as to the good of full membership. The preservation of a relation of equality in respect of those goods is a recognition by society that each member of it is as valuable as any other and as worthy of respect, and that he has a right to derive benefits and advantages from it on the same terms as anybody else. Each member of society is thought of as equally entitled to enjoy to the full the style of life characteristic of his society; he is equally entitled freely to participate in it and equally entitled to be secure in his enjoyment of its advantages.

Preserving equality of access to the goods that define full community membership is a fundamental element of a just social structure. It is the first duty of a society. Unless this duty is satisfied, citizens who fall below the critical threshold in terms of their ability to command resources or take advantage of opportunities will be excluded from the community. They will be unable to enjoy the advantages society offers; advantages of patterns of consumption and the opportunity and ability to participate in certain types of highly valued relationships. Exclusion of this kind is damaging to self-respect. It does foster a sense of personal failure; a sense that it is futile to formulate goals worth pursuing. The social relationships associated with the processes of exclusion in a society which stresses material success bring home a feeling of inadequacy and a belief that one is less worthy of respect than others, that one is a person who doesn't count. A lack of self-respect is, in most cases, bad in itself, because it undermines that person's sense that he has a life worth living, abilities and talents in which he can take a pride, and undercuts his motivation to engage in worthwhile projects. But it is also unfair that individuals should subjectively accept the public evaluation of them as failures. According to citizenship theorists, many individuals are not simply outside society; they have been excluded from it. Exclusion suggests agency and a process through which some individuals are exploited or taken advantage of or just plain victimized. It is these individuals who have a claim to be entitled to receive compensation and for whom rights to welfare can be and are unequivocally claimed.

In such cases there appear to be strong reasons for adopting the language of rights. Rights are generally held by individuals. If one's moral objective is to respect the importance of individuals as such, then rights are a peculiarly apt device for doing so. Other principles such as the aim to 'minimize suffering' or to 'act benevolently' appear to be relatively indifferent to the claims of specific individuals. Individuals tend to be treated merely as the bearers of whatever is valued or disvalued but receive no recognition of being independently of value. It is for this reason that acting on a principle such as 'minimize suffering' can result easily in the neglect of some cases of extreme suffering which are very expensive to eradicate in favour of the elimination of less serious suffering which is relatively cheap to remove. In cases where compensatory treatment is due, it is due specifically to *individuals* who have been unjustly treated. Therefore the form of the principle is that individuals (who are suffering because of injustice) be treated justly in recognition of their status as individuals who are to be respected as full members of the community. What matters is that it is Tom, Dick and Harry who have been treated unjustly and the claiming of rights draws attention to this fact.

A second but related reason for adopting the language of rights here is that there is a connection between respect for persons and respecting their rights. As Feinberg argues:

> rights are especially sturdy objects to 'stand upon' a most useful sort of moral furniture . . . This feature of rights is connected in a way with the customary rhetoric about what it is to be a human being. Having rights enables us to 'stand up like men', to look others in the eye, and to feel in some fundamental way the equal of anyone. To think of oneself as the holder of rights is not to be unduly but properly proud, to have that minimal self respect that is necessary to be worthy of the love and esteem of others. Indeed, respect for persons . . . may simply be respect for their rights, so that there cannot be the one without the other: and what is called 'human dignity' may simply be the recognizable capacity to assert claims. To respect a person then, or to think of him as possessed of human dignity, simply is to think of him as a potential maker of claims.[6]

And, by extension, to respect someone as a fellow citizen is to respect him in the possession of those rights which are attached to the status of citizenship. It is reasonable to argue that to respect someone as a citizen is to guarantee those rights which would restore full membership of society in the event of his being excluded.

Thirdly, there is a link between having a right to something and being secure in one's enjoyment of it. To have a right to something is to be able to demand and expect that it is respected. Rights provide grounds for coercive intervention by the state, if this is necessary to protect them. There is, therefore, in a society which honours rights, reasonable certainty that those in need because of exclusion will receive their due. Not only can they be secure in this expectation, but they can demand its satisfaction. An important sense of equality can, in principle, be preserved. There is a significant difference between standing on one's rights and supplicating for charity. In the first place one receives only one's due. In the second one receives something, if one in fact receives anything, for which one might be expected to show gratitude. The objection to such relationships is that they are inappropriate to the facts of the case. Nobody need be grateful for receiving that to which they are entitled. Relationships in which expressions of gratitude are appropriate may be ones which are inherently unequal and involve unacceptable condescension, patronizing attitudes and subtle forms of social control.

Establishing and protecting rights implies a recognition that such relationships are not usually acceptable.

There is, therefore, a strong case for adopting the practice of rights in those cases where compensation is due. As suggested above, compensation is required if individuals are excluded from the benefits of the society of which they are members. This, of course, suggests agency – a process of exclusion – in which some are exploited or victimized. In chapter 2 I pointed out that part of Titmuss's argument for universal publicly provided services depended on the claim that identification of individual responsibility for these exploitative practices is not possible and that, therefore, a social response is necessary. It follows that a judgement of citizenship theory that takes all things into consideration needs to analyse how extensive exclusionary processes are. In doing so it is necessary to invoke social theories explaining, amongst other things, class formation, social and educational mobility, income distribution, and so forth. Citizenship theory is more plausible and morally defensible the greater the proportion of those individuals not participating in a society's way of life – whose non-participation is a consequence of being subject to exclusionary processes. For these individuals compensation claims are an appropriate basis upon which to defend the welfare system.

But, as I have noted, not all claims can be treated as forms of compensation. If it is still desired to treat all need claims which are relevant to the welfare state as matters of justice it is necessary to adopt one or other or both of the following views. Either it is appropriate to treat all claims as if they were compensation claims, or all citizens have rights to receive what they need to respect their status as full members of society, irrespective of the reason why they lack resources and opportunity bases.

In order to deal with these possibilities it is necessary to consider the sorts of reasons which explain why people find themselves in need. Apart from those cases which can be assimilated to exclusion, there appear to be three types of causes of need. These are bad luck, personal incapacity or weakness and a lack of personal responsibility. Bad luck refers to a variety of circumstances. The idea is that one's plight is not one's fault but arose from conditions that it was not reasonable to foresee. But equally one is not a victim of a social process of exclusion or exploitation. Examples of bad luck include being orphaned, being deserted by a spouse and left holding the baby, being the innocent victim of a road accident, being born with a congenital handicap or developing an incurable and debilitating disease. Personal incapacity or weakness captures the sense that individuals vary in terms of their strength of will and competence as a decision-maker. Some individuals are less prudent than others, less able to defer gratification, and so forth. As a result of these variations in competence, some individuals find themselves unable to cope and unable to maintain themselves independently as full members of society. Finally, a lack of personal responsibility refers to cases of need created by the voluntary but imprudent action of someone who normally displays 'standard decision-making ability'. Included here, by way of example, would be some unmarried mothers and some persons who caused accidents in which they were injured.

How are these cases to be treated? First, these categories are not watertight. Many cases of decision-making incompetence can be ascribed to bad luck in the sense that someone was unluckly to be born into a family which failed to teach certain skills and attended a school which did nothing to improve matters. Here the argument might be that it is invidious to hold someone responsible for the consequences of weakness of the will or incompetence for which they are not responsible. It can be argued that the harm they suffer in not being a full member of society, although in a sense self-inflicted, is not something that they ought to be allowed to bear. Rather, their membership of the society is to be thought of as a sufficient reason to grant them the right to have that membership respected as full membership. This argument can be supplemented by pointing out that societies themselves sanction certain standards of success. I may be a miserable failure as an accumulator of income and wealth, though I would have been a success in a society in which making daisy-chains and peace were well rewarded. It is not my fault that my society rewards the former but not the latter, though I suffer the consequences. Perhaps I may have some claim to be compensated for the fact that the society in which I live is not one in which I can be independent.

Of relevance here is a third argument which stems from the importance of ignorance. One might well agree that need is created in different ways and that the way in which it is created could have a bearing upon the way it is met and the moral reasons for meeting it. But for public policy purposes it is too difficult to identify into which category individual cases fall and to adjust treatment accordingly. In particular, for practical purposes, it is very expensive and difficult to identify cases where personal responsibility for need exists. Moreover, the kinds of investigation required to identify where this is so are so intrusive that they unacceptably violate the rights to privacy of at least those who are not personally responsible for their condition. Thus even where there is a *prima facie* case for treating cases of 'voluntary' indigency in terms of charity, it may be morally unacceptable to do so.

When the issues are put in this way, the standard citizenship response is to argue that most cases of need can be treated as if they grounded a case for compensation. Writers such as Titmuss and Townsend spend considerable efforts in attempting to demonstrate that the vast majority of cases of need are the result of exclusionary social process. If this is so, the financial and moral cost of identifying genuinely voluntary cases is a high one and not one that is worth paying. In those cases where need is recognized to be the result of personal incompetence, citizenship theory relies directly on the claim that being a member of society is sufficient to ground a right to have that membership respected as full membership. Here the claim is that it is unjust to allow someone to suffer the consequences of his own inadequacies when remedial action is possible. The injustice exists not in the reasons why he falls out of society but in the fact that he remains outside it. His rights as a full member of society are violated by the inaction of society which fails to take the appropriate steps to readmit him. And a similar argument is available, of course, to cope with examples of need created by bad luck.

This resolution of the issue seems adequate to most defenders of the citizenship view. It should be noted, however, that the response to the problem of the creation of need by voluntary action for which the individual is personally responsible is purely pragmatic. It turns on the argument that the costs attached to the identification and differential treatment of these individuals are too high to pay. It does not mean that the approach is necessarily indifferent to the criticism that some persons may take advantage of their citizenship rights to exploit, abuse and free ride on the system. The granting of rights to welfare is consistent with a general duty to maintain oneself as an independent member of the community, as Robson and Marshall emphasize.

A difficulty this creates, however, is how one should react to those clear cases where need is created by a lack of personal responsibility. Consider, for example, the case of someone who participates in a sport such as hang-gliding in which accidents are frequent and tend to be serious when they occur. Clearly being a hang-glider is not an essential ingredient of most societies' way of life and the risks involved are not the standard risks of normal life in these societies. Suppose also that a national health service exists. An accident occurs and a hang-glider is brought in requiring very expensive surgery and intensive care. Should the health service treat his claims as on a par with someone who suffers similar injuries in an industrial accident which was nobody's fault? What happens if there is a conflict between their claims caused by scarce resources? Does the hang-glider have a right to be treated or not? A possible answer, and perhaps the right one, is that his claim against the society would not involve demanding a right but supplicating for charity. Of course, had he taken out insurance against such an accident the case would be different.

It may seem that cases like the hang-glider are relatively uncommon and, therefore, have few normative implications for the terms upon which provision is made. Provision where rights appear, *prima facie*, to be an inappropriate basis are either not identifiable or rare. But is this the case? It seems clear that a substantial proportion of medical costs in advanced industrial societies are incurred for the treatment of diseases which were, in a sense, voluntarily incurred. Included here are some or most cases of smoking- and alcohol-related diseases as well as heart attacks, and so forth, brought on by a lack of exercise and poor diet. Is it appropriate to regard provision for these cases as required to satisfy rights or as cases of charity? First, provision would obviously be tailored to satisfy rights if those in need had contributed to a fund to pay for the costs of treatment. These sorts of cases identify an area where insurance-based schemes organized on actuarial principles might be appropriate even within citizenship theory. Note, however, that it might be possible to regard taxes on tobacco and alcohol as satisfying this condition. Secondly, rights-based delivery might be justified if the analogy with a prodigal father is pursued. Whether this would satisfy basic intuitions is doubtful. More likely, in the absence of the relevant insurance mechanisms, these cases would appear to fit within a charity model. There may be a humanitarian obligation to aid in such cases but these individuals cannot demand as a right that they be treated in the same way and on the same terms as those who may properly be claiming their rights.

The most satisfactory moral basis for citizenship theory is one in which a system of duties exists alongside or underlies the structure of citizenship rights. Social rights could properly be claimed only if the claimant had fulfilled his duties. These might be identified as specific applications of a principle that each citizen had a duty to maintain himself as an independent member of the society. Thus, for example, each person would have a duty to maintain his health and seek gainful employment, if he can. Generally, there would be a presumption that these duties are honoured and invidious methods of determining whether they had been would be ruled out. Within this scheme it would be possible to allow some contracting out of these duties by charging individuals (through insurance or taxation) for the costs which are implied. If these costs are not paid, then the person in need may properly be treated as an object of charity.

This revision to the basis of citizenship theory is necessary if the theory is to carry moral conviction. The reason is that any morally satisfying theory of social policy provision must take account of the processes of need-creation, since this has a bearing on the morally appropriate methods and basis of response. The fact of need, independently of how the need was created, does not provide a sufficient ground upon which a normative defence of need meeting policies can be founded. This is recognized by citizenship theory itself when it identifies processes of exclusion and the requirements of compensation. It is reasonable to extend the account to cater for those cases where a genuine personal responsibility for the existence of need does exist. Thus, in summary, the most defensible version of citizenship theory holds that rights to welfare exist if (1) compensation is due or (2) it is not the fault of the person that he is in need because of bad luck or incompetence, but not (3) if he is genuinely and personally responsible for his condition. These conditions would apply subject to a pragmatically-based acknow-ledgement that identifying cases as falling under (1), (2) or (3) can be difficult and that cases should be presumed to fall under (1) or (2) rather than (3). A sense of duty or community would be relied on to prevent or minimize abuse of the system.

In the discussion so far I have suggested that both the rights to welfare and the obligations to make available the resources to meet these rights are grounded in one's membership of the society. The relevant obligations extend so far as is necessary to establish a condition of common citizenship as defined by the idea of full membership of a community. Because these obligations are correlated to welfare rights it is possible to justify coercion to enforce them. The obligations are strict obligations. A full defence of citizenship theory needs to show that these obligations are themselves morally acceptable. One way of doing this is to show that the establishment of the obligations in question does not violate more fundamental moral rights or claims of persons or citizens. In effect it is necessary to balance the moral claims of recipients against those of donors. In doing so it is necessary to identify the moral character of donors' claims to discover whether they permit, both in principle and in particular circumstances, imposing upon them the obligations which protecting welfare rights would require.

Moral Obligation in Citizenship Theory

Much of the relevant argument has already been put forward in this book. I have attempted to show that a strict obligation to aid does not conflict with more basic rights of individuals. I sought to displace the claim that an individual is entitled to full control in the use and disposition of whatever he has acquired justly and that, therefore, a system of taxation, which is used to gather the necessary social policy resources, is a form of institutionalized theft. The upshot of my discussion was that a system of taxation is not a grotesque violation of the distinctness and separateness of persons tantamount to treating some persons merely as instruments to the purposes of others, nor a system which gives some property rights in the bodies of others, in a way morally equivalent to a scheme of forced labour. Rather, I suggested, a system of taxation which allows individuals unrestricted freedom of choice of occupation and effort has much less extreme moral implications than that. Individuals have no claim in justice to keep full control of all they acquire through market transactions and the tax system can be organized to balance the legitimate interests of taxpayers and welfare recipients.

Provided that I am right in this, a *prima facie* case exists for regarding the duty to support a welfare scheme as a strict obligation. Turning this *prima facie* case into something more substantial involves direct substantive argument. It requires a demonstration that the basic interests protected by the relevant rights are more substantial than those threatened by the correlative obligations. In other words, the consequences of not recognizing rights which protect each individual's status as a full member of society must be shown to be more serious than the consequences of establishing a strict obligation to pay taxes. Much of this book has been concerned with the moral costs of the former in terms of the damage to self-respect, injustice, an unfair distribution of life chances, and so forth. What is important is to recognize that the relevant system of taxation does not impose obligations so substantial that the status of taxpayers as full members of the community is threatened by them.

The argument that meeting one's social obligations through a system of taxation does not involve serious moral costs draws on the principles discussed above. Hence it cannot be claimed that an individual is being treated unfairly or unjustly if the taxes he pays are either a reflection of the general social contribution made to his personal wealth or are a payment of compensation which is to be distributed to the 'exploited'. In these cases, what is taken is only what he has no claim to keep. No disrespect is shown to the net contributor by making him pay taxes.

The more difficult cases are the 'as if compensation' cases and cases of bad luck and personal incompetence which do not fall directly under the compensation principle. These are more difficult because the necessary taxation does involve depriving someone of what he has a *prima facie* right to keep. Here it is necessary to show that this *prima facie* right is overridden by the obligation to assist the needy. In these circumstances the moral importance of restoring someone to full membership of the community must be assessed in the light of the moral costs involved here. A system of taxation does restrict the freedom of the taxpayer and forces him to behave in ways he would not in the absence of taxes. Inevitably one is involved here in the weighing and balancing of different moral costs and this implies that there is a point at which the moral costs of a further increase in the tax burden would be intolerable. It is not possible to give an unambiguous indication of when that point would be reached, but it must be remembered that generally the cost of permitting someone to be excluded from society is likely to be greater than the cost of taxation. Allowing a citizen to be cut off from the community is more serious than a marginal limitation on personal disposable income.

My discussion of the moral basis of a citizenship approach has tried to draw attention to the role played in it by the idea of membership of the community. The claims of recipients, I have suggested, are rooted directly in their membership of society. It is because they are members of society that they have a claim to be treated as full members of it. Similarly it is because someone is a member of society that he has obligations to his fellow citizens regardless of whether he has consented to them. Finally, it is the idea of being a full member of society that provides the benchmark for the theory of justice which underlies my account. Thus, if some individuals benefit from a social process which pushes others below the benchmark, compensation is owed. If someone, through no fault of his own, finds himself below the benchmark, then he has a claim in justice to be raised up to it.

The reasons for relying on this kind of framework are reasonably clear. It allows, at least in principle, a more concrete specification of what is necessary to satisfy it than could be provided by a more abstract human rights approach. It focuses directly on particular societies as defining the context within which the claims of individuals have their bearing. Thirdly, it provides a workable alternative to those neutral, non-discriminatory or non-partisan accounts of need which I suggested earlier were not available. If a framework of need-satisfying policies is necessarily going to discriminate between different conceptions of the good life there may be strong reasons for preferring ones which guarantee the status of individuals as full members of their societies than those which do not.

So far the discussion has concentrated on the character of the moral arguments which constitute the foundation of the citizenship approach. I have stressed the importance of a sociologically defined notion of a society's way of life and the rights and obligations of members of the community. The impression this may have created is that the role played in the theory by the notion of community is restricted. Rights and obligations are held *qua* member of the community and the object of public policy is to guarantee, in so far as this is possible, the participation of each individual in the society's way of life. It might be thought, therefore, that the concept of 'community' is being used illegitimately in that no necessary reference is made to the existence of sentiments or attitudes of community possessed by its members. Hence, it could be argued that citizenship theory represents nothing more than a scheme of mutual insurance, predicated upon highly risk-averse individuals, into which it is in the self-interest of each member of society to contract.

In chapters 2 and 3 I criticized the idea that citizenship theory can be treated as a form of insurance. I pointed out that a welfare system organized according to citizenship principles would be systematically redistributive, in ways insurance schemes are not, because it redistributes between groups facing similar risks. Put bluntly, it discriminates against the well-off, the skilled, the person with adaptable talents and a high standard of decision-making ability, the person in a healthy job in attractive regions of the country, in favour of the poor, the unskilled, the poorly educated, the imprudent, and the person who lives in dirty or unfashionable regions of the country. It would be in the interest of persons in the former categories to contract out of the universal schemes and opt into actuarially sound insurance policies which are based on more selectively defined categories.

If this is correct the better off have a choice. Either they are coerced into the scheme, or they recognize the moral reasons underlying it, set aside self-interest and participate willingly. The only way to avoid the conclusion that a communitarian vision based on right intentional relationships underlies support for the welfare system is to deprive individuals of the knowledge required to predict the categories into which they will fall in society. If this can be done the universal scheme may be regarded as being equally in the interests of each member of society. This is the hypothetical contract solution. It does not work. First, the fact that it would have been in your self-interest to join the universal scheme in certain hypothetical circumstances does not mean that it *is* in fact in your self-interest to do so. If one wants to use a self-interest model then what counts is actual self-interest. The only reason that anyone would accept hypothetical self-interest as relevant is if he accepted that certain kinds of knowledge ought to be ruled out as unfair or immoral to possess in assessing what is in one's interest. But then one is using a morally circumscribed notion of self-interest which is itself controversial. Here one also runs the risk that in attempting to identify a scheme which would be equally in each individual's interest to join one is forced to exclude morally relevant information. Secondly, one falls foul of the difficulties in demonstrating that hypothetical contracts can be morally binding, and of the problem of identifying principles of rational choice which yield unique solutions, in the face of differing degrees of risk aversion amongst the population.

Citizenship theory is a communitarian theory. It acknowledges that public authority must be deployed according to moral principles. The appeal to community is an appeal to values to constrain self-interest. The goal is a political system in which citizens take an expansive view of their obligations to their fellows; a system in which the social order is not conceived purely instrumentally as a mechanism to be exploited for personal gain. Citizens are not expected to hold the community to ransom by extracting the highest price possible as a condition of their providing services. The community belongs to everyone equally, though not everyone is in the same position individually to derive advantages from it. Social justice requires that the benefits of social cooperation be fairly distributed, that those who are excluded be included.

The welfare state as it exists today does not live up to a citizenship ideal. It is mired in self-interest and services often confirm rather than overcome exclusion. In a society founded on personal achievement measured by economic success, welfare institutions cannot alone overcome the stigma of dependency. This can occur only where a wider moral vision corresponding to the principles of citizenship theory forms part of the constitution of everyday life. The political challenge facing the citizenship strand of social democracy is to regenerate this moral vision both in the institutions of the welfare state and the minds of its citizens. There is indeed a vital role for the market place in this and for recognizing the validity of the pursuit of private advantage. But private advantage must be constrained by public purposes, the market by the need to protect our fellows' standing in our community. As the decade of 'new right' social experiments unfolds and *its* economic and moral failures become daily more apparent, the agenda of citizenship theory appears ever more practicable.

The forging of some kind of consensus on the moral legitimacy of the pattern of market outcomes is inescapable. As I argued in chapter 6, the issue of social justice cannot be dodged by relying on allegedly neutral principles defining fair procedures. Some kind of moral defence of outcomes must be offered even by the new right. The difficulties of developing an acceptable degree of agreement on the legitimacy of those outcomes face equally *all* political theories which seek to raise the exercise of public authority above the deployment of naked power. In the contest for the hearts and minds of democratic citizens, citizenship theory has more to offer than its competitors. As the dusk falls on Thatcherism, social democracy spreads its wings.

Notes

Chapter 1 The 'New Right': Assailing the Welfare State

1 C. A. R. Crosland, *The Future of Socialism* (Jonathan Cape, London, 1956).
2 W. Beveridge, *Social Insurance and Allied Services* (Beveridge Report) (H.M.S.O, Cmnd 6404, London, 1942), p. 7.
3 P. Taylor-Gooby, *Public Opinion, Ideology and State Welfare* (Routledge and Kegan Paul, London, 1985), p. 64 ff.
4 See, for example, P. Taylor-Gooby, *Public Opinion, Ideology and State Welfare*, ch. 4; D. Heald, *Public Expenditure* (Martin Robertson, Oxford, 1983).
5 For example, F. A. Hayek, M. Friedman and (insofar as a common view emerges) the Institute of Economic Affairs take this view.
6 See, for example, D. Friedman, *The Machinery of Freedom: Guide to Radical Capitalism* (Harper and Row, New York, 1973).
7 A helpful discussion of this brand of 'neo-conservatism' is to be found in A. Gamble, 'The free economy and the strong state: the rise of the social market economy', in *The socialist Register 1979*, eds R. Miliband and J. Saville (Merlin Press, London, 1979).
8 S. Brittan, *Capitalism and the Permissive Society* (Macmillan, London, 1973).
9 R. Nozick, *Anarchy, State and Utopia* (Basic Books, New York, 1974).
10 F. A. Hayek, *Law, Legislation and Liberty*, vols I and II (Routledge and Kegan Paul, London, 1973, 1976).
11 For example, R. Posner, *Economic Analysis of Law* (Little Brown, Boston, 1977).
12 Hayek, *Law, Legislation, and Liberty*, vol. I, p. 51.
13 Ibid., p. 42.
14 F. A. Hayek, *The Constitution of Liberty* (Routledge and Kegan Paul, 1960), p. 133.
15 Hayek, *Law, Legislation, and Liberty*, vol. i, p. 54.
16 M. Friedman, *Capitalism and Freedom* (University of Chicago Press, Chicago, 1962), p. 195.
17 Hayek, *Constitution of Liberty*, p. 20.
18 Ibid., pp. 321–2.
19 For very helpful discussions of this see R. Goodin, 'Freedom and the welfare

state: theoretical foundations' and P. Jones, 'Freedom and the redistribution of resources', both in *Journal of Social Policy*, ii, 1982, pp. 146–76 and 217–38 respectively.

20 Hayek, *Constitution of Liberty*, p. 17.

21 Ibid., p. 83.

22 Hayek, *Law, Legislation, and Liberty*, vol. II, p. 32.

23 Hayek, *Constitution of Liberty*, p. 84.

24 Friedman, *Capitalism and Freedom*, p. 69.

25 This analysis draws heavily upon Nozick, *Anarchy, State and Utopia*, and the extensive literature associated with libertarianism.

26 This part of the analysis draws heavily upon M. Cranston, *What Are Human Rights?* (The Bodley Head, London, 1973).

27 My account is based on standard treatments in leading economic texts such as R. Lipsey, *An Introduction to Positive Economics* (Weidenfeld and Nicolson, London, 1966); and also on Posner, *Economic Analysis of the Law*. The discussion of these questions in D. Heald, *Public Expenditure* (Martin Robertson, Oxford, 1983) is very helpful.

28 Friedman, *Capitalism and Freedom*.

29 See J. Obler, 'Private giving in the welfare state', *British Journal of Political Science*, ii, 1981, p. 17.

30 R. Sugden, 'Hard luck stories: the problem of the uninsured in a laissez-faire society', *Journal of Society Policy*, ii, 1982, pp. 201–16.

31 The pamphlets of the Institute of Economic Affairs are the best summary of this wisdom. See also Hayek, *Constitution of Liberty* and Freidman, *Capitalism and Freedom*.

32 P. A. Samuelson, 'The pure theory of public expenditure', *Review of Economics and Statistics*, 36, 1954, pp. 387–89.

33 Particularly important in this area is the work of J. M. Buchanan and G. Tullock, *The Calculus of Consent* (University of Michigan Press, Ann Arbor, 1962); and W. A. Niskanen, *Bureaucracy and Representative Government* (Aldine-Atherton, Chicago, 1971). Useful too are the papers in *The Taming of Government*, IEA Readings 21, (Institute of Economic Affairs, London, 1979); and S. Brittain, 'The economic contradictions of democracy', *British Journal of Political Science*, 5, 1, 1975. Heald, *Public Expenditure*, provides an excellent and more detailed account of state failure than I provide here.

34 W. A. Niskanen, *Bureaucracy and Representative Government* (Aldine-Atherton, Chicago, 1971), p. 38.

35 S. Brittan, 'The economic contradictions of democracy', *British Journal of Political Science*, 5, 1, 1975, pp. 129–61.

Chapter 2 Citizenship and the Welfare State: Rejecting the Market

1 T. H. Marshall, *Social Policy in the Twentieth Century*, 4th edn, (Hutchinson, London, 1975), p. 84.

2 R. M. Titmuss, *Essays on 'The Welfare State'*, 2nd edn, (Unwin University Books, London, 1963), p. 39.

3 R. M. Titmuss, *Commitment to Welfare* (Pantheon Books, New York, 1968), p. 22.
4 Ibid., p. 199.
5 Marshall, *Social Policy*, p. 85.
6 W. A. Robson, *Welfare State and Welfare Society: illusion and reality* (George Allen and Unwin, London, 1976), p. 140.
7 P. Townsend, Letter, *The Manchester Guardian*, 19 May 1985.
8 R. M. Titmuss, *The Gift Relationship: from human blood to social policy* (George Allen and Unwin, London, 1970).
9 See G. Room, *The Sociology of Welfare: social policy, stratification and political order* (Blackwell and Martin Robertson, Oxford, 1979), and the studies discussed therein.
10 Titmuss, *Commitment to Welfare*, p. 140.
11 R. Mishra, *The Welfare State in Crisis: social thought and social change* (Wheatsheaf Books, Brighton, 1984), contains a good introductory discussion of this question.
12 Titmuss, *Commitment to Welfare*, p. 133.
13 Ibid.
14 See F. I. Michelman, 'Property, utility, and fairness', *Harvard Law Review*, 80, 1968, p. 1165.
15 Titmuss, *Commitment to Welfare*, p. 142.
16 Ibid., p. 134.
17 Ibid., p. 163.
18 Ibid., p. 134.
19 Ibid., p. 129.
20 Ibid.
21 Ibid.
22 Ibid., p. 134.
23 See chapter 4.
24 F. Hirsch, *The Social Limits to growth* (Routledge and Kegan Paul, London, 1977), p. 18.

Chapter 3 Citizenship and the Welfare State: Needs, Rights and Community

1 T. H. Marshall, *Social Policy in the Twentieth Century*, 4th edn, (Hutchinson, London, 1975), p. 201.
2 See, for example, the discussion of need in T. H. Marshall, 'Value problems in welfare-capitalism', reprinted in *The Right to Welfare and Other Essays* (Heinemann, London, 1981), p. 115.
3 Quoted in R. Plant, H. Lesser and P. Taylor-Gooby, *Political Philosophy and Social Welfare: essays on the normative basis of welfare provision* (Routledge and Kegan Paul, London, 1980), p. 21.
4 R. M. Titmuss, *Social Policy: an introduction* (George Allen and Unwin, London, 1974), p. 10.

5 R. M. Titmuss, *Commitment to Welfare* (George Allen and Unwin, London, 1968), p. 122.
6 T. H. Marshall, *The Right to Welfare*, and *Sociology at the Crossroads and Other Essays* (Heinemann, London, 1963).
7 W. A. Robson, *Welfare State and Welfare Society: illusion and reality* (George Allen and Unwin, London, 1976).
8 Marshall, 'Citizenship and social class' in *Sociology at the Crossroads and Other Essays*, p. 74.
9 Ibid., p. 107.
10 Ibid., p. 100.
11 Ibid.
12 Robson, *Welfare State and Welfare Society*, p. 63.
13 Marshall, 'Citizenship and social class', p. 74.
14 Cited in Marshall, *The Right to Welfare*, p. 43.
15 P. Townsend, *Poverty in the United Kingdom* (Penguin, London, 1979), p. 31.
16 Ibid., p. 57.
17 Ibid., p. 50.
18 Titmuss, *The Gift Relationship: from human blood to social policy* (George Allen and Unwin, London, 1970), p. 224.
19 Marshall, *The Right to Welfare*, p. 91.
20 Ibid., p. 88.
21 Marshall, 'Citizenship and social class', p. 87.
22 Ibid., p. 95.
23 Ibid., p. 96.
24 Marshall, *The Right to Welfare*, p. 31.
25 Ibid.
26 D. Miller, 'Constraints on freedom', *Ethics*, 94, 1968, p. 66.
27 P. Jones, 'Freedom and the redistribution of resources', *Journal of Social Policy*, 11, 1982, p. 217; and R. Goodin, 'Freedom and the welfare state: theoretical foundations', *Journal of Social Policy*, 11, 1982, p. 149.
28 See, for example, G. A. Cohen, 'Capitalism, freedom and the proletariat' in *The Idea of Freedom: essays in honour of Sir Isaiah Berlin*, ed. A. Ryan, (DUP, Oxford, 1979).
29 Titmuss, *The Gift Relationship*, p. 13.
30 Ibid., p. 108.
31 Ibid., p. 13.
32 Marshall, *The Right to Welfare*, p. 109.
33 Ibid., p. 107.
34 R. Plant in R. Plant, H. Lesser and P. Taylor-Gooby, *Political Philosophy and Social Welfare*, p. 232.
35 Ibid., p. 214.
36 Titmuss, *The Gift Relationship*, p. 12.
37 Ibid., p. 47.
38 Ibid., p. 238.
39 P. Singer, 'Freedoms and utilities in the distribution of health care' in *Markets and Morals*, ed. G. Dworkin, (Halsted Press, New York, 1977).
40 Titmuss, *The Gift Relationship*, p. 243.

41 Marshall, 'Citizenship and Social Class', p. 87.
42 D. Watson, *Caring for Strangers: an introduction to practical philosophy for students of social administration* (Routledge and Kegan Paul, London, 1980), p. 24.
43 Ibid., ch. 3.
44 Ibid., p. 14.
45 Marshall, *The Right to Welfare*, p. 124.
46 Ibid., p. 135.
47 Ibid.

Chapter 4 Altruism, Rights and Integration

1 R. M. Titmuss, *The Gift Relationship: from human blood to social policy* (George Allen and Unwin, London, 1970).
2 R. Plant, H. Lesser and P. Taylor-Gooby, *Political Philosophy and Social Welfare: essays on the normative basis of welfare provision* (Routledge and Kegan Paul, London, 1980), p. 243.
3 J. Parker, *Citizenship and Social Policy* (Macmillan, London, 1975), p. 156.
4 D. Watson, *Caring for Strangers: an introduction to practical philosophy for students of social administrations* (Routledge and Kegan Paul, London, 1980), ch. 4.
5 Titmuss, *The Gift Relationship*, p. 74.
6 Ibid., p. 239.
7 Ibid., p. 212.
8 For a spirited defence of Titmuss, see P. Singer, 'Altruism and commerce: a defence of Titmuss against Arrow', *Philosophy and Public Affairs*, 2, 3, 1973.
9 Helpful discussions of the relationships between rights and self-respect are to be found in R. Peffer, 'A defense of rights to well-being', *Philosophy and Public Affairs*, 8, 3, 1978 and P. Jones, 'Rights, welfare and stigma' in *Social Welfare: why and how?*, ed. N. Timmes, (Routledge and Kegan Paul, London, 1980).
10 Titmuss, *The Gift Relationship*, p. 239.
11 Ibid., p. 74.
12 E. Powell, *Still to Decide* (Elliot Right Way Books, London, 1972), p. 27.
13 Ibid., p. 14.
14 J. H. Goldthorpe, 'Social inequality and social integration in modern Britain' in *Poverty, Inequality, and Class Structure*, ed. D. Wedderburn, (CUP, Cambridge, 1974), and J. H. Goldthorpe, 'The current inflation: towards a sociological account', in *The Political Economy of Inflation*, ed F. Hirsch and J. H. Goldthorpe, (Martin Robertson, London, 1978), ch. 9.
15 Ibid. and F. Hirsch, *Social Limits to Growth* (Routledge and Kegan Paul, London, 1977). But see John Gray's essay in A. Ellis and K. Kumar, *Dilemmas of Liberal Democracies: studies in Fred Hirsch's social limits to growth* (Tavistock Publications, London, 1983).
16 See especially J. H. Goldthorpe, *Social Mobility and Class Structure in Modern Britain* (Clarendon Press, Oxford, 1980).
17 Prominent works include P. Taylor-Gooby and J. Dale, *Social Theory and*

Social Welfare (Edward Arnold, London, 1981); I. Gough, *The Political Economy of the Welfare State* (Macmillan, London, 1979); and J. O'Connor, *The Fiscal Crisis of the State* (St. James Press, London, 1973). Good reviews of the principal arguments may be found in: R. Mishra, *The Welfare State in Crisis: social thought and social change* (Wheatsheaf Books, Brighton, 1984); V. George and P. Wilding, *Ideology and Social Welfare* (Routledge and Kegan Paul, London, 1976); N. Furniss and T. Tilton, *The Case for the Welfare State: from social security to social equality* (Indiana University Press, 1977); and G. Room, *The Sociology of Welfare: social policy, stratification and political order* (Blackwell and Martin Robertson, Oxford, 1979).

18 R. Golding and S. Middleton, *Images of Welfare* (Martin Robertson, Oxford, 1982), p. 59.
19 Ibid., p. 5.
20 Cited in J. Mack and B. Lansley, *Poor Britain* (George Allen and Unwin, London, 1985), p. 206.
21 Cited ibid., p. 210.
22 Cited ibid., p. 206.
23 Ibid., p. 215.
24 P. Taylor-Gooby, *Public Opinion, Ideology and State Welfare* (Routledge and Kegan Paul, London, 1985).
25 Ibid., pp. 38ff.
26 Ibid., ch. 2.
27 Ibid., p. 113.
28 R. Pinker, *Social Theory and Social Policy* (Heinemann, London, 1971), pp. 141–42.
29 Cited in P. Spicker, *Stigma and Social Welfare* (Croom Helm, St. Martin's, London, 1984). p. 46.
30 Ibid., p. 182.
31 Ibid., p. 120.
32 D. Donnison, 'Liberty, equality, and fraternity' in *Talking About Welfare: readings in philosophy and social policy*, eds N. Timms and D. Watson, (Routledge and Kegan Paul, London, 1976).
33 D. Miller, 'Arguments for Equality', *Midwest Studies in Philosophy*, 7, 1982, p. 73.
34 Quoted as an epigraph to D. Wedderburn (ed.), *Poverty, Inequality and Class Structure* (CUP, Cambridge, 1974).

Chapter 5 Equality

1 R. H. Tawney, *Equality* (Unwin Books, London, 1964), ch. 4.
2 C. A. R. Crosland, *The Future of Socialism* (Jonathan Cape, London, 1956).
3 E. F. M. Durbin, *The Politics of Democratic Socialism: an essay in social policy* (Routledge and Kegan Paul, London, 1948).
4 B. Abel-Smith, *Freedom in the Welfare State* (Fabian Tract, London, 353, 1964).

5 R. M. Titmuss, *Commitment to Welfare* (George Allen and Unwin, London, 1968), p. 116.
6 K. Joseph and J. Sumption, *Equality* (J. Murray, London, 1979).
7 See the discussion of Hayek in ch. 1.
8 R. Nozick, *Anarchy, State and Utopia* (Basic Books, New York, 1974).
9 W. Letwin, *Against Equality* (Macmillan, London, 1983).
10 See, for example, T. H. Marshall, *Social Policy in the Twentieth Century*, 4th edn, (Hutchinson, London, 1975), p. 201.
11 In particular, W. A. Robson, *Welfare State and Welfare Society: illusion and reality* (George Allen and Unwin, London, 1976), ch. 4.
12 A. Weale, *Equality and Social Policy*, (Routledge and Kegan Paul, London, 1978), p. 22.
13 Ibid., p. 26.
14 Ibid.
15 Ibid., p. 27.
16 I. Berlin, 'The idea of equality', *Proceedings of the Aristotelian Society*, 56, 1955–6, p. 00.
17 Nozick, *Anarchy, State and Utopia*, ch. 7.
18 B. Williams, 'The idea of equality' in *Philosophy, Politics and Society*, series II, (Blackwell, Oxford, 1962), p. 110.
19 Ibid., p. 127.
20 See M. Walzer, *Spheres of Justice* (Basic Books, New York, 1983), ch. 3; and A. Gutmann, *Liberal Equality* (CUP, Cambridge, 1980), ch. 4.
21 Nozick, *Anarchy, State and Utopia*, p. 234.
22 J. Raz, 'Principles of equality', *Mind*, 87, 1978, p. 333.
23 Ibid.
24 D. Miller, 'Arguments for equality', *Midwest Studies in Philosophy*, 7, 1982, p. 73.
25 Tawney, *Equality*, p. 15.
26 Ibid., p. 46.
27 See, for example, T. H. Marshall, 'Value problems of welfare-capitalism', in *The Right to Welfare and Other Essays* (Heinemann, London, 1981), p. 135.
28 For example, Tawney, *Equality*, p. 113.
29 Ibid., p. 49.
30 Raz, 'Principles of equality', p. 327.
31 Ibid., p. 328.
32 Albert Weale argues for a principle like this in *Equality and Social Policy*, leaving the level of acceptable risk to be determined by the political system.

Chapter 6 Market Exchanges and Welfare Rights

1 R. Posner, 'The ethical and political basis of the efficiency norm in common law adjudication', *Hofstra Law Review*, 8, 1980, p. 492.
2 This point has been frequently noted as a criticism of social contract theories relying on tacit or hypothetical consent.

3 See R. Dworkin, 'The original position' in *Reading Rawls: critical studies of a theory of justice*, ed. N. Daniels (Oxford, Blackwell, 1975).

4 See, for example, J. L. Coleman, 'Efficiency, utility, and wealth maximization', *Hofstra Law Review*, 8, 1980, p. 524.

5 D. Miller, 'Justice and property', *Ratio*, 22, 1, 1980, p. 1; and T. Scanlon, 'Nozick on rights, liberty and property', *Philosophy and Public Affairs*, 6, 1, 1976.

6 D. Miller, 'Justice and property'.

7 R. Plant, H. Lesser, and P. Taylor-Gooby, *Political Philosophy and Social Welfare: essays on the normative basis of welfare provision* (Routledge and Kegan Paul, London, 1980), ch. 4.

8 See G. A. Cohen, 'Capitalism, freedom and the proletariat', in *The Idea of Freedom: essays in honour of Sir Isaiah Berlin*, ed. A. Ryan (OUP, Oxford, 1979).

9 L. Becker, *Property Rights: philosophic foundations* (Routledge and Kegan Paul, London, 1977).

10 J. R. Kearl, 'Do entitlements imply that taxation is theft', *Philosophy and Public Affairs*, 7, 1, 1977, pp. 74–81.

11 A. Ryan, 'Utility and ownership' in R. G. Frey, ed., *Utility and Rights*, ed. R. G. Frey (Blackwell, Oxford, 1985).

12 H. L. A. Hart, 'Are there any natural rights?', *Philosophical Review*, 64, 1964, pp. 175–91.

13 For a more extensive discussion of these questions see R. Peffer, 'A defense of rights to well-being', *Philosophy and Public Affairs*, 8, 3, 1978; D. Watson, *Caring For Strangers: an introduction to practical philosophy for students of social administration* (Routledge and Kegan Paul, London, 1980); and Plant et al., *Political Philosophy and Social Welfare*, ch. 4.

14 Plant et al., *Political Philosophy and Social Welfare*.

15 M. Cranston, *What Are Human Rights?* (The Bodley Head, London, 1973), has popularized this argument. For knock-down criticism, see Plant et al., *Political Philosophy and Social Welfare*, and Watson, *Caring For Strangers*.

16 Plant et al., *Political Philosophy and Social Welfare*, p. 76.

Chapter 7 Need

1 T. Scanlon, 'Preference and urgency', *Journal of Philosophy*, 72, 1975, p. 655.

2 R. Plant, H. Lesser and P. Taylor-Gooby, *Political Philosophy and Social Welfare: essays on the normative basis of welfare provision* (Routledge and Kegan Paul, 1980), p. 51.

3 Ibid.

4 A. Weale, *Equality and Social Policy* (Routledge and Kegan Paul, London, 1978), p. 70.

5 Discussion in D. Miller, 'Social justice and the principle of need', in *The Frontiers of Political Theory*, eds M. Freeman and D. Robertson (Harvester Press, Brighton, 1980) is very helpful on this and other points.

6　Weale, *Equality and Social Policy*, p. 79.
7　B. Barry, *Political Argument* (Routledge and Kegan Paul, London, 1965), especially pp. 48–9.
8　Plant et al., *Political Philosophy and Social Welfare*, chs 2 and 3.
9　D. Miller, *Social Justice* (Clarendon Press, Oxford, 1976), ch. 4.
10　Plant et al., *Political Philosophy and Social Welfare*, chs 3 and 4.
11　Ibid., p. 51.
12　J. Rawls, *A Theory of Justice* (OUP, Oxford, 1972), pp. 90 ff.
13　Weale, *Equality and Social Policy*, pp. 45–53.
14　Miller, *Social Justice*, p. 127.
15　Ibid., p. 128.
16　Ibid.
17　Ibid., p. 134.
18　Plant et al., *Political Philosophy and Social Welfare*, p. 35.
19　D. Z. Phillips and H. O. Mounce, 'On morality's having a point', *Philosophy*, 40, 1965, p. 308.
20　See ibid., p. 131, note 16.
21　See ibid., p. 130, note 11.
22　Plant et al., *Political Philosophy and Social Welfare*, p. 46.
23　Ibid., p. 38.
24　Ibid.
25　Ibid., p. 43.
26　F. Michelman, 'Constitutional welfare rights and a theory of justice' in *Reading Rawls: critical studies of a theory of justice*, ed. N. Daniels (Blackwell, Oxford, 1975).
27　Weale, *Equality and Social Policy*, p. 49.
28　T. Nagel, 'Rawls on justice', in *Reading Rawls: critical studies of a theory of justice*.

Chapter 8　Reconstructing Citizenship Theory

1　Support for this is found in the survey data reported in J. Mack and S. Lansley, *Poor Britain* (George Allen and Unwin, London, 1985).
2　P. Townsend, *Poverty in the United Kingdom* (Penguin, London, 1979).
3　See, for example, P. Townsend, *Poverty in the United Kingdom*.
4　For a similar view, see L. Thurow, 'Government Expenditures: Cash or In-Kind Aid?', *Philosophy and Public Affairs*, 5, 4, p. 361.
5　See J. LeGrand, *The Strategy of Equality* (Allen and Unwin, London, 1982).
6　J. Feinberg, 'The nature and value of rights', *Journal of Value Inquiry*, 4, 4, 1970, p. 252.

Bibliography

Abel-Smith, B., *Freedom in the Welfare State*, Fabian Tract 353, London, 1964.

Barry, B., *Political Argument*, Routledge and Kegan Paul, London, 1965.

Becker, L., *Property Rights: philosophic foundations*, Routledge and Kegan Paul, London, 1977.

Berlin, I., 'Equality as an ideal', *Proceedings of the Aristotelian Society*, 56, 1955–6, pp. 301–26.

Beveridge, W., *Social Insurance and Allied Services* (Beveridge Report), H.M.S.O, Cmnd 6404, London, 1942.

Brittan, S., *Capitalism and the Permissive Society*, Macmillan, London, 1973.

Brittan, S., 'The economic contradictions of democracy', *British Journal of Political Science*, 5, 1, 1975, pp. 129–61.

Buchanan, J. M. and Tullock, G., *The Calculus of Consent*, University of Michigan Press, Ann Arbor, 1962.

Cohen, G. A., 'Capitalism, freedom, and the proletariat' in *The Idea of Freedom: essays in honour of Sir Isaiah Berlin*, ed. A. Ryan, OUP, Oxford, 1979.

Coleman, J. L., 'Efficiency, utility, and wealth maximization', *Hofstra Law Review*, 8, 1980, pp. 509–53.

Cranston, M., *What Are Human Rights?*, The Bodley Head, London, 1973.

Crosland, C. A. R., *The Future of Socialism*, Jonathan Cape, London, 1956.

Daniels, N., (ed.), *Reading Rawls: critical studies of a theory of justice*, Blackwell, Oxford, 1975.

Deacon, A. and Bradshaw, J., *Reserved for the Poor: the means test in British social policy*, Blackwell and Martin Robertson, Oxford, 1983.

Donnison, D., 'Liberty, equality, and fraternity' in *Talking About Welfare: readings in philosophy and social policy*, eds N. Timms and D. Watson, Routledge and Kegan Paul, London, 1976.

Durbin, E. F. M., *The Politics of Democratic Socialism: an essay in social policy*, Routledge, London, 1948.

Dworkin, R., 'The original position' in *Reading Rawls: critical studies of a theory of justice*, ed. N. Daniels, Blackwell, Oxford, 1975.

Ellis, A. and Kumar, K., *Dilemmas of Liberal Democracies: studies in Fred Hirsch's social limits to growth*, Tavistock Publications, London, 1983.

Feinberg, J., 'The nature and value of rights', *Journal of Value Inquiry*, 4, 1970, pp. 243–57.

Friedman, D., *The Machinery of Freedom: guide to radical capitalism*, Harper & Row, New York, 1973.

Friedman, M., *Capitalism and Freedom*, University of Chicago Press, Chicago, 1962.

Furniss, N. and Tilton, T., *The Case for the Welfare State: from social security to social equality*, Indiana University Press, London, 1977.

Gamble, A., 'The free economy and the strong state: the rise of the social market economy', in *The Socialist Register 1979*, eds R. Miliband and J. Saville, Merlin Press, London.

George, V. and Wilding, P., *Ideology and Social Welfare*, Routledge and Kegan Paul, London, 1976.

Golding, P. and Middleton, S., *Images of Welfare*, Martin Robertson, Oxford, 1982.

Goldthorpe, J. H., 'Social inequality and social integration in modern Britain' in *Poverty, Inequality, and Class Structure*, ed. D. Wedderburn, OUP, Cambridge, 1974.

Goldthorpe, J. H., *Social Mobility and Class Structure in Modern Britain*, Clarendon Press, Oxford, 1980.

Goodin, R., 'Freedom and the welfare state: theoretical foundations', *Journal of Social Policy*, 11, 1982, pp. 146–76.

Gough, I., *The Political Economy of the Welfare State*, Macmillan, London, 1979.

Gutmann, A., *Liberal Equality*, CUP, Cambridge, 1980.

Hart, H. L. A., 'Are there any natural rights', *Philosophical Review*, 64, 1964, pp. 175–91.

Hayek, F. A., *Law, Legislation and Liberty*, vols. I and II, Routledge and Kegan Paul, London, 1973, 1976.

Hayek, F. A., *The Constitution of Liberty*, Routledge and Kegan Paul, London, 1960.

Heald, D., *Public Expenditure*, Martin Robertson, Oxford, 1983.

Hirsch, F., *The Social Limits to Growth*, Routledge and Kegan Paul, London, 1977.

IEA Readings 21, *The Taming of Government*, Institute of Economic Affairs, London, 1979.

Jones, K., Brown, J., and Bradshaw, J., *Issues in Social Policy*, 2nd edn, Routledge and Kegan Paul, London, 1983.

Jones, P., 'Rights, welfare, and stigma' in *Social Welfare: why and how?*, ed. N. Timms, 1980.

Jones, P., 'Freedom and the redistribution of resources', *Journal of Social Policy*, 11, 1982, pp. 217–38.

Joseph, J. and Sumption, K., *Equality*, J. Murray, London, 1979.

Kearl, J. R., 'Do entitlements imply that taxation is theft', *Philosophy and Public Affairs*, 7, 1, 1977, pp. 74–81.

Le Grand, J., *The Strategy of Equality: redistribution and the social services*, George Allen & Unwin, London, 1982.

Letwin, W., *Against Equality*, London, Macmillan, 1983.

Lipsey, R., *An Introduction to Positive Economics*, Weidenfeld and Nicolson, London, 1966.

Mack, J. and Lansley, S., *Poor Britain*, George Allen and Unwin, London, 1985.

Marshall, T. H., 'Citizenship and social class' in *Sociology at the Crossroads and Other Essays*, Heinemann, London, 1963.

Marshall, T. H., *Sociology at the Crossroads and Other Essays*, Heinemann, London, 1963.

Marshall, T. H., *Social Policy in the Twentieth Century*, 4th edn, London, Hutchinson, 1975.

Marshall, T. H., *The Right to Welfare and Other Essays*, Heinemman, London, 1981.

Michelman, F., 'Property, utility, and fairness', *Harvard Law Review*, 80, 1968.

Michelman, F., 'Constitutional welfare rights and a theory of justice' in *Reading Rawls: Critical studies of a theory of justice*, ed. N. Daniels, Blackwell, Oxford, 1975, pp. 1165–258.

Miller, D., 'Social justice and the principle of need' in *The Frontiers of Political Theory*, eds M. Freeman and D. Robertson, Harvester Press, Brighton, 1980.

Miller, D., *Social Justice*, Clarendon Press, Oxford, 1976.

Miller, D., 'Arguments for Equality', *Midwest Studies in Philosophy*, 7, 1982, pp. 73–87.

Miller, D., 'Constraints on freedom', *Ethics*, 94, 1983, pp. 66–83.

Mishra, R., *The Welfare State in Crisis: social thought and social chance*, Wheatsheaf Books, Brighton, 1984.

Nagel, T., 'Rawls on justice' in *Reading Rawls: critical studies of a theory of justice*, ed. N. Daniels, Blackwell, Oxford, 1975.

Niskanen, W. A., *Bureaucracy and Representative Government*, Aldine-Atherton, Chicago, 1971.

Nozick, R., *Anarchy, State and Utopia*, Basic Books, New York, 1974.

Obler, J., 'Private giving in the welfare state', *British Journal of Political Science*, 11, 1981, pp. 17–49.

O'Connor, J., *The Fiscal Crisis of the State*, St. James Press, London, 1973.

Parker, J., *Citizenship and Social Policy*, Macmillan, London, 1975.

Peffer, R., 'A defense of rights to well-being', *Philosophy and Public Affairs*, 2, 3, 1978.

Phillips, D. Z. and Mounce, H. O., 'On morality's having a point', *Philosophy*, 40, 6, 1965, pp. 308–19.

Pinker, R., *Social Theory and Social Policy*, Heinemann, London, 1971.

Plant, R., Lesser, H., and Taylor-Gooby, P., *Political Philosophy and Social Welfare: essays on the normative basis of welfare provision*, Routledge and Kegan Paul, London, 1980.

Posner, R., *Economic Analysis of the Law*, Little Brown, Boston, 1977.

Posner, R., 'The ethical and political basis of the efficiency norm in common law adjudication', *Hofstra Law Review*, 8, 1980, pp. 487–509.

Powell, E., *Still to Decide*, Elliot Right Way Books, London, 1972.

Rawls, J., *A Theory of Justice*, OUP, Oxford, 1972.

Raz, J., 'Principles of equality', *Mind*, 87, 1978, pp. 321–42.

Robson, W. A., *Welfare State and Welfare Society: illusion and reality*, George Allen and Unwin, London, 1976.

Room, G., *The Sociology of Welfare: social policy, stratification and political order*, Blackwell and Martin Robertson, Oxford, 1979.

Ryan, A., 'Utility and ownership', *Utility and Rights*, ed. R. G. Frey, Blackwell, Oxford, 1985.

Samuelson, P. A., 'The pure theory of public expenditure', *Review of Economics and Statistics*, 36, 1954, pp. 387–9.

Scanlon, T., 'Preference and urgency', *Journal of Philosophy*, 72, 1975, pp. 655–669.

Scanlon, T., 'Nozick on rights, liberty and property', *Philosophy and Public Affairs*, 6, 1, 1976, pp. 3–26.

Singer, P., 'Altruism and commerce: A defence of Titmuss against Arrow', *Philosophy and Public Affairs*, 2, 3, 1973, pp. 312–20.

Singer, P., 'Freedoms and utilities in the distribution of health care' in *Markets and Morals*, ed. K. Dworkin, Halsted Press, New York, 1977.

Spicker, P., *Stigma and Social Welfare*, Croom Helm, St. Martin's, London, 1984.

Sugden, R., 'Hard luck stories: the problem of the uninsured in a laissez-faire society', *Journal of Social Policy*, 11, 1982, pp. 201–16.

Tawney, R. H., *Equality*, London, Unwin Books, 1964.

Taylor-Gooby, P., *Public Opinion, Ideology and State Welfare*, Routledge and Kegan Paul, London, 1985.

Taylor-Gooby, P. and Dale, J., *Social Theory and Social Welfare*, Edward Arnold, London, 1981.

Thurow, L. C., 'Government expenditures: cash or in-kind aid?', *Philosophy and Public Affairs*, 5,4, pp. 361–81. .

Timms, N. and Watson, D. (eds), *Talking About Welfare: readings in philosophy and social policy*, Routledge and Kegan Paul, London, 1976.

Timms, N. (ed.), *Social Welfare: why and how?*, Routledge and Kegan Paul, London, 1980.

Titmuss, R. M., *Essays on 'the Welfare State'*, 2nd edn, Unwin University Books, London, 1963.

Titmuss, R. M., *Commitment to Welfare*, George Allen and Unwin, London, 1968.

Titmuss, R. M., *The Gift Relationship: from human blood to social policy*, George Allen and Unwin, London, 1974.

Titmuss, R. M., *Social Policy: an introduction*, George Allen and Unwin, London, 1974.

Townsend, P., Letter, *The Manchester Guardian*, 19 May, 1985.

Townsend, P., *Poverty in the United Kingdom*, Penguin, London, 1979.

Walzer, M., *Spheres of Justice*, Basic Books, New York, 1983.

Watson, D., *Caring for Strangers: an introduction to practical philosophy for students of social administration*, Routledge and Kegan Paul, London, 1980.

Weale, A., *Equality and Social Policy*, Routledge and Kegan Paul, London, 1978.

Wedderburn, D. (ed.), *Poverty, Inequality and Class Structure*, OUP, Cambridge, 1974.

Williams, B., 'The idea of equality' in *Philosophy, Politics and Society*, series II, Blackwell, Oxford, 1962.

INDEX